**Mildred Newcomb** is Professor Emerita of English at Ohio Wesleyan University.

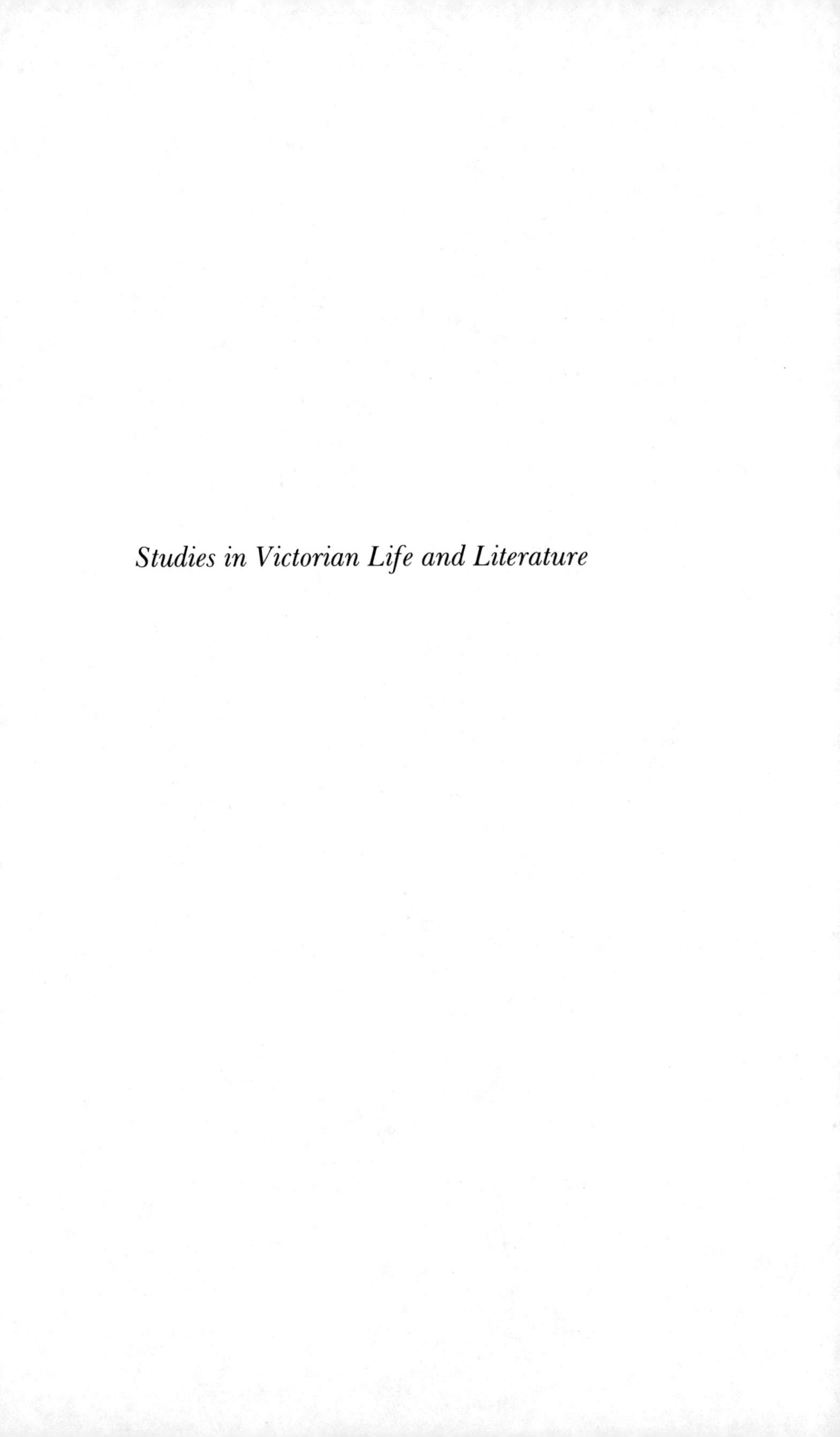

*Studies in Victorian Life and Literature*

# THE IMAGINED WORLD OF *Charles Dickens*

MILDRED NEWCOMB

OHIO STATE UNIVERSITY PRESS

*Columbus*

Library of Congress Cataloging-in-Publication Data

Newcomb, Mildred, 1914–
The imagined world of Charles Dickens / Mildred Newcomb.
p. cm.
Bibliography: p.
Includes index.
ISBN 0–8142–0482–1 (alk. paper)
1. Dickens, Charles, 1812–1870—Criticism and interpretation.
2. Imagination in literature. I. Title.
PR4588.N39 1989
823'.8—dc19 88–32682
CIP

The paper in this book meets the guidelines for permanence and durability of the Committee on Production Guidelines for Book Longevity of the Council on Library Resources.

Printed in the U.S.A.

9 8 7 6 5 4 3 2 1

*To my mother,*
*who never failed*
*to give me encouragement*

*and*

*To Jan and Kay,*
*who supported and sustained me*
*throughout the enterprise*

This Proclamation rendered Mr. Inspector additionally studious, and caused him to stand meditating on river-stairs and causeways, and to go lurking about in boats, putting this and that together. But, according to the success with which you put this and that together, you get a woman and a fish apart, or a Mermaid in combination. And Mr. Inspector could turn out nothing better than a Mermaid, which no Judge and Jury would believe in (*OMF,* bk. I, ch. 3)

—*Dickens on Research*

# *Contents*

# *Preface*

I WOULD LIKE especially to express my gratitude for guidance and assistance to Dr. Richard D. Altick, who initially suggested to me that I write my dissertation on Dickens and who has given me good advice and counsel ever since. His unflagging confidence in the study and his willingness to spend much time in reading and criticizing, as well as to assist the completion of the project in any way possible, have been invaluable.

Special gratitude goes also to Dr. Jeannette E. Stanton, now Emeritus Professor of Psychology at Ohio Wesleyan University, whose readings and rereadings of the complete manuscript have resulted in much greater clarity and coherence than would otherwise have been possible. The different perspectives she brought to the reading also led to extended perceptions on my part that have contributed substantially to the discussions.

In addition, several other readers have given hours of reading and careful criticism, which I have heeded to the improvement of the manuscript. Dr. Benjamin T. Spencer (Emeritus) and Dr. Michael Kearns, both of the Ohio Wesleyan University English faculty, have astutely read and criticized selected chapters, for which I thank them. Finally, I wish to express special appreciation for the careful readings and suggestions of the two anonymous readers for the Ohio State University Press. I trust that they can see the difference their efforts have made.

In fact, in view of the contributions of all of these collaborators, I shudder to think what the manuscript would have been without them.

All citations from the novels and stories of Dickens refer to either the Clarendon or the Oxford Illustrated editions of his works. I have used the Clarendon Editions of *David Copperfield* (*DC*), *Little Dorrit* (*LD*), *Martin Chuzzlewit* (*MC*), and *The Mystery of Edwin Drood* (*MED*). The remainder of the novels are from the Oxford Illustrated Editions: *Bleak House* (*BH*), *Dombey and Son* (*DS*), *Great Expectations* (*GE*), *Hard Times* (*HT*), *Nicholas Nickleby* (*NN*), *The Old Curi-*

*osity Shop* (*OCS*), *Our Mutual Friend* (*OMF*), *Oliver Twist* (*OT*), and *A Tale of Two Cities* (*T2C*). References to the short stories are from the Oxford Illustrated volumes entitled *Christmas Books* and *Christmas Stories* and are identified in the text by story title. To preserve the circumstances of original publication, the titles of stories that originally appeared as books are underlined.

## *Chronological Listing of Dickens Works Used*

|  |  |
|---|---|
| 1836–7 | *The Pickwick Papers* |
| 1837–9 | *Oliver Twist* |
| 1838–9 | *Nicholas Nickleby* |
| 1840–1 | *Master Humphrey's Clock* |
| 1840 | *The Old Curiosity Shop* |
| 1841 | *Barnaby Rudge* |
| 1843 | <u>A Christmas Carol</u> |
| 1843–4 | *Martin Chuzzlewit* |
| 1846 | <u>The Battle of Life</u> |
| 1846–8 | *Dombey and Son* |
| 1848 | <u>The Haunted Man</u> |
| 1849–50 | *David Copperfield* |
| 1850 | "A Christmas Tree" |
| 1851 | "What Christmas Is as We Grow Older" |
| 1852 | "The Poor Relation's Story" |
| 1852–3 | *Bleak House* |
| 1853 | "Down with the Tide" |
| 1853 | "Nobody's Story" |
| 1854 | *Hard Times* |
| 1855–7 | *Little Dorrit* |
| 1859 | *A Tale of Two Cities* |
| 1859 | "The Haunted House" |
| 1860–1 | *Great Expectations* |
| 1864–5 | *Our Mutual Friend* |
| 1866 | "Mugby Junction" |
| 1870 | *The Mystery of Edwin Drood* |

# *Introduction*

IT IS NOW just short of a half century since Edmund Wilson's essay, "Dickens: The Two Scrooges," touched off a profusion of studies examining some aspect of Dickens's imagination. In 1977, Robert Newsom reported that by that time it had "become the favorite subject, explicit or implicit, of modern critical studies" (*Dickens on the Romantic Side of Familiar Things.* [New York: Columbia University Press, 1977], p. 47). Now, in 1989, I believe that I can most appropriately introduce the guiding principles of my own late entry into the field by reviewing such related critical literature, and by adding commentary on the contributions of those who have preceded me into print. It is therefore my purpose in this essay to attempt a modest review of this criticism in order to trace and evaluate major trends and developments during these 48 years, particularly as they bear upon *The Imagined World of Charles Dickens.*

As a matter of fact, I consider that a number of quite disparate investigations must be crowded into the tent under the general rubric of "Studies of Dickens's Imagination." Most critics have made little effort to define this Protean term, which slips easily into a number of guises, but have let its meaning develop as an offspring of the approaches they employ. Although I shall myself consistently differentiate between "imagination" and "fancy," most critics use the terms almost interchangeably, though often with the suggestion that fancy is an exercise of the imagination rather than the imagination itself. Sometimes imagination is conceived as a faculty of the mind, sometimes as a way of processing phenomenal data, and sometimes as a repository of "imaginative" responses to such data that have produced an inner world of their own. I have relied upon all three concepts, with the weight of discussion falling obviously on the third.

I should like to produce a stipulative definition of imagination to clarify my own critical approaches and to point my discussion of other critics. The basic element in the controlling definition is the *figurative image.* This image creates a subjective interpretation of phenomena, which becomes a "felt experience" resulting from some kind of momentary fusion, synthesis, or other accommodation of the two worlds of outer and inner perception (neither of which, for Dickens, can be ignored). The former, in Kantean terms, furnishes images extended in space; the latter adds extension in time. Through these interpretations of life experiences a "philosophy of life"/belief system/encompassing "myth"/*Weltanschauung* develops by which the perceiver lives, having personally defined the nature of "reality" in a phenomenal world. The studies I have included in this review concern themselves in some fashion with some or all of these aspects of the imagination.

All of the studies under review share with mine certain further characteristics. They all explore at length Dickens's detailed imagery, which is the most salient feature of his writing. More will be said of this imagery as we go along. Secondly, all accept without question the primacy of the literary text. One of the stable advances made in this period (thanks to the New Critics) is that even the most extraneously oriented of critics gives more than passing acknowledgment to the literary text. On the other hand, even the most textually oriented of critics (thanks to the later critical reactions against the excesses of those same New Critics) no longer attempts to divorce it from its biographical/historical context.

And, finally, all of the critics represented here grant a special power to language that lifts "literature" above "écriture" in these latter egalitarian and nihilistic days of language analysis (see Murray Krieger, "Literature vs. Ecriture: Constructions and Deconstructions in Recent Critical Theory," (*Studies in the Literary Imagination,* XII [1979], pp. 1–17). Most Dickens scholars have sought to account for the singular power and energy of his writing. John Gross, in a 1962 essay, observed that "no one has ever shown to the full why his language crackles with such electricity" ("Dickens: Some Recent Approaches," in *Dickens and the Twentieth Century.* John Gross and Gabriel Pearson, eds. [London: Routledge & Kegan Paul, 1962], p. xv). His metaphor is perfect, and I believe his statement still holds, primarily because there *is* no one answer. But many partial answers appear in investigations of widely varying natures. Most of these studies locate the igniting spark in some combination of recognition and surprise produced in the reader's imaginative responses. Most critics acknowledge the interrelationship of author, text, and reader. Some explain the electricity in terms of language's tapping into the unconscious or prelingual experience commonly shared, culturally or universally, by author and reader. Others find the charge in the creations of rhetoric—wit, irony, and so on. Few any longer indicate belief that language is making contact with unseen principalities and powers in any mystic sense, though for many of us the power of language continues to have "spiritual" significance.

Some of the studies under review are, like *The Imagined World,* what I would call "comprehensive." Truly comprehensive studies, I should think, attempt to review some aspect of the Dickens imagination *in toto* after careful reading either of all of the Dickens novels or of a sufficient body of them to warrant generalization. Many of these carry their intent in their titles, which frequently read *The* [*Something*] *of Charles Dickens* or *Charles Dickens and* [*Something*]. "Imagination" and "World" appear variously combined in a number of titles, a fact which I found particularly frustrating in titling the present work. Comprehensive studies flourished in the two fertile decades from 1960 to 1980, turning around the hub of the centennnial year. Other studies, however brief or limited, have also been significant. Whereas articles and books from 1939–59 laid foundations to be either developed or challenged, since 1980, the trend has been toward "small" studies that examine a very limited question or a single novel or story.

Although the Dickens imagination is so fertile and its products so overwhelmingly abundant, its limits are after all confined to a quite finite, if extensive, body of material for critics to respond to. We must all circle around the same geography in our explorations rather than set out to explore new lands. This fact both enriches and sets limits about what we will achieve. Despite all efforts to make an exact science of any literary criticism, it must, as Anatole France observed in *La Vie Littéraire* (1888), forever remain an art, like the "objects" it analyzes. If a poem or a poet sustains a relation to science, he wrote, "it is to one that is blended with art, that is intuitive, restless, forever unfinished." While the best criticism works carefully and faithfully to its conclusions through the inductive process that has come to be called the "scientific method," what is being studied is not comparable to the objects of science. With them, each technological advance—micro or macro—that extends our sense modalities brings into our phenomenal perception new knowledge about the "thing in itself," which was there all the time but which we had no previous access to. In contrast, the object on the printed page has no existence beyond its phenomenal presence. If I labor this point, it is because I think that literary critics sometimes forget it. If they learned long ago the futility of asking how many children Lady Macbeth had, they may still (as Garrett Stewart does in his generally excellent book, *The Trials of Imagination* [see "Bibliographical Essay"]) create for Little Nell an extended psychic life and then base conclusions on it. Where it exists, such extrapolation is a problem of Dickens criticism, though it has its own fascination.

A related problem attaches to deductive or "centripetal" conclusions, which may tell more about the belief systems of their authors than about Dickens. First, a critic so oriented seeks for evidence to support previously formed conclusions (and almost surely in the "God's plenty" of a Dickens novel, one can find quotable scripture for conclusions that might greatly have surprised Dickens himself). I believe that this has to some degree particularly skewed the investigations of Marxist and psychoanalytic critics. The second horn of the dilemma is that sometimes critics have patiently and with brilliant results followed the inductive route through their analyses only to take a tremendous "leap of faith" to arrive at preordained conclusions.

A final "problem," which has grown larger with the body of existing criticism itself, is the very natural tendency of critics to quote and react to the work of other critics. One result is an ever-increasing sophistication of language and concepts that may lead critics finally to talk only with each other. More destructive of good criticism is that some studies contain almost more references to other studies (the new version of overwhelming footnotes) than they do to Dickens—a phenomenon I have come to call the "critical fallacy" after the example of Bernard De Voto, who charged the fiction writers of the 1920s with the "literary fallacy": basing novels more on other novels than upon life.

This essay, however, is intended as an appreciation of the good criticism coming out of the past fifty years, not as a cavil against its weaknesses. The best criticism, in my view, does not pretend to bring new knowledge to bear on the reading of Dickens, nor to make advances for others to build on as science does. Rather, it functions very much as "creative" literature itself does. Whereas the creation of felt experience in literature sends an active reader back to prelinguistic interpretations and therefore grants an opportunity to relive experience as if it were all new, so the best Dickens criticism sends the reader back to Dickens to read again as if for the first time.

Most critics, it turns out, assemble much the same data and try to answer similar questions. One encompassing question is how to categorize this writer who evades categorization. Although Dickens himself would probably turn "satirist" at the question thus put, he would equally probably fall to with enthusiasm if it were considered a problem of arriving at exactly the right name for himself: always a matter of supreme importance to him. Is he a symbolist, an allegorist, a realist, a social critic, a poet, a super-naturalist, a Bible-Christian, a humanist, an existentialist? All of these and many more names have been proposed, and most have been objected to with some argument of oversimplification or over-reading. Using Dickens's (and Browning's) own method of getting at the truth, perhaps if we surround him with enough names, we shall finally in some sense "have" him.

A second encompassing question inquires into the degree of conscious control Dickens exerted over his novels. The evidence points strongly in opposite directions, creating a continuum along which critics may stand. Particularly in early criticism, there seemed to be almost a consensus that Dickens's achievements were a happy product of his simply letting the work write itself. Dickens himself, of course, frequently attested to the fact that he wrote what flowed to the point of his pen. Out of such evidence came belief in his art—or his artlessness—as the product of "unconcious" or "automatic" writing processes. This interpretation was aided by the obvious restrictions imposed by the very conditions of serial publication, which rendered total advance planning impossible. When the evidence came pouring in, particularly with the research of Butt and Tillotson (*Dickens at Work* [London: n.p., 1957]) into Dickens's extensive habitual working plans, that he did indeed think out his novels with great care, the pendulum began to swing in the opposite direction. More recent critics credit even the "apprentice" novelist of *Pickwick Papers* with a degree of total control in which I simply cannot believe. Others are made uneasy by the subject of "the role of the unconscious mind in art," and move quickly away from it. Surely some way must be found to reconcile the two equally compelling views.

No critic of Dickens's imagination can long escape discussion of the metaphysical question: What is real? All of our critics begin with rejection of simple mimesis, the photographic imitation of external reality. If Dickens is a realistic novelist (and most if not all will agree that he is), he has to be so in some other sense. In coming to grips with this question, we confront an imposing series of irreducible pairings: this "versus" that, or "between" this and that. It may well be that Dickens of all writers confronts the reader with the most formidable array of basic polarities; of dualities to be bridged only by the processes and unique powers of the imagination: fact/fancy, waking/sleeping, alive/dead, animate/inanimate, conscious/unconscious, sane/mad, the "actual"/dream or hallucination or fantasy or delusion. His ultimate dualisms are the age-old questions of good/evil, order/chaos, body/mind, appearance/reality. Or, in terms Dickens would never himself have used, phenomenal/noumenal. These questions have insistently invaded most studies of Dickens's imagination. The most ambitious study that directly addresses the question is John Romano's instructive book, *Dickens and Reality* (New York: Columbia University Press, 1978 [see "Bibliographical Essay"]). The soundest analyses, I believe, conclude that the continued preservation of these polarities in some kind of balanced tension is a vital function of the imagination.

We come at last to the pivotal question whose answers provide the bases for dealing with all other questions: What do we make of the figurative imagery? The question demands attention because of three qualities that seem to define the Dickensian style. First, the characteristic repetitive imagery is too insistent to be ignored—repetitive, yet so varied in its manifestations that it conveys the impression of tremendous imaginative creativity rather than of limitation. Second, the piling up of detail, which produces not only the abundant feasts prepared for every possible occasion but also many a scene crowded with people and things, is a Dickens trademark. And, finally, the associational and analogical significance of much of Dickens's imagery has sent critics along still different lines of inquiry.

The three seminal essays most frequently cited from the first decade or so of our review chart directions for us to follow in assessing what critics have made of the figurative language. The first of these was written by Edmund Wilson, who pointed criticism in a psychoanalytic direction. "Edmund Wilson," (wrote Lionel Trilling in his essay "Art and Neurosis," *The Liberal Imagination* [New York: Viking Press, 1950]), "in his striking phrase, 'the wound and the bow,' has formulated for our time the idea of the characteristic sickness of the artist, which he represents by the figure of Philoctetes, the Greek warrior who was forced to live in isolation because of the disgusting odor of a suppurating wound and who yet had to be sought out by his countrymen because they had need of the magically unerring bow he possessed" (p. 158). Wilson's essay on Philoctetes (which gave him the title for his book) concluded the volume, which began with "Dickens: The Two Scrooges." Wilson's discussion in the latter essay describes the "wounds" creating the "suppurating" sore of Dickens's "obsessions," which in turn drew him in the direction of the criminal, the rebel, and the outlaw, and drove him into isolation from "normal" society. Later psychoanalytic criticism has itself departed from what Leonard Mannheim referred to in 1983 as Wilson's "rather disingenuously set forth" study of Dickens. In pointing out that Wilson's thesis led him to ignore the "ambivalence" between the attraction of the criminal/rebel and the love of law and order that balances Dickens's outlook, he draws attention to the distortions early Freudian psychoanalysis invites when applied to literary artists. (Mannheim's essay summarizing psychoanalytic criticism to that date is worth reviewing: "Dickens and Psychoanalysis: A Memoir," *Dickens Studies Annual,* 11 [1983] pp. 335–45.)

While other critics might account for the repeated images in some other way, those psychoanalytically inclined who follow Wilson have, like him, continued to declare for them a psychopathic origin indicating mental abnormality. In addition, the language of psychoanalysis ("obsession," etc.) has likewise influenced the thinking of many critics who would perhaps deny any psychoanalytic affiliations. When, for example, they describe Dickens's extraordinarily vivid imagery as "hallucinatory" or "hypnagogic," they carry on the myth of Dickens's "abnormal" responses to sensory stimuli.

It is interesting, I think, to speculate in this vein on a treatment of the imagery that might well have been applied to Dickens, but which was largely bypassed, perhaps partly as a result of Wilson's essay. This is the method of Caroline Spurgeon, who produced an engrossing study, *Shakespeare's Imagery and What It Tells Us* (New York: Cambridge Univ. Press, 1952), by retracing Shakespeare's footsteps to observe what he would have observed in his surrounding world to make his associations and create his similes and metaphors. Spurgeon's study may seem innocent and perhaps ingenuous beside the psychoanalytic probings, but who is to say that it is less valid?

Critics who are avowedly psychoanalytic have found further support for their views in the recurrent presence of dreams, dreaming, and dream-like states in Dickens's works. Taken as projections from his unconscious, they invite efforts to understand the author, both as man and writer, by putting together the dream images, the biographical facts, and a necessary measure of speculation to "diagnose" a patient who may not have existed. Sometimes these studies are quite illuminating, while others suffer from a complaint that has been diagnosed as the result of being written by people who know either too little about psychology or too little about literature.

The second seminal essay coming out of the 1940s is likewise psychologically oriented, but charts a different course for criticism to follow: Warrington Winters's "Dickens and the Psychology of Dreams," *PMLA* 63 (Sept. 1948), pp. 984–1006. This essay describes Dickens as himself a nineteenth-century psychologist fully aware of the phenomena about which he wrote and trying to grasp their significance. It presents him, not as a potential patient for Freud, but possibly as one of his forerunners—one of those to whom he might have been referring in later life when, on the occasion of his seventieth birthday, he said: "The poets and philosophers before me discovered the unconscious. What I discovered was the scientific method by which the unconscious can be studied." (Quoted in Lionel Trilling, "Freud and Literature," *The Liberal Imagination,* p. 32. By this time Freud himself had long since modified his views on the connection between art and neurosis.) Seen in this light, Dickens, with his careful observations, may well have been one of those writers who helped Freud formulate his theories, though I have not yet found direct reference to that influence.

Winters points out that earlier critics rejected any notion of Dickens as psychologist, quoting George Gissing, for instance, as typical of previous opinion: "Of psychology—a word unknown to Dickens—we, of course, have nothing; to ask for it is out of place" (*Charles Dickens,* [London: Blackwell and Son, Ltd., 1898]). (Long before, George Eliot's famous comment in *The Natural History of German Life* [1857] had contributed to the widely held complementary view that Dickens lacked both interest in psychological matters and psychological content in his writing. While praising his gift for rendering "with the utmost power . . . the external traits of our town population," she lamented that "if he could give us their psychological character—their conceptions of life, and their emotions—with the same truth as their idiom and manners, his books would be the greatest contribution Art has ever made to the awakening of social sympathies.") Winters made abundantly clear that both views were spectacularly false, and later criticism has profitably extended his insights.

In my opinion, however, the question of influence or of applied psychology is much less important than a point made by Trilling in the previously quoted essay: "To pass from the reading of a great literary work to a treatise of academic psychology," he writes, "is to pass from one order of perception to another, but the human nature of the Freudian psychology is exactly the stuff upon which the poet has always exercised his art" (p. 32). The definition of psychology has widened with this concept of "human nature" to include "normal" as well as "abnormal" psychic processing in the "stuff" to be considered as psychological. The fundamental links between psychology and literature have been forged in the matrix of their common source in language: poetic work and dream work involve remarkably similar processes. They further share a belief that the most important thing to comprehend about the human psyche is the process of development. The only thing worth writing about, Browning recorded in the preface to *Sordello,* is the development of the soul. Dickens shared this idea. So did Jung and the other myth psychologists (who might phrase it as the "search for the Great Man within" or as the "process of individuation"), as well as the "developmental psychologists," who would call it "maturation," or the process of "growing up." Although some Dickens critics of other persuasions still shy nervously away from the whole field of psychological criticism, studies of the natural relationships between psychology and poetry can produce richly interactive insights.

A second critical intepretation of Dickens's imagery finds a particular stimulus in the provocative terms of our third seminal essay, George Orwell's "Charles Dickens" (*Inside the Whale* [London, 1940]). Although much of his discussion, as he explains in part V, has concentrated on Dickens's "message," which he acknowledges may have angered some readers, and although he continues to assert that "all art is propaganda" (p. 157), in the latter portions of the essay he tries to answer the question, "Why do *I* care about Dickens?" What is inimitable in Dickens? He concludes that "the thing that cannot be imitated is his fertility of invention, which is invention not so much of characters, still less of 'situations,' as of turns of phrase and concrete details. The outstanding, unmistakable mark of Dickens's writing is the *unnecessary detail*" (p. 159, emphasis Orwell's). The examination of this "unnecessary detail" continues to engage the attention of critics, who still employ Orwell's term as a clue to Dickens's unique quality. Their conclusions, of course, show why it was *not* unnecessary. Orwell concludes that its aggregate force is to give us the "face" of Dickens himself: "the face of a man who is always fighting against something, but who fights in the open and is not frightened, the face of a man who is *generously angry*—in other words, of a nineteenth-century liberal, a free intelligence, a type hated with equal hatred by all the smelly little orthodoxies which are now contending for our souls" (p. 171).

Critics after Orwell have arrived at different conclusions dictated by the routes they have followed. To mention but two, Taylor Stoehr (see "Bibliographical Essay") finds that Dickens's typical use of such rhetorical devices as anaphora and metonomy both orders and connects his details to produce active effects on characterization and plotting. In a quite different vein, Harry Marten (also see "Bibliographical Essay") shows how the details assemble, by contiguity and composition, into a visual picture which, like the engravings of Hogarth, bursts with significance.

The final way of examining Dickens's imagery has its roots in traditional literary analysis, placing Dickens among those masters of rhetoric and style who employ virtuoso techniques to play the language like a finely tuned instrument. It is inconceivable that any critic of literature would exclude this way of looking at literature, whatever his other leanings. By and large, critics in this mode "hear" the language, which at other times they "see." Their discussions of "voice" and "tone" further indicate the felt relationships between literature and music.

The intellectual quality of this approach is apparent, for the detection and appreciation of wit and irony require the resources of the mind, not the feelings. Most Dickens critics of this inclination are quick to point out, however, the radical difference between him and the "metaphysical poets" with their studied conceits. What language critics seem to admire most in Dickens is the natural spontaneity, life, and gusto of his language. Recent critics seem to agree that the particular nature and virtue of Dickens's imagery is a complex interplay of association (metonomy) and analogy (metaphor), which creates the wit and irony that spark the Dickens style.

Finally, with regard to the "Bibliographical Essay" at the end of this book, I must acknowledge a set of personal criteria for the evaluation of the selected studies. I chose most of the items because they had some immediate bearing on this study, although a few appear primarily because of the insistence of their titles. (Criticism I have actually used in formulating my discussions is acknowledged and documented in the text and in the endnotes.) Assessing the various studies, I find that my agreements or arguments with their writers are traceable in part to harmony or lack of it between our perceptual and intellectual belief systems. I hope that I am not more easily satisfied with the evidence and lines of reasoning for judgments I agree with or more demanding and critical of those with which I disagree—but it may be so.

I believe that as critics we are all at our best when we are carefully tapping along some chosen vein of inquiry with the tools appropriate to our method; we are at our weakest when we stake out large claims for what we have discovered. In making those claims, we must also be prepared for the inevitable later "assayers" to tell us whether they think we have struck gold or pyrite. These comments are intended both as apologia and as a statement of expectation.

# I

## *The Argument of the Book*

THIS BOOK explores the perceptual universe of Charles Dickens as revealed in the non-discursive parts of his writings and as frequently supported by discursive statement. In his book *The Problem of Style,* J. Middleton Murry analyzes the special kind of thought produced by the creative writer through images and particularized details. The creative literary artist, Murry explains, "does not generalize; or rather, his generalization is not abstract." Because the artist's attitude to life is "predominantly emotional, his thoughts partake much more of the nature of residual emotions, which are symbolized in the objects which aroused them, than of discursive reasoning." Objects and episodes from experience form impressions that accumulate to become a "coherent emotional nucleus" consolidating into a "kind of speculative thought which differs from the speculative thought of the philosopher by its working from particular to particular." Murry concludes that "it is by virtue of this mysterious accumulation of past emotions that the writer, in his maturity, is able to accomplish the miracle of giving to the particular the weight and force of the universal."[1]

This is Dickens's gift: "to accomplish the miracle of giving to the particular the weight and force of the universal." An absorbed reader working from the "particular to particular" of a writer's imagined world comes to view experience through that author's eyes, to develop a similar emotional nucleus, to share for the time what Murry calls the writer's "mode of experience." The reader shares this imaginative experience and receives complex meaning with unmediated comprehension, as one adept in a foreign language will understand its meaning without translation.

To apprehend Dickens's mode of experience—his way of perceiving the world—one must turn, not to the discursive statements so well adapted to the "speculative thought" of the philosopher, but rather to the non-discursive materials that show rather than tell, that paint a picture without explaining its significance. In such materials one studies, not what Dickens said he thought, but rather *how his mind worked* in unifying experience to wrest order from chaos: the *manner, style,* or *mode* of his imaginative functions.

The Dickens mode of experience can be visualized as a figured tapestry or pictorial scroll interpreting life. In it are contained allegorical people, emblematic places and things, key epithets that provide attitudinal and emotional coloring. All of these are caught in moments of crucial and universal meaning: of birth, of death and threat of death, of crisis, of transition. In their selection and combination, they make a sprawling interpretative tapestry to which Dickens pragmatically referred the data of continuing experience and by which he judged it. That he did so is inferred from the works themselves—within those expressed artistic interpretations of life are found the materials for reconstructing his perceptual universe.

Now, if, as Murry claims, "the great writer does not really come to conclusions about life," then how is it possible for that writer first to formulate and then to communicate anything about life that is not as fragmented and chaotic as the original raw experience?

The answer seems to life in the creation of *Gestalten,* defined by Richard Ohmann as "arbitrary ways of breaking up the flux" by intuitively associating, selecting, and ordering chaotic materials.[2] Each gestalt, a gathering together of discrete elements of felt experience into a pattern or composition viewed as somehow complete, is different from "real" experience in that it has already been selected and *shaped* into a picture by an individual consciousness. Such sense gestalten are the primitive analogues that give abstract ideas their contact with concrete reality.[3] Suzanne Langer explains:

> The laws that govern this sort of articulation are altogether different from the laws of syntax that govern language. The most radical difference is that visual forms are not discursive. They do not present their constituents successively, but simultaneously, so the relations determining a visual structure are grasped in one act of vision. Their complexity, consequently, is not limited, as the complexity of discourse is limited, by what the mind can retain from the beginning of an apperceptive act to the end of it. . . . An idea that contains too many minute yet closely related parts, too many relations within rela-

> tions, cannot be "projected" into discursive form; it is too subtle for speech.[4]

But not too subtle for art, which can present simultaneously all the parts of a complex picture. The Dickens mode of experience, the tapestried imagination, might now be conceived as a comprehensive gestalt, a composition of many harmoniously united patterns.

It is the function of literary art, says Langer, voicing what seems like consensus, to create "the illusion of life." And "the prose fiction writer, like any other poet, fabricates an illusion of life entirely lived and felt."[5] Success in creating this illusion depends upon the writer's ability to recreate the conditions of the original experience: to include in fiction internally felt reactions to the externally imposed objects of experience. Internal and external realities blend into an implicit interpretation of experience that weaves the sense images and impressions from the inner world through descriptions of the external world. This is the illusion of life entirely lived and felt.

It is crucial to understand this function of the writer, for while the unmistakable sign of life and vitality is *diversity*, there is an equally insistent human drive—reflected in language—toward unity. The very identity of established language depends upon its ability to categorize, to simplify, to abstract, to eradicate the multiple differentiations that make ordering the chaotic world stuff of raw perceptions so difficult, and then to freeze meaning at its most advanced stage of abstraction. From its beginnings, language places progressively rigid bonds upon an individual's consciousness, and one's spirit must constantly struggle against this restricting tyranny of the word, which determines attitudes, memory, even what can be thought about.

It is a basic function of the writer to keep sensitivity alive in the reader and to awaken the possibility of other and richer choices than those the reader has already made through interpretation of experience. Hence the literary artist must destroy—or circumvent—entrenched patterns of unity before alternative ones can even be entertained. Yet the writer must employ the same language, already over-unified, that frustrates the communication efforts of the ordinary person. The artist's problem is how to reassert multiplicity, diversity, and abundance: to recharge language itself by surprising it back to its creative sources, reviving its dead metaphors and revitalizing its clichés. In Murry's words: "Every work of enduring literature is not so much a triumph of language as a victory over language: a sudden injection of life-giving perceptions into a vocabulary that is, but for the energy of the creative writer, perpetually on the verge of exhaustion."[6] Whatever else may or may not be claimed for Dickens, he had an unquestioned faculty for recharging language to create the "illusion of life entirely lived and felt."

The secret of this ability in Dickens lies first in his image-making mind. His figurative images develop into patterns and enlarge into allegories that encompass the extended meaning of his insights. In the process, furthermore, a chaotic "reality" may intrude itself, asserting its independence from any formal control by exploding the very patterns that have made communication possible.[7] This radical intrusion becomes a further "sudden injection of life-giving perceptions."

Sometimes Dickens's imagery is simply associational, but most frequently it is also analogical. It is important to differentiate between the precise term *analogy* and the less discriminating word *symbol,* for a certain kind of symbol is never found in Dickens.[8] (Perhaps some of the critics who have protested against a symbolic reading of his works sense the blurred perception it fosters.) The more one studies his analogies, the less they look like symbols in the restrictive sense. It tends to be the nature of symbols not simply to suggest, but to substitute for the thing they represent and then to be that thing dependably; their occurrence is a kind of shorthand signifying the interchangeability of symbol and thing. These symbols are frequently qualitatively different from the thing they stand for. Although they *may* originate in image and analogy, they do not necessarily do so, but are often arbitrary and alogical.

Mr. Twemlow of *Our Mutual Friend* illustrates the different nature of the typical Dickens "symbol." We first meet him as

> an innocent piece of dinner-furniture that went upon easy castors and was kept over a livery stable-yard in Duke Street, Saint James's, when not in use. . . . [H]e was in frequent requisition and at many houses might be said to represent the dining-table in its normal state. . . . Sometimes, the table consisted of Twemlow and half-a-dozen leaves; sometimes, of Twemlow and a dozen leaves; sometimes, Twemlow was pulled out to his utmost extent of twenty leaves. . . . This evening the Veneerings give a banquet. Eleven leaves in the Twemlow; fourteen in company all told. (*OMF,* ch. 2)

Twemlow is clearly an elaborately developed symbol, but hardly a simply understood one. First, he has symbolic meaning only for certain characters, such as the Podsnaps and the Veneerings, who are themselves satirized by their utilitarian reduction of another person to a useful thing. Twemlow takes on this symbolic value for them through analogy with their other ostentatious possessions, also to be dragged out on state occasions when they wish to impress each other. Second, and perhaps more important, Dickens as narrator further ridicules these characters by providing Twemlow with a complicated character, concerned with his own anxieties and problems, which has nothing to do with the dining-table symbolism. Indeed, in all likelihood, Mr. Twemlow has no notion that he is so viewed by his "friends," and would be horrified to realize it.

In Dickens's analogical symbols, then, a qualitative likeness is perceived between attributes of two different things. When the likeness ceases to exist, the image is abandoned, for it has life only in the likeness. Even when simile slips into metaphor, the awareness of similarity rather than substitution remains. Without the need for consistency demanded by symbolic identity, the emotional ground under these images is free to shift in response to the immediate context. As a consequence, a reader following Mr. Twemlow through the chapter in which he is introduced has no trouble dissociating him from the dining-table "symbol."

Furthermore, as John Killham notes,[9] the conscious remembering of one analogy for too long may even interfere with the meaning of a later analogy. For example, "fire" is, for Dickens, a recurring analogical image indicative primarily of life. But sometimes fire may be supportive, sometimes destructive of life. A rigidly symbolic reading of Dickens might find some frustration here. A reader free to respond completely to the immediate context, however, will find only the residual memory of an alternative possibility communicating the complexity of exprience in which fire has such ambiguous meanings. The arbitrary symbol simplifies, the analogy diversifies.

Furthermore, an imaginative intellect constantly sees new analogues for the same thing, or sees in the old analogy new implications that produce new interpretations. Analogies are thus natural and more universal than symbols, less strained and idiosyncratic—and much more likely to be old and worn. Their age and common usage, however, is not in itself a count against them: their very strength lies in their power to strike fire in the consciousness of a reader by suddenly touching a forgotten experience and flashing from it a moment of insight. Therefore to blame Dickens for lack of originality in his analogical language is to miss a very important point: the unexpected recognition itself creates part of the life illusion.

Dickens's ability to create this life illusion is not explained completely, however, by the analogizing quality of his imagination. Equally characteristic is its primitive picture-making quality, whereby a complex, totally felt experience repeatedly finds instantaneous expression through a configuration—a gestalt—of associated images. The supposed puzzle of the insistently recurring images in Dickens's work has provoked unnecessarily bizarre solutions. The images recur simply because they existed whole in their creator's consciousness from the moment of their inception. If they initially appeared as "Ur-choices" (see note 2) for the man in synthesizing chaotic world stuff, they remain as tools for the artist in ordering experience, part of the unquestioned assumptions by which their owner lives. None of them may be considered to have vacated his mind completely at any given moment, and they recur in various configurations like the chips of colored glass in a kaleidoscope, changing intensity, shape, and focus with each emerging pattern.

The following chapters will isolate and scrutinize in turn the various groupings of associated images that seem to constitute Dickens's perceptual universe. Chapters II and III consider the river and marsh configurations, which place human life in the perspective of eternity. These are configurations of mystery and uncertainty, filled with reminders of the great unknown preceding birth, brooding over life, and following death. Although they seem to suggest attitudes related principally to death, in Dickens's view they actually point toward life, for they provide the larger perspective necessary for full understanding of life's meanings.

The remaining configurations primarily suggest attitudes toward temporal life. Death is timeless; life is inseparable from time. Chapter IV explores the relationship between sensitivity to time and capacity for life. Chapters V through VIII, which complete the analysis of Dickens's mode of experience, then trace the development of a synthesized human life through its various stages to its ideal achievement of full humanity. Among the guiding configurations, one discovers, are embodied many lures and dangers lying in wait to freeze an individual at an immature stage, or to transform a person into a monster.

Throughout these chapters, I have chosen the sharpest, clearest, and best-developed delineations of each pattern for the most emphatic treatment. It must be understood, however, that the patterns seldom appear thus baldly and completely isolated within the total context of a novel. More often they will be partial, displaced, or disguised by the inventive fancy.[10] One may, for example, catch brief or subliminal glimpses of the marsh or the river anywhere; and it is not unusual for a number of configurations to interplay briefly or at length in the portrayal of a single person or event. In proceeding into the later chapters, the reader should try to carry actively forward the perceptions of the earlier chapters to perceive the whole interwoven pattern. In chapter IX, I shall myself attempt to synthesize the various configurations into the encompassing gestalt—the total allegory—that constitutes Dickens's imagined world.

Although I do not believe that this imagined world changed in substance once an interpretation was imprinted on his consciousness, it appears clear that Dickens steadily grew in his ability to use, control, and manipulate that world. Three of the early novels—*Pickwick Papers, Nicholas Nickleby,* and *Barnaby Rudge*—are singularly free of figurative language and therefore have little or no relevance to this study. All of the others, beginning with *Oliver Twist,* are rich in the imaginative materials on which this book is based. If at first, as seems likely, Dickens simply wrote down the thoughts and impressions that flowed into his mind, he learned to use the images of his perceptual world with increasing complexity and subtlety. In attempting to harness these powerful imaginative resources, he launched into experiments leading to impressive advancements in craftsmanship. His forays into both expressionistic and impressionistic writing amazingly anticipate twentieth-century writers concerned, like him, with conveying existential reality.

# II

## *The River and the Marsh*

THE APPROACH to the Dickens mode of experience lies along the river and stretches into the marsh. Between them, the river and marsh configurations shape the background against which the drama of human life is played out. Many of their related images reflect the twinned themes of time and death, for whenever one contemplates an individual against the perspective of eternity, attention is drawn both to the brevity of each life and to its sharply defined final boundary. Dickens makes this sensitivity to time—ultimately attentiveness to one's own mortality—the critical test of life in his characters: its presence connotes a full capacity for living, while indifference to time is the mark of the dead or moribund. The river, like time, continuously flows with change; the marsh, like eternity, is static and unmoving. "Tempus fugit" issues glibly from human lips. The image clusters connected with the river and with the marsh through which it flows restore complex life to the dead metaphor in the dead language.

### 1

Dickens belongs to a long line of allegorists in viewing individual human life as a linear journey through time from birth to death—resistless, adamant, irreversible. Sometimes this journey lies, like Dante's, through a darkening wood;[1] most frequently, however, it is down a river from source to sea. This river, at its idyllic "garden" source far upcountry, is meandering and pure. As it moves toward the ocean, however, it gathers such force and speed that by the time it flows through the city and under the city bridges toward the marsh, it heaves and ebbs with the tidal flow of the nearby sea, and roils darkly with the debris it has gathered along its course. Dickens develops these features of the river as one interpretation of the human relationship to time and death.[2]

In the allegorical "Nobody's Story"[3] (Christmas story for 1853), a partial picture of this river introduces the story:

> He lived on the bank of a mighty river, broad and deep, which was always silently rolling on to a vast, undiscovered ocean. It had rolled on, ever since the world began. It had changed its course sometimes, and turned into new channels, leaving its old ways dry and barren, but it had ever been on the flow, and ever was to flow until Time should be no more. Against its strong, unfathomable stream nothing made head. No living creature, no flower, no leaf, no particle of animate or inanimate existence, ever strayed back from the undiscovered ocean. The tide of the river set resistlessly toward it; and the tide never stopped, any more than the earth stops in its circling round the sun.

Sometimes the river analogy applies primarily to general human life, sometimes to the individual life; but most often, as here, it shifts back and forth between the two. Although "Nobody" lives on the bank of the river, each "living creature" is understood to travel down its course. The vague point of view ambiguously identifies the reader with both Nobody on the bank and the life carried along in the water, since no "living creature" can escape its tide. Thus, at times the individual may live beside the river, but at other times the river may itself be construed as "the living waters" of human life.

A fuller perspective of the river occurs in *Our Mutual Friend* as Betty Higden wanders through the country just before her death:

> In those pleasant little towns of Thames, you may hear the fall of the water over the weirs, or even, in still weather, the rustle of the rushes; and from the bridge you may see the young river, dimpled like a young child, playfully gliding away among the trees, unpolluted by the defilements that lie in wait for it on its course, and as yet out of hearing of the deep summons of the sea. It were too much to pretend that Betty Higden made out such thoughts; no; but she heard the tender river whispering to many like herself, "Come to me, come to me! When the cruel shame and terror you have so long fled from, most beset you, come to me!" (*OMF,* bk. III, ch. 8)

Although it were indeed too much to pretend that Betty Higden made out such thoughts, Dickens takes care that the reader shall do so: that one shall imagine the pure young river, unhurried and carefree in an idyllic pastoral landscape; the polluted and rushing river as it approaches the imperiously calling sea; the bridge from which the river may be observed; the siren lure of the water to a troubled human being. As with much of the Dickens imagery, the physical reality depicted, though indispensable, is expressionistic.[4] Betty Higden, looking down at the river from the bridge, completes in her person the analogy set up in the inverted simile. If the young river in which she is reflected is like a dimpled child, she in turn reflects the "old" river. She looks through eyes that have seen both the river and humanity in their polluted lower reaches, and she herself is fast approaching the summoning sea. Betty's experience attests to the fact that corruption and defilement lie in wait not only for the literal river; human life itself, individually or collectively, moves along in a stream, gathering pollution about it as it grows more concentrated and hurried. For this reason, the heavily populated city along the river is corrupt and defiled. Below the city bridge, the presence of death is felt as an ambiguously guilty or unnatural thing (as in the suggested suicide).

The image of the bridge is conspicuous in the total picture of the lower river. From above (as for Betty Higden, or "you"), it furnishes a view of the river for those in a mood to contemplate. From below, its shadowy arches hover threateningly overhead. From above, the city bridge provides a junction for the two streams of human life, the individual and the collective. The stream of humanity flows back and forth, coming and going across the bridge with the river flowing below it. But at any moment an individual may detach from that stream to peer more or less thoughtfully down toward the river with its awful implications, not only for that person, but also for the entire indifferent stream. The individual may or may not at the moment be completely aware of the implications. The view from the bridge is obscured in *Bleak House,* for example, when "Chance people on the bridges [peep] over the parapets into a nether sky of fog, with fog all round them" (*BH,* ch. 1).

But the view is clear for Master Humphrey of *The Old Curiosity Shop,* an old man with leisure for thought, who is led to speculate at length about "the stream of life that will not stop":[5]

> the crowds for ever passing and repassing on the bridges . . . where many stop on fine evenings looking listlessly down upon the water, with some vague idea that by-and-by it runs between green banks which grow wider and wider until at last it joins the broad vast sea—where some halt to rest from heavy loads, and think, as they look

> over the parapet, that to smoke and lounge away one's life, in a dull, slow, sluggish barge, must be happiness unalloyed—and where some, and a very different class, pause with heavier loads than they, remembering to have heard or read in some old time, that drowning was not a hard death, but of all means of suicide the easiest and best. (*OCS*, ch. 1)

Master Humphrey seems ominisciently aware of the river's implications for everybody in these fancied musings. For each thought, in its own way, says to the pausing wayfarer: "Come to me, come to me!" toward either actual death or the "drowned" death-in-life of the lotus eater on the barge.

Although the death association seems to occur with any bridge, city bridges carry the heaviest weight of meaning. It is important that the city (often London) lies near the sea. In *The Mystery of Edwin Drood,* a picture develops that brings together upper and lower river, city, bridges, and death. After an idyllic summer boat trip up the river for Mr. Tartar and his friends "came the sweet return among delicious odours of limes in bloom, and musical ripplings; and, all too soon, the great black city cast its shadow on the waters, and its dark bridges spanned them as death spans life, and the everlastingly-green garden seemed to be left for everlasting, unregainable, and far away" (*MED,* ch. 22). The "great black city" here is Cloisterham (Rochester) rather than London, but here too the river is "already heaving with a restless knowledge of its approach towards the sea." The location of the city along the lower river possesses double significance, for by now the river is running very fast, with a sense of urgency; it also seems that the city itself, with its streams of humanity, is responsible for the debris and pollution loading the river. If the "chance people" on the bridge in *Bleak House* had been able to see through the fog, they would know that the river "rolls defiled among the tiers of shipping and the waterside pollutions of a great (and dirty) city" (*BH,* ch. 1). But the impenetrable fog in which they stand prevents their sensing either the urgent message of the rolling water for themselves, or the responsibility they might have for its condition.

David Copperfield, however, catches all such implications. He and Mr. Peggotty, he writes, were following the desperate Martha through the river streets of London in the vicinity of Blackfriars Bridge. Instead of going across the bridge, as he had expected, she led them away from the peopled thoroughfare along the river bank choked with refuse waiting to fall over the brink into the water.

David comments on how quickly she moved "when she got free of the two currents of passengers setting towards and from the bridge" (*DC,* ch. 47). They made their way through a dreary neighborhood, where "a sluggish ditch deposited its mud at the prison walls," where "carcases of houses . . . rotted away" and "the ground was cumbered with rusty iron monsters." Here:

> Slimy gaps and causeways, winding among old wooden piles, with a sickly substance clinging to the latter, like green hair, and the rags of last year's handbills offering rewards for drowned men fluttering above high-water mark, led down through the ooze and slush to the ebb tide. There was a story that one of the pits dug for the dead in the time of the Great Plague was hereabout, and a blighting influence seemed to have proceeded from it over the whole place. Or else it looked as if it had gradually decomposed into that nightmare condition, out of the overflowings of the polluted stream.
>
> As if she were a part of the refuse it had cast out, and left to corruption and decay, the girl we had followed strayed down to the river's brink, and stood in the midst of this night-picture, lonely and still, looking at the water. (ch. 47)

In the light of this discussion, the implications of this passage begin to shift subtly back and forth through levels of significance. On the first level, Martha, viewing the scene, finds an analogy between the river and her own life. "'I know it's like me!'" she exclaims. "'I know that I belong to it. I know that it's the natural company of such as I am! It comes from country places, where there was once no harm in it—and it creeps through the dismal streets, defiled and miserable—and it goes away, like my life, to a great sea, that is always troubled—and I feel that I must go with it!'" She therefore feels the urge to throw herself into the river to become another piece of debris drawn along by the ebbing tide: the lifeless human body adding the final corruption as the river approaches the sea. Then David adds: "I have never known what despair was, except in the tone of those words. 'I can't keep away from it. I can't forget it. It haunts me day and night. It's the only thing in all the world that I am fit for, or that's fit for me. Oh, the dreadful river!'" Martha's strong sense of personal guilt leads her to her conclusions.

But what of the other stream that David fancies has cast her out, the "polluted stream"? In his view (the second level), the river is not her life, but that other stream of indifferent humanity: the guilt is not hers, but theirs in thus abandoning her to death. Beyond these two layers of meaning, human guilt does not go. But the "corruption" present in the disinterred or floating bodies is the final defilement by death itself. Independent of human iniquity, yet vile and terrible, it projects the meaning onto a third level of significance to question the source of human suffering itself, and also to provide firm warning of the destination to which time brings everyone.

The value of these multilayered images of impending death lies in their power to evoke the questions of human guilt and suffering in all their complexity, and to make it difficult to rest on glib answers. A similar unsettling uncertainty attends a passage from *Our Mutual Friend.* Here again, two outside observers, Eugene and Mortimer, are making their way down to the riverside to investigate the supposed drowning of John Harmon: "The wheels rolled on, and rolled down by the Monument, and by the Tower, and by the Docks; down by Ratcliffe, and by Rotherhithe; down by where accumulated scum of humanity seemed to be washed from higher grounds, like so much moral sewage, and to be pausing until its own weight forced it over the bank and sunk it in the river" (*OMF,* bk. I, ch. 3). Once more, what forces the human debris into the river? Is it pushed in, as suggested by "moral sewage," or does it fall by its own weight of corruption? The question remains open. What stands sure is that below the city bridge, corruption points with vague accusation, like Mr. Tulkinghorn's finger of Allegory in *Bleak House.*

Dickens's craftsmanship was not always in command of this multilayered imagery at the expressive level. The author was going into his late thirties when he wrote *David Copperfield;* he was less than twenty-five when he began *Oliver Twist.* Yet Martha is already imaginatively prefigured in Nancy of the youthful novel. The difference in craftsmanship in their presentation is noteworthy. Like Martha, Nancy looks back with regret upon a life that separates her from "virtuous" women to such an extent that they righteously shrink away from her. Like Martha, she considers herself beyond redemption. Nonetheless, she is determined to save innocent Oliver from Fagin and Bill Sikes and thus makes arrangements for periodic rendezvous with Rose Maylie and Mr. Brownlow. "'Every Sunday night, from eleven until the clock strikes twelve,' said the girl without hesitation, 'I will walk on London Bridge if I am alive!'" (*OT,* ch. 40). As we shall see, the unhesitating choice of place illustrates the way in which Dickens's own experience led him to interweave the river-bridge analogy and Nancy's approaching murder.[6]

Two Sundays later, unknowingly followed by Noah Claypole, Nancy makes her way toward the bridge: "The church clocks chimed three quarters past eleven as two figures emerged on London Bridge" (ch. 46). A very dark night, "and at that hour and place there were few people stirring. Such as there were, hurried quickly past: very possibly without seeing, but certainly without noticing, either the woman, or the man who kept her in view." These two "crossed the bridge, from the Middlesex to the Surrey shore."[7] Just before the arrival of Rose and Brownlow, "the heavy bell of St. Paul's tolled for the death of another day."

Nancy, afraid to talk on the public bridge, leads Rose and Brownlow to a flight of steps "which, on the Surrey bank, form a landing-stairs from the river." The scene is carefully, even laboriously, described.

> These stairs are a part of the bridge; they consist of three flights. Just below the end of the second, going down, the stone wall on the left terminates in an ornamental pier or pedestal facing towards the Thames. At this point the lower steps widen, so that a person turning that angle of the wall is necessarily unseen by any others on the stairs who chance to be above him, if only a step. (ch. 46)

Noah, who has slipped ahead of them, pauses in this angle, "as there seemed no better place of concealment, and, as the tide being out, there was plenty of room."

Visually imagined, this scene suggests the total bridge picture. The configuration on the bridge is that of indifferent passing stream and detached individuals, with Noah at one point even "leaning over the parapet" to conceal his figure from the girl (like the "chance people" in *Bleak House* "peering over the parapet" into the concealing fog). The descent upon the stairs moves the visual scene below the bridge, and imagination supplies the shadowed arches looming above. Brownlow asks Nancy why she has brought them to "'this dark and dismal hole,'" and she replies that all day she has had "'horrible thoughts of death, and shrouds with blood upon them.'" Reading a book, "'I'll swear I saw "coffin" written in every page . . . —aye, and they carried one close to me, in the street to-night.'"

Whether the introduction of the associational bridge imagery in this chapter of *Oliver Twist* was unconscious on the part of the young author, whether he feared that his readers would miss the implications, or whether he purposely built the effect rhetorically, the insertion of the tolling bells and the macabre fears reenforces meanings that the more accomplished craftsman in later books would entrust to the river-bridge imagery alone. Evidently, the young writer had not yet assimilated the separate elements into a well-defined, self-supporting analogical unit.

Nancy's confidants, fearing for her future after she has made her revelations about Fagin and Bill, urge her to come with them to begin a new life. But she chooses to return, for she feels chained to her old life although she hates it.

> "What," cried [Rose], "can be the end of this poor creature's life!"
>
> "What!" repeated the girl. "Look before you, lady. Look at that dark water. How many times do you read of such as I who spring into the tide, and leave no living thing, to care for, or bewail them. It may be years hence, or it may be only months, but I shall come to that at last." (ch. 46)

Like Martha once more, she clearly considers "the dreadful river" to be "the only thing in life that I am fit for." By daylight on that very morning, Bill Sikes murders Nancy, fulfilling her premonition of a violent death, a fate to which she, at the least, acquiesces.

As in Martha's case, whose was the guilt? Bill killed her, to be sure, but what held her to the life to which she felt chained? Once more, Dickens has left nothing here for the "imagination" to grasp, for he has already had Nancy answer these questions in the earlier conversation with Rose. "'I must go back,'" she explains. "'Whether it is God's wrath for the wrong I have done, I do not know; but I am drawn back to him through every suffering and ill-usage: and should be, I believe, if I knew that I was to die by his hand at last'" (ch. 40). Nancy accepts her guilt, but what does she mean by: "I am drawn back to him through every suffering and ill-usage"? Here is more than a suggestion of layered meaning. Are she and Bill perpetrators or victims of the suffering and ill-usage that draws them together? To emphasize the ambiguity, she has just explained to Rose that her situation might have been quite altered had indifferent humanity earlier shown her the compassion communicated now by Rose. "'If I had heard [such words] years ago, they might have turned me from a life of sin and sorrow; but it is too late, it is too late!'"

Thus at discursive length Dickens piles up and spells out in *Oliver Twist* the death-associated meanings of the bridge and the lower river. At the other extreme, these meanings are so muted that they are almost subliminal, as in the following passage from *Bleak House,* where contrasting images are innocently separated by the chapter division. Jo has temporarily paused from his incessant "moving on" toward his death. He sits "munching and gnawing" near St. Paul's Cathedral.

> There he sits, the sun going down, the river running fast, the crowd flowing by him in two streams—everything moving on to some purpose and to one end—until he is stirred up and told to "move on" too.
>
> Chapter 20
>
> The long vacation saunters on towards term-time like an idle river very leisurely strolling down a flat country to the sea. Mr. Guppy saunters along with it congenially. (*BH*, chs. 19, 20)

The urgency of time running out permeates the first sentence: Jo's personal river drawing fast to the sea, the streams of people flowing indifferently past him in two directions, until someone casts him out (like Martha) and moves him on away from the main current of people preoccupied with "some purpose," while all thoughtlessly move on "to one end." With the next sentence, Mr. Guppy, finny inhabitant of the main stream, saunters along, complacently unconscious of approaching "term-time," through a "leisurely" pastoral scene literally set in that same London. He may even be one of the "crowd flowing by" Jo. Multilayered irony cuts sharply between the two chapters: Jo, the innocent doomed child, belonging to and yet cast out from the corrupt stream in which Guppy moves; Guppy pursuing his childlike course along the innocent up-country river without thought of responsibility; and the actual river, unnoticed by Jo, Guppy, or the crowd, though it is "running fast" past the little scene. The function of the river cluster is pivotal for the ironic accents with their implicit warning, later in the story to be made most abundantly explicit as Jo proves his universal brotherhood by democratically sharing his disease: the indifferent river of humanity can ill afford to ignore the corruption and urgency of the river beside which Jo sits momentarily.

At all times the river flows fast as it approaches the sea, but it flows fastest when the tide is ebbing; now of all times and between the tidal boundaries of all places is a human body likely to be found floating among the other refuse. Part of the impact of the analogy to life arises, as usual, from the fact that the statement is literally true. Mr. Crisparkle, joining the search for Edwin Drood, uses this fact to guide him: "No search had been made up here, for the tide had been running strongly down . . . and the likeliest places for the discovery of a body, if a fatal accident had happened under such circumstances, all lay—both when the tide ebbed, and when it flowed again—between that spot and the sea" (*MED*, ch. 16). If a body exists anywhere in the river, most likely it will be here. But the meaning quickly spills over into the terrifying knowledge that a human body in the river is a somehow guilty thing. Who in reading of this does not find reenforced the presentiment that Edwin Drood has been foully murdered?

Gaffer Hexam makes a living from knowing where a body may be found. In the first chapter of *Our Mutual Friend*, he and his daughter Lizzie are abroad on the river at a crucial time, for "the tide, which had turned an hour before, was running down" (*OMF*, bk. I, ch. 1). Lizzie, guiding the boat, watches her father's face to catch his signalled directions, and "in the intensity of her look there was a touch of dread or horror." Somehow, if her father is not the cause of her horror, he is in some way implicated. The man is completely absorbed by the immediate situation, but whatever the business at hand, he trusts the girl to guide the boat according to his signals. This situation calls forth Lizzie's reaction of terror as the light from the setting sun "glanced into the bottom of the boat, and touching a rotten stain there which bore some resemblance to the outline of a muffled human form, coloured it as though with diluted blood." The "rottenness" of this stain has no literal referent. The description is furnished by the girl's suggestible state of mind: the affective value of the statement is a deepened suggestion of human involvement in some horrible act.

Although the surface hint throughout this chapter suggests that Gaffer might himself be a murderer, and although Dickens makes the most of the uncertainty in the later accusations against the man, he is not as a matter of fact guilty of the charge—nor does Lizzie herself harbor the clear suspicion. The guilt invoked is more profoundly the vague guilt implicit in the image clusters of the lower river and the ebbing tide. Lizzie's feelings of terror are heightened by her father's matter-of-factness. He reasons with her, pointing out her ingratitude to the provident river, and the impossibility of hurting a lifeless body. To him, the human body is merely valuable salvage drifting among the other debris, and after this successful expedition, he glances with nothing but satisfaction over the stern "at something the boat had in tow." The girl, however, has "pulled the hood of the cloak she wore over her head and over her face."

The course of the river, then, provides a persistent pattern of images suggestive of the course of human life. Although its irreversible movement from source to sea relates it to time, the river and time are not the same. A highly charged passage from *Our Mutual Friend* dramatically illustrates their interlaced yet separable meanings. Bella is on a train rushing her to the bedside of Eugene Wrayburn, who is expected to die momentarily.

> Then, the train rattled among the house-tops, and among the ragged sides of houses torn down to make way for it, and over the swarming streets, and under the fruitful earth, until it shot across the river: bursting over the quiet surface like a bombshell, and gone again as if it had exploded in the rush of smoke and steam and glare. A little more, and again it roared across the river, a great rocket: spurning the watery turnings and doublings with ineffable contempt, and going straight to its end, as Father Time goes to his. To whom it is no matter what living waters run high or low, reflect the heavenly lights and darknesses, produce their little growth of weeds and flowers, turn here, turn there, are noisy or still, are troubled or at rest, for their course has one sure termination, though their sources and devices are many. (*OMF,* bk. II, ch. 11)

Then into a carriage, and "the nearer they drew to the chamber where Eugene lay, the more they feared that they might find his wanderings done." Finally, Bella sits by the bedside with the others, silently waiting: "And now, in this night-watch, mingling with the flow of the river and with the rush of the train, came the questions into Bella's mind again . . ."

Within the images of train and river here associated, two ways of looking at time are portrayed.[8] One of these pictures presents time as a metronomic and objective measurement of duration. This is the train rushing straight through the night at unvarying rate. The other picture, of the turning and doubling river, presents the relative and subjective measurement of duration. However long and leisurely a summer day may seem to Guppy, it is still only twenty-four hours long. All the "watery turnings and doublings" by which an individual may gain the illusion that time has stopped cannot negate the objective fact that it actually carries him along at exactly the same rate.[9]

Thus the muted ironic warning contained in the juxtaposed passages from *Bleak House* receives in *Our Mutual Friend* a more direct and rhetorical statement. Human life, it reiterates, may sometimes meander and dawdle with a quite unwarranted sense of leisure, while time thunders relentlessly across it at the same pace whether the river is far up country or close to the sea. Although a

Guppy or a Gaffer does not see it, the warning flows along under their noses. The more thoughtful among mankind, however, feel with Lizzie the terror of its threat and, like Bella, are led to question the course of their lives.

## 2

The marsh assemblage of images implies the mystery shrouding the beginning and end of temporal existence. These images form an ambiguous grouping in which the origins and destiny of every individual are darkly linked in the unknown preceding birth and following death. Life comes up out of the sea through the marsh; it is drawn back through the marsh into the sea. Water, air, land, and stones mix confusedly here. The picture is a landscape only—not a seascape—for visibility ceases this side of the point where the land finally disappears. One hears and feels the sea in the winds surging inland, but it is not clearly seen.

The marsh, then, borders the sea. Long lines stretch across it: the river, the edge of the sea, streaks in the sky, occasional stepping-stones. It is a featureless waste, broken only where some man-made structure rears up blackly against the sky, or where some living creature passes momentarily across it. It is a place of fog, darkness, cold, wet, east wind and implacable wintry weather. Time is of no consequence in this world where it is perpetually twilight or nighttime. Such life as the marsh affords has come up out of sea and mud. It is primitive and threatening: reptiles, amphibians, and huge monsters; cold-blooded, mindless, sometimes savage. These creatures lurch and waddle and limp and jerk in a fearful parody of the rhythmic grace of life. An aura of vague guilt pervades the marsh. The only colors here are black, gray, and the lurid red or purple of violence, often brought together in the red sunrise or sunset. At the edge of the marsh the graveyard lies in the shadow of the vaguely suggested church. The church/graveyard itself is an uneasy border between life and the ambiguous marsh country.

This is recognizably the land where the reader first meets Pip, "a small bundle of shivers growing afraid of it all and beginning to cry" (*GE*, ch. 1). Although *Great Expectations* is narrated by a grown-up Pip who at first expects to look back on his childish view of things with a mixture of amusement and condescension, his detachment quickly vanishes as memory draws him back to *be* again that child; for however intellectually superior the adult may be to his childish concepts, their emotional impact upon him is as compelling as ever.[10] What has created his terror? Pip recreates his impressions for the reader:

> Ours was the marsh country, down by the river, within, as the river wound, twenty miles of the sea. My first most vivid and broad impression of the identity of things seems to me to have been gained on a memorable raw afternoon towards evening. At such a time I found out for certain that this bleak place overgrown with nettles was the churchyard; and that Philip Pirrip, late of the Parish, and also Georgiana Wife of the Above, were dead and buried; and that Alexander, Bartholomew, Abraham, Tobias, and Roger, infant children of the aforesaid, were also dead and buried; and that the dark flat wilderness beyond the churchyard, intersected with dikes and mounds and gates, with scattered cattle feeding on it, was the marshes; and that the low leaden line beyond was the river; and that the distant savage lair from which the wind was rushing was the sea; and that the small bundle of shivers growing afraid of it all and beginning to cry was Pip. (ch. 1)

This memorable raw afternoon brings to birth Pip's first real apprehension of his own identity as a mortal human being as he finds out "for certain" what the graveyard and the marsh mean. The flat, ritual intonations induced by the repeated words—"that"/"and that" (repeated seven times) and "dead and buried"/"dead and buried"—well convey his chilling certainty regarding the bleak "identity of things." The father and mother and little brothers, no longer comfortably interchangeable with the letters on a tombstone or with "five little stone lozenges" were all real people, "dead and buried," to whom he himself is ominously linked. His origin and his destiny lie together in the graveyard. Simultaneously he feels a fearful relationship between himself and the sea, unseen but sensed in the wind across the marsh. The darkness, the flatness, the low leaden line (all somehow the negation of life) bring close that "distant savage lair" from which not only the wind but all kinds of monstrous creatures might momentarily emerge.

In this setting, Pip has his encounter with "the fearful man," who will be more fully discussed in the next chapter. All of Pip's impressions of the convict Magwitch are derived from, magnified by, and indelibly recorded on his consciousness by association with this marshland. At the end of the episode, his fear of the man himself is not sufficiently engrossing to prevent a last sweeping glance across the total landscape:

> The marshes were just a long black horizontal line then, as I stopped to look after him; and the river was just another horizontal line, not nearly so broad nor yet so black; and the sky was just a row of long red lines and dense black lines intermixed. On the edge of the river I could faintly make out the only two black things in all the prospect that seemed to be standing upright; one of these was the beacon by which the sailors steered—like an unhooped cask upon a pole—an ugly thing when you were near it; the other a gibbet, with some chains hanging to it which had once held a pirate. (ch. 1)

The Dickens language and imagery everywhere show a lively apprehension that diversity is a basic quality of life and an indispensable sign of life: the monotony[11] of the marsh bespeaks its lifelessness. It is appropriately significant that the only features breaking this monotony—"the only . . . things in all the prospect that seemed to be standing upright"—are manmade intrusions: gravelike mounds and mound-like humps, a gibbet, and a lighthouse that is, perhaps not surprisingly, an "ugly thing." Since human life does not really belong in the marsh, its representations there are all ominously cold and deathlike things. When young David Copperfield comes down to Yarmouth for the first time, however, he finds he would welcome even these dark evidences of life. He reports:

> I was quite tired, and very glad, when we saw Yarmouth. It looked rather spongy and soppy, I thought, as I carried my eye over the great dull waste that lay across the river, and I could not help wondering, if the world were really as round as my geography book said, how any part of it came to be so flat. But I reflected that Yarmouth might be situated at one of the poles, which would account for it.
>
> As we drew a little nearer, and saw the whole adjacent prospect lying a straight low line under the sky, I hinted to Peggotty that a mound or so might have improved it,[12] and also that, if the land had been a little more separated from the sea, and the town and the tide had not been quite so much mixed up, like toast and water, it would have been nicer. (*DC*, ch. 3)

Thus innocently the frozen ("at one of the poles") featureless landscape and the mounds have glancingly foreshadowed the death association.[13]

The mounds of the marsh are obviously death emblems, frequently employed and running through other clusters to which they are appropriate. The marsh lighthouse (the beacon of *Great Expectations*, "an ugly thing when you are near it"), though less obvious, is even more insistent. It has an especially ominous value, for while mounds are fulfilling their intended function by containing death, the lighthouse makes a promise of safety it does not fulfill; it is surrounded by death and may sometimes deceptively lure people to it.

For Pip, the ugly lighthouse becomes indelibly associated with his first impressions of the convict Magwitch. Many years later it likewise becomes identified with his last desperate effort to save the life of his benefactor. Even though the trip down the river has seemed to start auspiciously ("The crisp air, the sunlight, the movement on the river, and the moving river itself—the road that ran with us, seeming to sympathize with us, animate us, and encourage us on—" [*GE,* ch. 54]), the presence of "two or three amphibious creatures" (typical of marsh life) as Herbert and Pip cast off from the Temple Stairs into the falling tide become foreboding signs. Gradually apprehension grows when "by imperceptible degrees, as the tide ran out, we lost more and more of the nearer woods and hills, and dropped lower and lower between the muddy banks . . ." Now the country around begins to lose its differentiated features and the banks form a monotonous, muddy continuation of the river. Pip recalls:

> It was like my own marsh country, flat and monotonous, and with a dim horizon; while the winding river turned and turned, and the great floating buoys upon it turned and turned, and everything else seemed stranded and still. . . . [S]ome ballast-lighters, shaped like a child's first rude imitation of a boat, lay low in the mud; and a little squat shoal-lighthouse on open piles stood crippled in the mud on stilts and crutches; and slimy stakes stuck out of the mud, and slimy stones stuck out of the mud, and red landmarks and tidemarks stuck out of the mud, and an old landing-stage and an old roofless building slipped into the mud, and all about us was stagnation and mud.
>
> We pushed off again, and made what way we could. It was much harder work now, but Herbert and Startop persevered, and rowed, and rowed, and rowed, until the sun went down. By that time the river had lifted us a little, so that we could see above the bank. There was the red sun, on the low level of the shore, in a purple haze, fast deepening into black; and there was the solitary flat marsh; and far away there were the rising grounds, between which and us there seemed to be no life, save here and there in the foreground a melancholy gull. (ch. 54)

This complex mingling of the marsh features and colors brings violence and death very close. Of particular interest at the moment is the little shoal-lighthouse, which "on open piles stood crippled in the mud on stilts and crutches." A deceptive lighthouse, through no fault of its own: the promises of safety are shipwrecked around its broken foundations as the ballast lighters "shaped like a child's first rude imitation of a boat" lie low in the mud.

The two references to red, the violent color associated with the marsh, are noteworthy in the neighborhood of the lighthouse. This color has its own little family of associations that play back and forth together throughout Dickens's writings and which need to be discussed before the ugly lighthouse can be fully explored. In the passage above, the "red sun" stands in ominous contrast to the earlier bright, cheerful sunlight that filled Pip with hope.

The appearance of the red sun(set) marks the entry into the night and violence of the marsh country, for to the sensitive person it suggests both destructive fire and spilled blood. It heightens the terror felt by Lizzie Hexam in the beginning of *Our Mutual Friend,* for instance. She steers her father's boat as it cruises the river on its obscurely threatening business. Suddenly,

> a slant of light from the setting sun glanced into the bottom of the boat, and, touching a rotten stain . . . coloured it as though with diluted blood. This caught the girl's eye, and she shivered.
>
> "What ails you?" said the man, immediately aware of it, though so intent on the advancing water; "I see nothing afloat."
>
> The red light was gone, the shudder was gone,[14] and his gaze, which had come back to the boat for a moment, traveled away again. (*OMF,* bk. I, ch. 1)

The red light of the setting sun and the association with spilled blood—suggested to Lizzie, though lost on her father—fuse and fade together.[15]

Later in the story, Lizzie is waiting beside the river for her father, who has been gone all night. The concentrated terror of the opening scene has given way to a haunting fear surrounding her thoughts of him. Appropriately: "The white face of the winter day came sluggishly on, veiled in a frosty mist, and the shadowy ships in the river slowly changed to black substances; and the sun, blood-red on the eastern marshes behind darks masts and yards, seemed filled with the ruins of a forest it had set on fire" (bk. I, ch. 6). At dawn, that other boundary of the night, the sun is also red. Here it trails in its wake the two violent associations of spilled blood and destructive fire.[16]

Still another variation occurs later in the book when Rogue Riderhood is stalking the murderously inclined Bradley Headstone, who is rowing along the river.

> The boat went on, under the arching[17] trees, and over their tranquil shadows in the water. The bargeman skulking on the opposite bank of the stream, went on after it. *Sparkles of light showed Riderhood when and where the rower dipped his blades, until, even as he stood idly watching, the sun went down and the landscape was dyed red.* And then the red had the appearance of fading out of it and mounting up to Heaven, as we say that blood, guiltily shed, does. (*OMF,* bk. IV, ch. 1. Emphasis mine.)

The italicized sentence shows the Dickens style at its poetic best, as the images coalesce differently in the imagination from the way in which they are physically presented. The "sparkles of light" flashing when and where the rower dipped his "blades" turn to red drops on a knife or dagger before the reader's eyes, while spilled blood stains the landscape.[18] The conventional analogy of the next sentence reduces the felt thought to the banality frequently evident when Dickens abandons his images and lapses into discursive explanation of their meaning. This passage from one of the last novels illustrates that, despite the evidences of developing craftsmanship in compression, economy, and control, Dickens never learned dependably to rely on presentation—on "showing": he might well occasionally add the damaging pedestrian explanation in late as in early works.[19]

It is now possible to discuss the ugly lighthouse, which is frequently drawn into the configuration of red sun, fire, and blood. Sometimes its red light imitates the red sun to designate it as a siren beacon luring into the marsh. Sometimes unlighted itself, it draws redness to itself, as in the unspecified "red landmarks and tidemarks" that are neighbors to the crippled lighthouse observed by Pip.

In *The Mystery of Edwin Drood,* the reader gradually comes to realize that John Jasper lives in an ugly lighthouse. Literally, to be sure, his dwelling is "an old stone gatehouse crossing the Close, with an arched thoroughfare passing beneath it." But:

> Through its latticed window, a fire[20] shines out upon the fast-darkening scene, involving in shadow the pendent masses of ivy and creeper covering the building's front. As the deep Cathedral-bell

> strikes the hour, a ripple of wind goes through these at their distance, like a ripple of the solemn sound that hums through tomb and tower, broken niche and defaced statue, in the pile close at hand. (*MED,* ch. 2)

Already the description contains oblique allusions to the lower river in the suggestion of the arched bridge with a stream flowing under it. The fire, barred by the lattice, is not cheery, but creates obscuring shadows. The "rippling" wind carries a hint of the sea, its connotations of death enhanced by the companion ripple of solemn sound humming through tombstones and stone representations of life. But these are only suggestive wisps. Midway through the story, the allusion becomes pointed. Jasper and Durdles, about to make a midnight excursion into the crypt of the cathedral, pause to glance around them: "The whole expanse of moonlight in their view is utterly deserted. One might fancy that the tide of life was stemmed by Mr. Jasper's own gatehouse. The murmur of the tide is heard beyond; but no wave passes the archway, over which his lamp burns red behind his curtain, as if the building were a Lighthouse" (ch. 12). Jasper's gatehouse, then, stands on the edge of the graveyard, the borderland beyond which life does not go. His lighthouse with its red light and ambiguous meaning is of the marsh: an ugly beacon surrounded by death.

On the evening Edwin will disappear, a terrible storm arises. As it continues through the night, John Jasper's gatehouse light "burns" reassuringly.

> The red light burns steadily all the evening in the lighthouse on the margin of the tide of busy life. Softened sounds and hum of traffic pass it and flow on irregularly into the lonely Precincts; but very little else goes by, save violent rushes of wind. It comes on to blow a boisterous gale. (ch. 14)

Further on:

> No such power of wind has blown for many a winter night. Chimneys topple in the streets, and people hold to posts and corners, and to one another, to keep themselves upon their feet. The violent rushes abate not, but increase in frequency and fury until at midnight, when the streets are empty, the storm goes thundering among them rattling at all the latches, and tearing at all the shutters, as if warning the people to get up and fly with it, rather than have the roofs brought down upon their brains.

> Still, the red light burns steadily. Nothing is steady but the red light. (ch. 14)

Despite the reassuring lighthouse, morning reveals the devastation all about, while time discloses that Edwin has vanished mysteriously sometime during the tempestuous night: the ominous steadiness of the deceptive red light has signaled not safety, but destructive violence.

In the last pages of the novel, left incomplete but clearly approaching its crisis, Mr. Datchery, one of Dickens's indefatigable bloodhounds, has appeared mysteriously on the scene. Convinced of Jasper's guilt in the disappearance of his nephew, Datchery has his own interpretation of the lighthouse: "John Jasper's lamp is kindled, and his lighthouse is shining when Mr. Datchery returns alone towards it. As Mariners on a dangerous voyage, approaching an iron-bound coast, may look along the beams of the warning light to the haven lying beyond it that may never be reached, so Mr. Datchery's wistful gaze is directed to this beacon, and beyond" (ch. 23). The "warning light" has no power to deceive Datchery with its steadiness. Its warning for him is different as he warily seeks a way past it to the "haven" that is sure evidence of Jasper's guilt, the end of the case.

The ugly lighthouse takes its place along with the gibbet and the mounds as a prominent feature in the perspective picture of the marsh, itself a monotonous design of long horizontal lines against which such human structures of violence and corruption jut guiltily into the sky. As monotony is the prevailing characteristic of the marsh, human affairs smelling of the marsh share this characteristic. A striking example appears in *Hard Times*, in the portrayal of Coketown, a displaced marsh town.[21]

> Let us strike the keynote, Coketown, before pursuing our tune.
>
> It was a town of red brick or of brick that would have been red if the smoke and ashes had allowed it; but as matters stood it was a town of unnatural red and black like the painted face of a savage. It was a town of machinery and tall chimneys, out of which interminable serpents of smoke trailed themselves forever and ever, and never got uncoiled. It had a black canal in it, and a river that ran purple with ill-smelling dye, and vast piles of buildings full of windows where there was a rattling and a trembling all day long, and where the piston of the steam-engine worked monotonously up and down like the head of an elephant in a state of melancholy madness. It contained several large streets all very like one another, in-

> habited by people equally like one another, who all went in and out at the same hours, with the same sound upon the same pavements, to do the same work, and to whom every day was the same as yesterday and tomorrow, and every year the counterpart of the last and the next. (*HT*, ch. 5)[22]

The affective description of this industrial town produced by the marsh images once more reveals the analogizing nature of Dickens's thought as his fancy finds appropriate contextual parallels for the originally conceived interpretation. The long lines of river and sky become streets stretching off monotonously in all directions. It is a town of red, black, gray, and purple, with its own appropriately polluted river. The buildings stand in "vast piles" reminiscent of the open piles of the little shoal lighthouse, and their guilty man-made chimneys rear up to belch corrupting "serpents" of smoke, later described as the "monstrous serpents of smoke" which, "submissive to the curse of all that tribe, trailed themselves upon the earth" (ch. 11). Coupled with the painted savage and the mindless elephant, they represent the typical life of the marsh. Chimneys, like lighthouses, do not really belong in the deadly marsh except when they are "ugly": promising a cheery fireside, they produce only smoke or destruction (cf. the toppling chimneys in *Edwin Drood*). Chimneys in Coketown, "for want of air to make a draught, were built in an immense variety of stunted and crooked shapes," like the crippled little shoal-lighthouse. The only people who live "in the innermost fortifications of that ugly citadel," Coketown, are amphibious marsh creatures, "walking against time toward the infinite world," and "generically called 'the Hands'—a race who would have found more favour with some people if Providence had seen fit to make them only hands, or, like the lower creatures of the seashore, only hands and stomachs" (ch. 10).[23]

Everything in this world moves monotonously and mechanically: drearily, wearily, "in a state of melancholy madness." Added to the monotony of place, the deadly monotony of undifferentiated marsh time makes today like yesterday and tomorrow like today.

The London of *Bleak House* is also a marsh town. In the introductory chapter, emphasis falls on the "implacable weather" of the marsh, its wintry season, and its typical time of day: late afternoon, when the shadows are lengthening and no kind of light can illumine clearly enough for visibility. Later on, lamps will be effective; earlier, the sun was bright and cheerful. But now all light is swallowed in twilight:

> Implacable November weather. As much mud in the streets as if the waters had but newly retired from the face of the earth, and it would not be wonderful to meet a Megalosaurus, forty feet long or so, waddling like an elephantine lizard up Holborn Hill. Smoke lowering down from chimney-pots, making a soft black drizzle, with flakes of soot in it as big as full-grown snowflakes—gone into mourning, one might imagine, for the death of the sun. Dogs, undistinguishable in mire. Horses, scarcely better; splashed to their very blinkers. Foot passengers, jostling one another's umbrellas in a general infection of ill temper, and losing their foot-hold at street-corners, where tens of thousands of other foot passengers have been slipping and sliding since the day broke (if this day ever broke), adding new deposits to the crust upon crust of mud, sticking at those points tenaciously to the pavements, and accumulating at compound interest. (*BH*, ch. 1)

Here the waddling reptile (the "elephantine lizard" imaginatively merging with the Coketown elephant) and the modern creatures abroad in "London, Michaelmas term lately over, and the Lord Chancellor sitting in Lincoln's Inn Hall," all slip and slide together through the eternal mud, the time between them completely canceled out. The guilty drizzle of smoke parodies snow in its flakes of soot, which, along with the fog rolling through the next paragraph, reduce vision to a blur. It is a "raw afternoon" with: "Gas looming through the fog in divers places in the streets, much as the sun may, from the spongey fields, be seen to loom by husbandman and ploughboy. Most of the shops lighted two hours before their time—as the gas seems to know, for it has a haggard and unwilling look." This eerily luminous gas, like the lighthouse and chimney, belongs here because of its gloomy failure to achieve its usual purpose. It "has a haggard and unwilling look," and may be seen "much as the sun may"—which is to say very little on this day of the sun's death.

If London is like the marsh, so is the Court of Chancery, with its own analogous images: its "groping" and "floundering"; with the "foggy glory" around the head of the Lord High Chancellor appropriately sitting on "such an afternoon," outwardly "directing his contemplation to the lantern in the roof, where he can see nothing but fog"; the members of the High Court "mistily engaged" and "tripping one another up on slippery precedents, groping knee-deep in technicalities," and running their heads against "walls of words"—or accumulated mud; the "crimson cloth and curtains" and "red table"; the "wasting candles" in the "dim" court where "stained glass windows lose their colour and admit no light," where the chancellor looks into "the lantern that has no light in it," and where "the attendant wigs are all stuck in a fogbank." All of these images establish the Court of Chancery as authentic marsh country "which gives to monied might the means abundantly of wearying out the right." The case of Jarndyce and Jarndyce, the most monotonously pre-eminent of the suits in chancery, "still drags its dreary[24] length before the court, perennially hopeless." This wounded snake, sluggish and crippled, looks quite at home in the surrounding marsh. Equally at home, "in the midst of the mud and at the heart of the fog, sits the Lord High Chancellor in his High Court of Chancery."

> "Mr. Tangle," says the Lord High Chancellor, latterly something restless under the eloquence of that learned gentleman.
>
> "Mlud," says Mr. Tangle. (ch. 1)

Thus innocently Dickens touches together two strands of meaning to create a titillating shock of recognition in the imaginative fusing of his Lordship and the obstructive mud.

The deadening effects of the marsh reach out beyond London to touch other places connected with the story. Esther's guardian, though he will have nothing to do with the suit, cannot escape being a Jarndyce.

> "The Jarndyce in question," said the Lord Chancellor, still turning over leaves, "is Jarndyce of Bleak House."
>
> "Jarndyce of Bleak House, my lord," said Mr. Kenge.
>
> "A dreary name," said the Lord Chancellor.
>
> "But not a dreary place[25] at present, my lord," said Mr. Kenge. (ch. 3)

The home of John Jarndyce is not of the marsh, even if its name foreshadows that he must suffer effects from the bleak House of Jarndyce. Lady Dedlock's "place" in Lincolnshire,[26] on the other hand, is itself a dreary place. "The waters are out in Lincolnshire. An arch of the bridge in the park has been sapped and sopped away. The adjacent low-lying ground for half a mile in breadth is a stagnant river with melancholy trees for islands in it and a surface punctured all over, all day long, with falling rain. My Lady Dedlock's place has been extremely dreary" (ch. 2). Lady Dedlock feels the dreary effects of the marsh directly, as will be seen in the next chapter.

Jarndyce, on the other hand, acquires his premonitions and apprehensions indirectly, carried along the east wind that blows through the marsh, bitter and cold. This is the wind David Copperfield observes working its chilling effects on Mr. Dick: "How many winter days have I seen him, standing blue-nosed, in the snow and east wind, looking at the boys going down the long slide . . ." (*DC*, ch. 17). Or, more ominously, it is the "black east wind" of The Haunted Man (Christmas book for 1848), which "would spin like a huge humming-top" through a frozen world. In the case of John Jarndyce, it is even more like the wind used to describe Mr. Twemlow in *Our Mutual Friend*, where Mr. Veneering's mirror reflects the little man confusedly trying to sort out Veneering's "old" friends: "grey, dry, polite, susceptible to east wind" (*OMF*, bk. I, ch. 2). Jarndyce, too, is susceptible to east wind, like Twemlow a kindly and warm human being troubled and easily chilled by marsh weather. In *Bleak House*, the people around Jarndyce, at first puzzled by his references to the east wind, soon come to accept them as merely his idiosyncratic way of stating alarm. Esther writes:

> "The little Jellybys," said Richard, coming to my relief, "are really—I can't help expressing myself strongly, sir—in a devil of a state."
>
> "She means well," said Mr. Jarndyce hastily. "The wind's in the east."
>
> "It was in the north, sir, as we came down," observed Richard.
>
> "My dear Rick," said Mr. Jarndyce, poking the fire, "I'll take an oath it's either in the east or going to be. I am always conscious of an uncomfortable sensation now and then when the wind is blowing in the east."
>
> "Rheumatism, sir?" said Richard.
>
> "I dare say it is, Rick. I believe it is . . ." (*BH*, ch. 6)

Ada and Esther interpret it differently, as Esther later explains:

> Ada and I agreed, as we talked together for a little while upstairs, that this caprice about the wind was a fiction and that he used the pretence to account for any disappointment he could not conceal, rather than he would blame the real cause of it or disparage or depreciate any one. We thought this very characteristic of his eccentric gentleness and of the difference between him and those petulant people who make the weather and the winds (particularly that unlucky wind which he had chosen for a different purpose) the stalking-horses of their splenetic and gloomy humours. (ch. 6)

Jarndyce's references to the east wind ordinarily have a whimsical and humorous look to them, giving him a lovable and eccentric character. But when he encounters the caged birds of Miss Flite, some of whose names indicate the wearying effects of the Chancery Court, the wind grows colder: "'This is a bitter wind!' muttered my guardian. . . . 'If ever the wind was in the east, . . . I think it's there today!'" (ch. 14). Attention in this exclamation, with its darkened tone, draws away from the speaker and more fittingly toward the thing he describes, with its source in the cold marshland: its prevailing east wind emblematizes the chill spirit of the marsh as a force in human affairs: blowing from the bleak wasteland across the entire world, this east wind carries with it everywhere the threat of frozen, guilty death.

Many of the images related to the marsh carry another common thread of meaning: in the marsh the elements have ceased to function in a natural way. In their natural state they nurture and sustain life, but in the unnatural state of the marsh they suspend it in a moribund atmosphere or threaten it with destruction. Water, fire (both light and heat), earth, and air malfunction or commingle to produce destructive paralysis or paralyzing destruction. Lighthouses lure to shipwreck; chimneys lean or topple. The sun either burns everything it touches, casts shadows, or "haggardly" fails to either light or warm the world. In weak imitation, the lamps and lanterns and candles of human creation waste futilely away. Fire burns threateningly or, in a fireplace, creates smoke rather than warmth. Water and earth turn into mud; earth and air become dust—and so on. In this unnatural setting, such "elemental" human structures as church and home similarly malfunction.

An extended example of natural elements gone awry opens *Little Dorrit,* where Dickens plunges the reader at once into a bewildering confusion of disjointed impressions. Caught between the "Sun and Shadow" of Marseilles, "broiling in the sun" of the "fierce August day," we arrive there along with all the other strangers "stared out of countenance" by the burning sun, the universal stare "making the eyes ache." The stare of this sun shining off every object creates an impenetrable, blinding surface. All of the anonymous inhabitants of Marseilles on this fierce day flee from its blinding stare into the equally obscuring shadowy recesses of houses, churches, or prison. This is not a "natural" sun enlivening a natural scene; rather, it malfunctions as the lighthouses of the marsh do. The city, which should, one would think, be a beehive of activity and life, hangs instead in the motionless suspension of the marsh. Outside the foul water of its harbor lies the natural world of the "beautiful sea," but a line of demarcation shows "the point which the pure sea would not pass" (*LD,* bk. I, ch. 1).

The churches of Marseilles also bear the marks of the marsh-bordering churches. The sun, which "grant it but a chink or keyhole . . . shot in like a white-hot arrow," cannot penetrate their walls: "The churches were the freest from it. To come out of the twilight of pillars and arches—dreamily dotted with winking lamps, dreamily peopled with ugly old shadows piously dozing, spitting, and begging—was to plunge into a fiery river, and swim for life to the nearest strip of shade." These churches lack effective light of any nature. They exist in a dream world filled with ominous images. Yet to leave their shadows for the sun or the "river"—unnaturally fiery—of the outside world exposes one to out-of-control elements. The prison, too, while shutting out the malfunctioning sun, has also effectively shut out the "light of day": "'Day? the light of yesterday week, the light of six months ago, the light of six years ago. So slack and dead!'"

In chapter 3, when Arthur Clennam comes "Home" to London and to the "House" in which he was reared, the city extending around him is, like Marseilles, a world suspended in time. He is surrounded by malfunctioning churches. "Maddening church bells of all degrees of dissonance" echo hideously around him, newly arrived on this Sabbath day. Also surrounding him are "Ten thousand responsible houses" frowning their disapproval, and "fifty thousand lairs" gasping for air in the "heart of the town [through which] a deadly sewer ebbed and flowed, in the place of a fine fresh river" (bk. I, ch. 3).

As the day dies around Clennam, sitting in a coffeehouse on this evening of his return home, the rain begins to fall, and the mud seems "to collect in a moment . . . and in five minutes to have splashed all the sons and daughters of Adam." Taking up his hat and buttoning his coat, Arthur walks out and into the unnatural rain. "In the country the rain would have developed a thousand fresh scents, and every drop would have had its bright association with some form of growth or life." But here, "it developed only foul stale smells."

Proceeding past St. Paul's and along the river, he passes through "a narrow alley leading to the river, where a wretched little bill, FOUND DROWNED, was weeping on the wet wall"; and now "he came at last to the house he sought": "a double-house, with long, narrow, heavily-framed windows. Many years ago, it had had it in its mind to slide down sideways; it had been propped up, however, [like the ineffectual little shoal-lighthouse] and was leaning on some half-dozen gigantic crutches." The House of Clennam is clearly tagged as a marsh dwelling.

Midway through the novel, Dickens reminds the reader of the suspended world through which the story is moving. It is now autumn, with darkness and night creeping up to the highest ridges of the Alps where several groups of weary travellers make their way upward through the Pass of the Great Saint Bernard toward the convent located in the frosty, rarified air at the top. They struggle through barrenness and desolation:

> Blackened skeleton arms of wood by the wayside pointed upward to the convent, as if the ghosts of former travellers overwhelmed by the snow haunted the scene of their distress. Icicle-hung caves and cellars built for refuges from sudden storms, were like so many whispers of the perils of the place; never-resting wreaths and mazes of mist wandered about, hunted by a moaning wind; and snow, the besetting danger of the mountain, against which all its defences were taken, drifted sharply down. (bk. II, ch. 1)

Arriving finally at the "weather-beaten structure" like "another Ark," which is the convent/inn at the top of the pass, the travellers are met by their "host," a "bright-eyed, dark young man of polite manners . . . who no more resembled the conventional breed of Saint Bernard monks than he resembled the conventional breed of Saint Bernard dogs." The convent, in fact, functions more as an "inn" than as a religious institution. Thus "rarified" is the representation of the church in the frosty world "up here in the clouds, [where] everything was seen through cloud, and seemed dissolving into cloud." Like Marseilles on that earlier fierce August day, up here is a dream world arrested in time, in this instance not by unbearable light and heat, but rather by equally unbearable darkness and freezing cold.

Through all of its manifestations in the novels, the static, timeless world of the marsh is a parody of "conventional" ideas about an eternity that contrasts with the temporality of life. Even if behind its images hovers the reality of a mysterious realm preceding birth and following death, the images themselves are analogies for human states of mind and action that imitate the state of death. The stony coldness of literal death is permanent. Under the proper circumstances, however, the frozen guilty death of the marsh world can be warmed and softened into the flexibility of life.

## 3

Although the river-marsh configurations have been treated separately so far, in actual practice they are frequently impossible to disentangle without diminishing their combined effect: a clear case where, as is very often true in the functional interplay of the configurations abstracted in this study, the whole is greater—richer and deeper—than the sum of its parts. Dickens provides a fine example of such a combination at the beginning of an obscure journalistic piece (also referred to in note 7), "Down with the Tide," a title itself alluding to marsh and lower river. Its first few paragraphs are reproduced here:

> A very dark night it was, and bitter cold; the east wind blowing bleak and bringing with it stinging particles from marsh, and moor, and fen—from the Great Desert and Old Egypt, may be. Some of the component parts of the sharp-edged vapor that came flying up the Thames at London might be mummy-dust, dry atoms from the Temple at Jerusalem, camels' footprints, crocodiles' hatching places, loosened grains of expression from the visages of blunt-nosed sphynxes, waifs and strays from caravans of turbaned merchants, vegetation from jungles, frozen snow from the Himalayas. O! It was very dark upon the Thames, and it was bitter bitter cold.
>
> "And yet," said the voice within the great pea-coat at my side, "you'll have seen a good many rivers too, I dare say?"
>
> "Truly," said I, "when I come to think of it, not a few. From the Niagara, downward to the mountain rivers of Italy, which are like the national spirit—very tame, or chafing suddenly and bursting bounds, only to dwindle away again. The Moselle, and the Rhine, and the Rhone; and the Seine, and the Saone; and the St. Lawrence, Mississippi, and Ohio; and the Tiber, the Po, and the Arno; and the—"
>
> Peacoat coughing, as if he had had enough of that, I said no more. I could have carried the catalogue on to a teazing length, though, if I had been in the cruel mind.
>
> "And after all," said he, "this looks so dismal?"
>
> "So awful," I returned, "at night. The Seine at Paris is very gloomy too, at such a time, and is probably the scene of far more crime and greater wickedness; but this river looks so broad and vast, so murky and silent, seems such an image of death in the midst of the great city's life, that—"

> That Peacoat coughed again. He *could not* stand my holding forth.
>
> We were in a four-oared Thames Police Galley, lying on our oars in the deep shadow of Southwark Bridge—under the corner arch on the Surrey side—having come down with the tide from Vauxhall. We were fain to hold on pretty tight though close in shore, for the river was swollen and the tide running down very strong. We were watching certain water-rats of human growth, and lay in the deep shade as quiet as mice; our light hidden and our scraps of conversation carried on in whispers. Above us, the massive iron girders of the arch were faintly visible, and below us its ponderous shadow seemed to sink down to the bottom of the stream. (*DT*)

Is it by coincidence that this bit of atmospheric reporting contains many of the characteristic images, analogies, and associational relationships of both river and marsh? On the night in question, Dickens was allegedly being given a guided tour of the facilities and activities of the River Police—his guide a matter-of-fact police officer made uneasy by the reporter's apparently rhetorical flights of fancy. His own half-rueful, half-amused acknowledgment of his guide's lack of appreciation masks the fact that, far from being whimsical, every detail belongs in a large picture carried permanently in the mind of the writer.[27]

The first paragraph reconstructs the marsh through a combination of real and fancied details, carefully conveying that not only the present, but also the whole dead past resides in this timeless world to be blown as dust across the living by the cold east wind. This, then, is the large setting for a night on the river. A middle setting emerges in paragraph three with the catalogue of rivers, which sends the reader's imagination out across the earth as it has already been sent out across time. Thus all time and space hang suspended around the little boat as the writer continues with the analogy toward which he has all this time been working: "This river looks so broad and vast, so murky and silent, seems such an image of death in the midst of the great city's life . . ."

Now the reporter moves in to describe the immediate scene with a series of carefully chosen details: the "deep shadow," reiterated as "deep shade" and "ponderous shadow"; the bridge; the reiterated arch, the swollen river and the "down with the tide" of the title twice repeated, once verbatim and once as "the tide running down very strong"; the hidden light, the faint visibility, the suggestion of human guilt as they watch "certain water-rats of human growth"; and finally, the imaginative following of the shadow as it "seemed to sink down to the [muddy] bottom of the stream." It seems clear that the complex assemblage of suggestive images from river and marsh reflects Dickens's desire to evoke the background against which to project his ensuing discussion of murder and suicide along the Thames.

Both river and marsh are needed in this picture because, while their connotations are similar in three important respects (their association with death; their ambiguous, vague guilt; their implicit warning), they are very different in their relationship to time. Whereas the warning of the rushing river is of time running out, the timeless world of the marsh, it will be shown, seems to warn even more against death-in-life than it does against the fact of literal death. Human life, it says, which like the marsh is cold, rigid, and monotonous, is no life at all. This warning will be more clearly delineated in the next chapter. Both river and marsh, by projecting the brief human life span against the cosmic background of eternity and infinity, stress the urgency for every individual to live fully each passing moment.

# III

## *Marsh Creatures*

AMPHIBIOUS PEOPLE, savages, and cold-blooded monsters are the travesties of human life to be found haunting river and marshland. Fully alive human beings, like the lighthouses and chimneys—emblems of the light and warmth of human society—do not belong here; even dead ones come no closer than the bordering graveyard. These marsh denizens are either for some reason subhuman, or else have been in some way dehumanized; that is, they may be drawn into the marsh either because they themselves share its characteristics, or because they have been blighted by it. The aura of ambiguous guilt continues to prevail here, where even the victim is usually not completely innocent. (Conversely, few villains are completely guilty.) The responsibility for a person's condition may rest upon that person, or upon society—or vaguely on both. This double source of guilt is doubly felt by a sensitive individual, such as Pip; whether the guilt is Pip's alone, or his as a representative of society—or both—he is always guilty. However civilized he may be, he is made to realize that he contains the savage and the monster within himself.

True marsh creatures are not this sensitive to their condition or they would struggle against it. But sometimes, with varying results, the marsh reaches outside itself, as in the cold east wind, to touch sensitive human beings. John Jarndyce is only chilled, but Lady Dedlock and other more susceptible people freeze or are blighted by this touch.

## 1

*Great Expectations,* with its initial physical setting in the marsh, is once again an obvious place to begin as we look for evidence of marsh dwellers. Pip, "growing afraid of it all and beginning to cry," suddenly hears a frightening confirmation of his terror:

> "Hold your noise!" cried a terrible voice, as a man started up from among the graves at the side of the church porch. "Keep still, you little devil, or I'll cut your throat!"
>
> A fearful man, all in coarse gray, with a great iron on his leg. A man with no hat, and with broken shoes, and with an old rag tied round his head. A man who had been soaked in water, and smothered in mud, and lamed by stones, and cut by flints, and stung by nettles, and torn by briars; who limped, and shivered, and glared, and growled; and whose teeth chattered in his head, as he seized me by the chin. (*GE,* ch. 1)

Has the "fearful man" come out of the grave or out of that "distant savage lair" described in the preceding chapter? Either origin would be appropriate for this gray, water-soaked, mud-smothered, shivering-cold, threatening creature. Vague suggestions of guilt surround him. Is he perpetrator or victim? The images hint at both: the great iron on his leg and his being lamed by stones and cut by flints suggest both guilt and martyrdom. In his savage figure are epitomized Pip's felt terror of the sea, the marsh, and the graveyard. Primitive creatures, it seems, still roam this world, and dead men may rise to haunt the living.

At the end of the episode between Pip and the "fearful man," the man looks across the "cold wet flat" with the wish that he might have been a "frog" or an "eel." As he lurches away into the marshes, hugging "his shuddering body in both his arms—clasping himself, as if to hold himself together—" he seems a monster from the primitive past; he is also somehow tied to Pip's individual past as he picks his way past the green mounds looking "as if he were eluding the hands of the dead people, stretching up cautiously out of their graves to get a twist upon his ankle and pull him in." Pip takes to his heels, but: "presently I looked over my shoulder, and saw him going on again towards the river, still hugging himself in both arms, and picking his way with his sore feet among the great stones dropped into the marshes here and there for stepping-places when the rains were heavy, or the tide was in."

The feeling of terror pervading this first chapter of *Great Expectations* intensifies with the simple action, "I looked over my shoulder," for looking over one's shoulder is a particularly fearful way of looking, experienced by all children and remembered by all adults as a fragile defense against shadowy pursuers. The pictorially affective value of the scene is further enhanced by the "great stones" dropped "here and there for stepping-places when the rains were heavy or the tide was in." Although neither condition prevails at the moment, the apparently chance comment superimposes them both upon the picture spread before the reader, so that the primitive creature, larger than ordinary men in order to utilize the "great" stepping-stones, appears to be making his rain-blurred way back into the flood-tided sea.

Pip's attention reverts to the marsh itself until drawn back to the man, who is now near the gibbet with the "chains hanging to it which had once held a pirate." Pip imagines that "the man was limping on towards this latter, as if he were the pirate come to life, and come down, and going back to hook himself up again."[1] The indelible marsh picture in Pip's mind is a flat, featureless world with lines stretching forward, back, right, and left as far as the eye can see. Against this background the three monolithic representations of humanity rear upward, black and distinct and ugly: the beacon, the gibbet, and the primitive monster. "It gave me a terrible turn," says Pip; ". . . now I was frightened again, and ran home without stopping."

This important day in Pip's life marks the beginning of the feeling of personal guilt that is to haunt him. Part of its power over him comes from his unwilling identification with this primitive criminal-martyr, who comes out of and returns to the mysterious marsh. Later, he will have much difficulty in reconciling this image of Magwitch with his image of his fairy godmother. Meanwhile, it takes the strongest of holds upon him.

Two important associations here attach to the figure of Magwitch. First, he is twice associated with stones, once lamed by them, and once picking "his way with his sore feet among the great stones." The cold stone and the frozen rigidity of death look much alike, and the stone association quickly suggests the connotations of the marsh—ambiguously, for the laming by stones, which causes Magwitch to limp like a marsh monster, also hints at the martyrdom of St. Stephen. This marking of marsh monsters or victims through a stone association is a frequent leitmotif in Dickens. Just as earlier we learned that Pip found it difficult to dissociate his brothers from "five little stone lozenges," so in other contexts people who are affectively "dead" become stony people.[2]

The second association attaches to the "old rag" tied round Magwitch's head, which imaginatively fuses with the cut throat immediately preceding it, as well as with the later suggestions that the convict is a temporarily revivified hanged man on his way back to the gibbet. The hangman's noose figures prominently in Dickens's depiction of marsh monsters.

The lower river of *Our Mutual Friend* provides another physical setting understandably alive with marsh creatures. Two of these are Gaffer Hexam and Rogue Riderhood, whose archetypal habitat, though they make their living on the surface of the river, is the muddy river bottom that merges with the marshland. Gaffer is much the more complex—and therefore more nearly human—of the two. His boat is "allied to the bottom of the river rather than the surface by reason of the slime and ooze with which it was covered, and its sodden state," and he himself is "half savage . . . with no covering on his matted head, with his brown arms bare to between the elbow and the shoulder, with a loose knot of a looser kerchief lying low on his bare breast in a wilderness of beard and whisker, with such dress as he wore seeming to be made out of the mud that begrimed his boat" (*OMF,* bk. I, ch. 1). The man, like the boat, seems entirely at home in this primeval world of slime and ooze. The only item of his dress emerging clearly from the mud is the loosely knotted kerchief, suggestive of the hangman's noose.

That Gaffer is not completely subhuman, however, is evident in his tender relationship to his daughter Lizzie. As a web of circumstantial evidence seems to tighten around her father, Lizzie grows extremely apprehensive and susceptible to suggestion: it is the evening of the day when she associated the red sunrise with blood and fire. Her father, angry at his runaway son, repeatedly strikes his knife wrathfully into the table as he discusses the situation with Lizzie. His daughter cannot contain a cry of horror as she begs him to put the knife down. Bewildered by her obvious fear, he questions her. "What should I hurt?" he asks.

> "Nothing, dear father. On my knees, I am certain, in my heart and soul I am certain, nothing! But it was too dreadful to bear; for it

> looked—" her hands covering her face again, "O it looked—"
> 
> "What did it look like?"
> 
> The recollection of his murderous figure, combining with her trial of last night, and her trial of the morning, caused her to drop at his feet, without having answered. (bk. I, ch. 6)

Now, in contrast to his earlier threatening appearance, Gaffer tries "with the utmost tenderness" to revive this "best of daughters," and failing in his efforts runs out the door with the empty brandy bottle clutched in his hands. But:

> He returned as hurriedly as he had gone, with the bottle still empty. He kneeled down by her, took her head on his arm, and moistened her lips with a little water into which he had dipped his fingers: saying fiercely, as he looked around, now over this shoulder, now over that:
> 
> "Have we got a pest in the house? Is there summ'at deadly sticking to my clothes? What's let loose upon us? Who loosed it?" (bk. I, ch. 6)

Ironically, as with Magwitch, what he seeks and fears as he looks over his shoulders is embodied in himself. His fierce and bewildered questions are vaguely accusatory, giving him the pathetic helplessness of an innocent, held semi-savage through no volition of his own. He is as complete a human being as circumstances have enabled him to be.

Gaffer's children also demonstrate his potential humanity. His daughter, Lizzie, is warmly and completely human; his son, Charley, stands somewhere between his father and his sister.

> There was a curious mixture in the boy, of uncompleted savagery, and uncompleted civilization. His voice was hoarse and coarse, and his face was coarse, and his stunted figure was coarse; but he was cleaner than other boys of his type; and his writing, though large and round, was good; and he glanced at the backs of the books, with an awakened curiosity that went below the binding. No one who can read, ever looks at a book, even unopened on a shelf, like one who cannot. (bk. I, ch. 3)

The boy foreshadows the man, for though his reading marks him as a potential human being with "awakened curiosity," the effects of the marsh stay upon him.

In contrast to Gaffer, Rogue Riderhood, though crafty, is a simple man with uncomplicated purposes. As he sets about his evil purpose of fastening the supposed murder of John Harmon upon Gaffer, Mortimer Lightwood and Eugene Wrayburn follow him and observe him closely.

> He went on before them as an ugly Fate might have done, and they kept him in view, and would have been glad enough to lose sight of him. But on he went before them always at the same distance, and the same rate. Aslant against the hard implacable weather and the rough wind, he was no more to be driven back than hurried forward, but held on like an advancing Destiny. There came, when they were about midway on their journey, a heavy rush of hail, which in a few minutes pelted the streets clear, and whitened them. It made no difference to him. A man's life to be taken and the price of it got, the hailstones to arrest the purpose must be larger and deeper than those. He crushed through them, leaving marks in the fast-melting slush that were shapeless holes; one might have fancied, following, that the very fashion of humanity had departed from his feet. (bk. I, ch. 12)

Gaffer was savage, but this man is a monster like the antediluvian reptiles, with impenetrable hide and shapeless feet crushing his unswerving way through the marsh, outside the movement of time, "no more to be driven back than hurried forward." He has the absentmindedness of obsessive, destructive purpose: heedless, impervious, implacable like the weather he ignores. Later on, Rogue is himself fished from the river into which so many in this book fall. Although he is unconscious and near death, it becomes apparent that he will not after all die: "the low, bad, unimpressible face is coming up from the depths of the river, or what other depths, to the surface again" (bk. III, ch. 3). The depths of the river, the depths of the marsh, the depths of death, the depths of time, the depths of depravity: all are conjured up by this reverberating sentence.

Rogue Riderhood seems to sense other marsh creatures. Later in the story he realizes the murderous intentions of Bradley Headstone and decides to lay a trap for the schoolmaster. Rogue suspects that Headstone is deliberately copying his dress so that evidence will point to him when the murder is committed. Rogue therefore decides to alter one article of his clothing.

> Rogue Riderhood went into his Lock-house, and brought forth, into the now sober gray light, his chest of clothes. Sitting on the grass beside it, he turned out, one by one, the articles it contained, until he came to a conspicuous bright red neckerchief stained black here and there by wear. It arrested his attention, and he sat pausing over it,

> until he took off the rusty colourless wisp that he wore round his throat, and substituted the red neckerchief, leaving the long ends flowing. "Now," said the Rogue, "if arter he sees me in this neck-hankecher I see him in a sim'lar neckhankecher, it won't be accident." (bk. IV, ch. 1).

Neither is the choice of a "neckhankecher" with its interplay of marsh colors an accident. It is related to the "loose kerchief" worn by Gaffer and to the hangman's noose. On the occasion already noted when Eugene and Mortimer are following Riderhood, the two exchange comments regarding their impression of him: "'Look at his hang-dog air,' said Lightwood, following." To which Eugene replies, "'It strikes me rather as a hang-*man* air. . . . He has undeniable intentions that way" (bk. I, ch. 12). Here, as elsewhere in *Our Mutual Friend,* an ambiguity of guilt hangs over Riderhood as it did over the others. Victim or sinner? Probably both. Regardless, he is an evil monster.

Both Gaffer the savage and Riderhood the monster belong among "those amphibious human creatures who appear to have some mysterious power of extracting a subsistence out of tidal water by looking at it" (bk. I, ch. 6). Their counterparts are sprinkled throughout Dickens's works. When the actual term "amphibious" occurs the reference is usually to anomalous creatures along the waterfront who, like Charley Hexam, are "hoarse" and "coarse" and "stunted." Unlike him, they are usually mud-covered, simple-minded, and singleminded, often seen in dogged pursuit of some undeviating purpose. Or, as with the "two or three amphibious creatures" around Temple Stairs when Pip and Herbert are getting into their boat, their presence merely implies the marsh setting. Sometimes savages or monsters, they are always a little less than human—reiterated reminders of that gray borderland between man and reptile.

The long parade of marsh monsters in the Dickens novels began many years before either *Great Expectations* or *Our Mutual Friend* was written. Fagin and Bill Sikes head the procession. Dickens introduces Fagin as "a very old shrivelled Jew, whose villainous-looking and repulsive face was obscured by a quantity of matted red hair. He was dressed in a greasy flannel gown, with his throat bare; and seemed to be dividing his attention between the frying-pan and a clothes-horse, over which a great number of silk handkerchiefs were hanging" (*OT,* ch. 8). This conspicuously bare throat begins a leitmotif between handkerchiefs and throats that runs through the book. An important stock-in-trade for the old master thief is the silk handkerchief; it is one of the first items he teaches his boys to filch with deftness. In any "Emporium of petty larceny" to be found in the narrow and dismal alley leading to Saffron Hill, these pilfered articles are offered for sale:

> In its filthy shops are exposed for sale, huge bunches of second-hand silk handkerchiefs, of all sizes and patterns; for here reside the traders who purchase them from pickpockets. Hundreds of these handkerchiefs hang dangling from pegs outside the windows, or flaunting from the doorposts; and the shelves, within, are piled with them. (ch. 26)

Quite understandably, Fagin and his companions have a very sensitive feeling about their throats.

In an early conversation between Sikes and Fagin, the former indulges in a bit of descriptive pantomime: "tying an imaginary knot under his left ear, and jerking his head over on the right shoulder; a piece of dumb show which the Jew appeared to understand perfectly" (ch. 13).[3] On a later occasion, Fagin finds it useful to remind Bolter of the one fact none of them forgets for long: "'Only think,' said the Jew, shrugging his shoulders and stretching out his hands; 'only consider. You've done what's a very pretty thing, and what I love you for doing; but what at the same time would put the cravat round your throat, that's so very easily tied and so very difficult to unloose—in plain English, the halter!'" (ch. 43). Thus Fagin shows his affinity to the marsh in this preoccupation with the gibbet.

On the "chill, damp, windy night" when he sets out to plan the robbery intended to ensnare the innocence of Oliver, Fagin slinks quickly down the street in the direction of Spitalfields.

> The mud lay thick upon the stones, and a black mist hung over the streets; the rain fell sluggishly down, and everything felt cold and clammy to the touch. It seemed just the night when it befitted such a being as the Jew, to be abroad. As he glided stealthily along, creeping beneath the shelter of the walls and doorways, the hideous old man seemed like some loathsome reptile, engendered in the slime and darkness through which he moved: crawling forth, by night, in search of some rich offal for a meal. (ch. 19)

He has now emerged as an undisguised marsh monster.

Fagin's fellow conspirator, Bill Sikes, is a savage monster rather than a loathsome reptile. He appropriately appears on the scene with a snarl on his lips:

> The man who growled out these words was a stoutly built fellow of about five-and-thirty, in a black velveteen coat, very soiled drab breeches, lace-up half boots, and grey cotton stockings, which enclosed a very bulky pair of legs, with large swelling calves; the kind of legs, that in such costume, always look in an unfinished and incomplete state without a set of fetters to garnish them. He had a brown hat on his head, and a dirty belcher handkerchief round his neck: with the long frayed ends of which, he smeared the beer from his face as he spoke; disclosing, when he had done so, a broad heavy countenance with a beard of three day's growth: and two scowling eyes; one of which, displayed various parti-coloured symptoms of having been recently damaged by a blow. (ch. 13)

With necessary adjustments for the change of environment, he looks much like the convict Magwitch. Bill develops, however, as a complete savage with none of the redeeming tenderness of Magwitch or even Gaffer Hexam. Late in the story, as he makes his murderous way home after learning that Nancy has betrayed him, his figure sheds all pretence to civilization: as with Rogue Riderhood, "the very fashion of humanity had departed from his feet."

> Without one pause, or moment's consideration: without once turning his head to the right, or left, or raising his eyes to the sky, or lowering them to the ground, but looking straight before him with savage resolution, his teeth so tightly compressed that the strained jaw seemed starting through his skin; the robber held on his headlong course, nor muttered a word, nor relaxed a muscle, until he reached his own door. (ch. 47)

Implacable and impervious to Nancy's pleas for mercy, Bill beats her face savagely with his pistol. Now, in melodramatic contrast to the halter-neckerchiefs throughout the novel, Nancy draws "from her bosom a white handkerchief—Rose Maylie's own" as she breathes a last prayer before Bill, like a primitive savage, "seized a heavy club and struck her down."

Nancy is dead, but poetic justice pursues her murderer. Quickly leaving the scene of the murder, Bill wanders aimlessly through the country, accompanied by a growing terror that the murdered girl is dogging his steps, "a ghastly figure following at his heels": "At times, he turned, with desperate determination, resolved to beat this phantom off, though it should look him dead; but the hair rose on his head, and his blood stood still: for it had turned with him and was behind him then. He had kept it before him that morning, but it was behind him now—always" (ch. 48). Three days later, "the very ghost of Sikes" appears at Jacob's Island. Here, "He laid his hand upon a chair which stood in the middle of the room, but shuddering as he was about to drop into it, and seeming to glance over his shoulder, dragged it back close to the wall—as close as it would go—ground it against it—and sat down" (ch. 50). Thus the fearful "look over the shoulder" intensifies into mortal terror, which will lead Bill to hang himself accidentally: "looking behind him on the roof," he "uttered a yell of terror": "'The eyes again!' he cried in an unearthly screech." The noose he has intended to slip under his armpits is instead around his neck as he plunges from the roof, finally to fulfill the prophecy of the ominous handkerchiefs.

Fagin will shortly fulfill the same prediction as he awaits his punishment in Newgate Prison where, at dawn, a bloodthirsty crowd gathers:

> A great multitude had already assembled; the windows were filled with people, smoking and playing cards to beguile the time; the crowd were pushing, quarrelling, and joking. Everything told of life and animation, but one dark cluster of objects in the very centre of all—the black stage, the crossbeam, the rope, and all the hideous apparatus of death. (ch. 52)

This brief description of the bloodthirsty crowd returns to a theme introduced earlier by Nancy and now to be fully developed in the melodramatic scenes leading to Bill's death: the ambiguity of guilt shared by a criminal and by the society that both has produced him and now casts him out.

When Bill arrives at the house on Jacob's Island, he plunges into a nightmare Hogarthian scene of grotesquely exaggerated images from the marsh and lower river. The tempo quickens in these scenes as a great crowd assembles, with "lights gleaming below, voices in loud and earnest conversation, the tramp of hurried footsteps—endless they seemed in number—crossing the nearest wooden bridge" (ch. 50). As things seem to go badly for Bill, the crowd roars in triumph. Faces hang from every window, and "Each little bridge (and there were three in sight) bent beneath the weight of the crowd upon it. Still the current poured on to find some nook or hole from which to vent their shouts, and only for an instant see the wretch." Someone spreads the report that an entrance has been made into the house.

> The stream abruptly turned, as this intelligence ran from mouth to mouth; and the people at the windows, seeing those upon the bridges pouring back, quitted their stations, and, running into the street,

> joined the concourse that now thronged pell-mell to the spot they had left: each man crushing and striving with his neighbour, and all panting with impatience to get near the door, and look upon the criminal as the officers brought him out. (ch. 50)

It has become appallingly clear that the bloodthirsty horde of people who come to revel in Bill's apprehension—this "stream" of indifferent humanity with its flooding currents from bridge and lower river—matches him in guilty loathsomeness.

The imaginative textural richness of this remarkable chapter recording Bill's death is, I believe, surpassed nowhere else in Dickens: an achievement largely of resonant imagery, which he has permitted to carry its message without any of the discursive explanation and moralizing to which he so often resorts in this early work. By projecting these events through a carefully designed point of view, Dickens has artfully conveyed the complexity of human guilt, fully felt. This point of view might be described as a movement shifting outward—from the inner torment and terror of the criminal individual, to the vengeful ardor of the pursuing mob, to the encompassing perspective of a remote spectator able to perceive and judge them all.[4]

Scarcely have Fagin and Bill departed from the scene (1839) before another marsh creature—Daniel Quilp—begins to prowl through the rambling pages of Dickens's next novel, *The Old Curiosity Shop* (1840). Although Quilp like his predecessors shows an affinity for the gibbet, he himself is much more like that other monolith of the marsh, the ugly lighthouse. His identity develops slowly. When Little Nell appears for the first time with the dwarf in tow, we note his "coarse hard beard," "discoloured fangs," "dirty white neckerchief," "grizzled black hair," and hands of "rough coarse grain" (*OCS*, ch. 27). These details, appropriate to many contexts, are not in themselves conclusive evidence of the marsh. The first trip to Quilp's Wharf adds a few more scraps:

> On the Surrey side of the river was a small rat-infested dreary yard called 'Quilp's Wharf,' in which [was] a little wooden counting-house burrowing all awry in the dust as if it had fallen from the clouds and ploughed into the ground. . . . On Quilp's Wharf, Daniel Quilp was a ship-breaker, yet to judge from these appearances he must either have been a ship-breaker on a very small scale, or have broken his ships up very small indeed. Neither did the place present any extraordinary aspect of life or activity, as its only human occupant was an amphibious boy in a canvas suit, whose sole change of occupation

> was from sitting on the head of a pile and throwing stones into the mud when the tide was out, to standing with his hands in his pockets gazing listlessly on the motion and on the bustle of the river at high-water. (ch. 4)

Quilp's Wharf (with the imaginative suggestion of pilings), the dreary yard on the Surrey side of the river, with its amphibious boy monotonously throwing stones into the mud at low tide, begins to associate Quilp somewhat more clearly with the marsh. The "little wooden counting-house burrowing all awry in the dust" looks irrelevant unless one holds actively in memory "a little squat shoal-lighthouse" that "stood crippled in the mud on stilts and crutches." Even these similarities might remain unnoted—or be summarily discounted—were it not for the immediate repetitious references to broken ships. As it is, memory stirs in a reader familiar with Dickens's novels.

Now comes a picture of Quilp at home, where he is a cruel tyrant. He forces his wife to sit beside him through the night while he smokes one cigar after another: "the small lord of the creation took his first cigar and mixed his first glass of grog. The sun went down and the stars peeped out, the Tower turned from its own proper colours to grey and from grey to black, the room became perfectly dark and the end of the cigar a deep fiery red, but still Mr. Quilp went on smoking and drinking in the same position" (ch. 4). As Quilp sits through the night surrounded by the marsh colors of gray, black, and fiery red, his ability to remain "in the same position" is highly suggestive of a creature somewhat less than human.

Quilp's description takes a new turn when, as he is preparing to leave the house the next day, he is surprised by his mother-in-law, Mrs. Jiniwin, making in the mirror "a horribly grotesque and distorted face with the tongue lolling out" (ch. 5). This is the face of a hanged man, particularly graphic because at the time he is looking into the mirror, "putting on his neckerchief," the only item of his dress mentioned.[5]

Quilp now makes his way again to Quilp's Wharf. Having taken a boat to the Surrey side, he "caused himself to be put ashore hard by the wharf, and proceeded thither, through a narrow lane which, partaking of the amphibious character of its frequenters, had as much water as mud in its composition, and a very liberal supply of both." The first thing Quilp sees upon his arrival is the amphibious boy, standing on his head. "And here it may be remarked, that between this boy and the dwarf there existed a strange kind of mutual liking."

Later in the story, Quilp has decided to set up bachelor quarters in an interesting room

> which, by reason of its newly-erected chimney depositing the smoke inside the room and carrying none of it off, was not quite so agreeable as more fastidious people might have desired. Such inconveniences, however, instead of disgusting the dwarf with his new abode, rather suited his humour; so, after dining luxuriously from the public-house, he lighted his pipe, and smoked against the chimney until nothing of him was visible through the mist but a pair of red and highly inflamed eyes, with sometimes a dim vision of his head and face. (ch. 50)

This malfunctioning chimney with which Quilp is identified as they smoke foggily together suggests the earlier occasion when he smoked a cigar rather than a pipe.[6] The picture of "red and highly inflamed eyes" seen through the "mist" coalesces fleetingly with the image of the ugly lighthouse. The opening paragraph of a much later chapter draws a pointed parallel to this scene with an interestingly inverted analogy: "A faint light, twinkling from the window of the counting-house on Quilp's Wharf, and looking inflamed and red through the night-fog, as though it suffered from it like an eye, forewarned Mr. Sampson Brass" (ch. 62). Here, finally, the total cluster—counting-house/lighthouse, smoke/fog, red eyes/red light—is brought strikingly together.

As Quilp sits, first with his cigar glowing fiery red through the dark; then with his red and inflamed eyes looming through the smoke; and finally with the inflamed, redly lighted window of his counting-house looming like an eye through the fog, the reasons for which he is known as a "ship-breaker" now seem much clearer. Both in his person and in his place of business, Quilp resembles the deceptive lighthouse, surrounded by death.

Like many other marsh creatures, Daniel Quilp meets his end in the cold dark water of the lower river, into which he accidentally falls as he is about to be apprehended. Behind him, the counting-house has been set afire by an overturned stove. Although "the strong tide filled his throat," he struggles desperately to save himself. Suddenly he makes out a black object he is drifting close upon. "The hull of a ship! He could touch its smooth and slippery surface with his hand. One loud cry now—but the resistless water bore him under it, carried him away a corpse" (ch. 67). The water

> toyed and sported with its ghastly freight, now bruising it against the slimy piles, now hiding it in mud or long rank grass, now dragging it heavily over rough stones and gravel, now feigning to yield it to its own element,[7] and in the same action luring it away, until, tired of the ugly plaything, it flung it on a swamp—a dismal place where pirates had swung in chains, through many a wintry night—and left it there to bleach.
>
> And there it lay, alone. The sky was red with flame, and the water that bore it there had been tinged with the sullen light as it flowed along. The place the deserted carcass has left so recently, a living man, was now a blazing ruin. There was something of the glare upon its face. (ch. 67)

The ominous inflammation of the red eye has spread to consume the ugly lighthouse itself and garishly light the last trip of the old ship-breaker, fittingly broken against a ship and carried by the river to the marshland where he belongs.

Magwitch, Hexam, Riderhood, Fagin, Sikes, and Quilp are a formidable troop of monsters developed in a somber setting. But it does not always suit Dickens's purposes to present his marsh creatures with so much solemnity. Sometimes he catches them deftly and suspends them momentarily wriggling on a rapier point before he tosses them aside. The result is satirical ridicule in which they are reduced to contemptible size.

David Copperfield, recalling an incident from his childhood, records what apparently he just "happened" to remember as the sequence of events on an occasion fraught with associational significance.

> Peggotty and I were sitting one night by the parlour fire, alone. I had been reading to Peggotty about crocodiles. I must have read very perspicuously, or the good soul must have been deeply interested, for I remember she had a cloudy impression, after I had done, that they were a kind of vegetable. I was tired of reading, and dead sleepy, but having leave, as a high treat, to sit up until my mother came home from spending the evening at a neighbour's, I would rather have died upon my post (of course) than have gone to bed. (*DC*, ch. 2)

Now, fearful that he will fall asleep, he engages Peggotty in an apparently irrelevant discussion about marriage that obviously makes her uneasy.

> I couldn't understand why Peggotty looked so queer, or why she was so ready to go back to the crocodiles. However, we returned to those monsters, with fresh wakefulness on my part, and we left their eggs in the sand for the sun to hatch, and we ran away from them, and baffled them by constantly turning, which they were unable to do quickly, on account of their unwieldy make, and we went into the water after them, as natives, and put sharp pieces of timber down their throats; and in short we ran the whole crocodile gauntlet. *I* did, at least, but I had my doubts of Peggotty, who was thoughtfully sticking her needle into various parts of her face and arms all the time.
>
> We had exhausted the crocodiles, and begun with the alligators, when the garden-bell rang. We went out to the door, and there was my mother, looking even unusually pretty, I thought, and with her a gentleman with beautiful black hair and whiskers, who had walked home with us from church last Sunday. (ch. 2)

This gentleman, Mr. Murdstone, pats David on the head and tries to ingratiate himself with the boy. David, however, is for some reason reluctant and suspicious. "'Come! let us be the best friends in the world!' said the gentleman, laughing. 'Shake hands!'"

This is an effective sequence of grim humor. Starting innocently with the child's book about reptiles and the child's questions about marriage, the two subjects become uneasily related in David's sleepy consciousness because of Peggotty's strange manner, and then (as he senses the reason for her uneasiness) they merge to produce growing nightmarish apprehensions about his mother and the whiskered laughing gentleman. Murdstone's relationship to the marsh is further signaled (as is Headstone's) by his name: as Aunt Betsey says, David's mother "goes and marries a Murderer—or a man with a name like it" (ch. 13).

Another "chance" association acquires similar heightened satirical meaning in *Our Mutual Friend,* on an occasion when Mr. Boffin, "the Golden Dustman," is visiting Venus's specialty shop (which features such wares as stuffed birds, artificial limbs, bones, and a "Hindoo baby in a bottle"). The unexpected appearance of Silas Wegg, who has earlier profited from Boffin's employment, precipitates an amusing sequence of events. At this point in the developing narrative, the reader has been led to believe that Boffin has lost his warm, human qualities and has become a dehumanized miser. Venus finds a quick way to hide him from the new visitor:

> "Hush! here's Wegg!" said Venus. "Get behind the young alligator in the corner, Mr. Boffin, and judge him for yourself. I won't light a

> candle till he's gone; there'll only be the glow of the fire; Wegg's well acquainted with the alligator, and he won't take particular notice of him. Draw your legs in, Mr. Boffin, at present I see a pair of shoes at the end of his tail. Get your head well behind his smile, Mr. Boffin, and you'll lie comfortable there; you'll find plenty of room behind his smile. He's a little dusty, but he's very like you in tone." (*OMF,* bk. III, ch. 14)

The indoctrinated reader, having to agree that "he's very like you in tone," is amused.

Upon being admitted into the shop, Wegg indulges in some accusatory comments about Boffin that lead to the authorial observation that many slanderers and traitors similarly "transform their benefactors into their injurers." Whereupon: "the yard or two of smile on the part of the alligator might have been invested with the meaning, 'All about this was quite familiar knowledge down in the slime, ages ago.'" It is now treacherous Mr. Wegg who is associated with the alligator. The shift from the ridiculous picture of Boffin to the ugly picture of Wegg is emphasized in what takes place after Wegg's departure.

> Mr. Boffin disengaged himself from behind the alligator's smile, with an expression of countenance so very downcast that it not only appeared as if the alligator had the whole of the joke to himself, but further as if it had been conceived and executed at Mr. Boffin's expense.
>
> "That's a treacherous fellow," said Mr. Boffin, dusting his arms and legs as he came forth, the alligator having been but dusty company. "That's a dreadful fellow."
>
> "The alligator, sir?" said Venus.
>
> "No, Venus, no. The Serpent." (bk. III, ch. 14)

In light of later revelations, when Boffin's fall turns out to have been a benevolent deception, the alligator indeed seems to have had the whole of the joke to himself at Boffin's expense, for the treacherous fellow has tricked the reader into laughing condescendingly at the good Golden Dustman. Wegg, however, is neatly reduced even lower by Boffin's correction of Venus: Wegg is not just a harmlessly smiling alligator; as a betrayer of goodness, he is the reptilian incarnation of evil itself.

Such then are the creatures to be found in the marsh. Insensitive, cold-blooded, unfeeling like their reptilian ancestors, true marsh creatures relentlessly seek the satisfaction of their own primitive appetites and desires, for thoughtless egocentricity lies at their center instead of a heart. When Pip finally grows aware of the great heart of Magwitch, he also realizes that the convict has been a victim of the marsh, rather than one of its monsters as he appears.

## 2

Even warm-blooded human beings are not safe from the destructive effects of the marsh, for a deadly miasma seeps out of its confines and spreads everywhere to infect those susceptible to its touch. This miasma is the monotony that, creeping with the fog through the opening chapter of *Bleak House,* also envelops Lady Dedlock in *ennui,* the smothering atmosphere surrounding those "In Fashion" being the same as that around those "In Chancery." Lady Dedlock has come up to London to escape her "dreary place" in Lincolnshire. "My Lady Dedlock says she has been 'bored to death'," though she lives "at the top of the fashionable tree," comments the narrator (*BH,* ch. 2).

To Dickens, a monotonous existence and the boredom attendant upon it are as destructive to human beings as the egocentrism of the marsh dwellers. Related to the marsh by its uniform grayness and pointless repetitions of lines and streets and days and actions (cf. the description of Coketown), a monotonous existence is the very negation of life. Sometimes people are thrust as victims into a monotonous existence, as with the amphibious boys or the "Hands" in Coketown, whose marshlike environment reduces them to primitive creatures seemingly without the passions and feelings that characterize humanity. More often, however, those touched by this miasma are people who for some reason *perceive* their lives as reduced to a meaningless existence of monotony and boredom. Such people may become "frozen" to the life-giving and warm-hearted emotions in such fashion that they resemble the cold-blooded creatures of the marsh. Lady Dedlock, it seems, has been thus affected:

> How Alexander wept when he had no more worlds to conquer, everybody knows—or has some reason to know by this time, the matter having been frequently mentioned. My Lady Dedlock, having conquered *her* world, fell, not into the melting, but rather into the freezing mood. An exhausted composure, a worn-out placidity, an equanimity of fatigue not to be ruffled by interest or satisfaction, are

> the trophies of her victory. She is perfectly well-bred. If she could be translated to Heaven tomorrow, she might be expected to ascend without any rapture. (ch. 2)

On "this muddy, murky afternoon," my Lady sits in her room in her town house with her husband and Mr. Tulkinghorn the lawyer. She is attempting lamely to explain away the unprecedented animation she has manifested in response to the handwriting on a paper tendered her by Tulkinghorn: "'Anything to vary this detestable monotony,'" she says. Mr. Tulkinghorn fears my Lady is ill, but Sir Leicester reassures him: "'She really has been bored to death down at our place in Lincolnshire.'"

Lady Dedlock's life, the narrator reports, has become a continual flight[8]—from Chesney Wold yesterday, to London today, off for Paris tomorrow. They are all the same to her. Day after tomorrow she flies back to Lincolnshire: "Weariness of soul lies before her, as it lies behind—her Ariel has put a girdle of it round the whole earth, and it cannot be unclasped" (ch. 12). A "weary manner," languor, and fatigue surround the figure of Lady Dedlock except on the rare occasions when for some reason, as in the exchange with Tulkinghorn, her interest is surprised into being. As Tulkinghorn sets about to "close in" on her, her freezing mood becomes more and more confirmed and finally closes completely about her. She is at last "as indifferent as if all passion, feeling, and interest had been worn out in the early ages of the world and had perished from its surface with its other departed monsters" (ch. 48).[9]

Yet the very fact that Lady Dedlock "fell into the freezing mood" implies that she has not always been the cold and haughty Lady who tries to fly from the weariness of soul that possesses her. That weariness, as she tells Esther, arises from guilty memory, which will not let her rest. She urges her daughter to see beneath the fashionable figure to the reality within: "'Think that the reality is in her suffering, in her useless remorse, in her murdering within her breast the only love and truth of which it is capable! And then forgive her, if you can; and cry to Heaven to forgive her, which it never can!'" (ch. 36). Her consciousness of guilt growing out of an experience in which she was part perpetrator, part victim (her guilty love affair and the desertion of her daughter) has made her susceptible to the miasma of the marsh and has turned the entire world for her into a gigantic monotonous wasteland, she herself becoming frozenly dehumanized, having "murdered" within her breast the capacity to feel human emotions. That they are not really dead is manifested by her animated response to the handwriting of her former lover.

From almost our first glimpse of her, Lady Dedlock is seen to be in the "clutch of the Giant Despair." This despair deepens through the course of the book as Tulkinghorn closes in on her. She longs for his death as a solution to her problems. When it providentially occurs, she learns that she has been "but wishing that all he held against her in his hand might be flung to the winds and chance-sown in many places. So, too, with the wicked relief she felt in his death. What was his death but the key-stone of a gloomy arch removed, and now the arch begins to fall in a thousand fragments, each crushing and mangling piecemeal!" (ch. 55). Lady Dedlock has acquired one more reason for self-accusation: her "wicked relief" in his death. Her despair is complete as the "terrible impression steals upon and overshadows her that from this pursuer, living or dead . . . there is no escape but in death." The crumbling of the "gloomy arch" has completed the process already in threatening operation long before when it was observed at the dreary place in Lincolnshire that "an arch of the bridge in the park has been sapped and sopped away" (see ch. II).

Lady Dedlock is not the only one in *Bleak House* who leads a weary, dreary life of dreadful monotony related to the emblematic marsh.[10] All of the suitors caught in the Jarndyce case reflect the stultifying effects of this deadly repetitiveness. Richard, for example, the counterpart "In Chancery" of Lady Dedlock "In Fashion," flits from profession to profession—rather than from city to city—as a relief from sameness and as a preliminary to falling victim to its deadly effects: "'It's monotonous,'" he explains to Esther and Ada as the reason for leaving Mr. Bayham Badger's; "'and to-day is too like yesterday, and to-morrow is too like to-day'" (ch. 17).

Three years after publication of *Bleak House,* Dickens produced in *Little Dorrit* another character remarkably similar to Lady Dedlock. This woman is Mrs. Clennam, who created and inhabits the marsh world in which Arthur grew up, and which still holds him captive.

On the evening Arthur arrives home, he is appropriately met at the door by the marsh creature Flintwinch. "'I doubt,' said Flintwinch, 'if your mother will approve of your coming home on the Sabbath'" (*LD,* bk. I, ch. 3). Arthur follows the crablike old man through the old house to the tomblike room where his mother sits paralyzed by the monotonous world surrounding her.

> There was a fire in the grate, as there had been night and day for fifteen years. There was a kettle on the hob, as there had been night and day for fifteen years. There was a little mound of damped ashes on the top of the fire, and another little mound swept together under the grate, as there had been night and day for fifteen years. There was a smell of black dye in the airless room, which the fire had been drawing out of the crape and stuff of the widow's dress for fifteen months, and out of the bier-like sofa for fifteen years. (bk. I, ch. 3)

The malfunctioning fire with its "mound" of damp ashes, the black smell in the room without air, and the repetitive drone of phrases point to the monotony of her existence as she sits "with her cold grey eyes and her cold grey hair, and her immovable face, as stiff as the folds of her stony headdress." As she explains to Arthur: "'The world has narrowed to these dimensions. . . . I have lost the use of my limbs. I never leave my room. . . . All seasons are alike to me. The Lord has put me beyond all that.'" The narrator adds that "her being beyond the reach of the seasons, seemed but a fit sequence to her being beyond the reach of all changing emotions."

Mrs. Clennam's Lord is the stern, unforgiving god of the Old Testament. Arthur remembers the "dreary" Sundays of his childhood: "when his mother, stern of face and unrelenting of heart, would sit all day behind a bible—bound like her own construction of it in the hardest, barest, and straitest boards . . . as if it, of all books! were a fortification against sweetness of temper, natural affection, and gentle intercourse." Now, she sits before him within "the gloomy labyrinth of her thoughts" (bk. I, ch. 3). Putting on her spectacles, she begins to read certain passages aloud from "a" book. Later, in "her frozen way," she speaks of herself as "'your infirm and afflicted—justly infirm and righteously afflicted—mother'" (bk. I, ch. 5). Her belief requires that her suffering must be the just consequence of wrongdoing, although it is not yet clear whether she knows what she is guilty of. In her affliction, she continues to find consolation in her religion.

> Great need had the rigid woman of her mystical religion, veiled in gloom and darkness, with lightnings of cursing, vengeance, and destruction, flashing through the sable clouds. Forgive us our debts as we forgive our debtors, was a prayer too poor in spirit for her. Smite thou my debtors, Lord, wither them, crush them; do Thou as I would

> do, and Thou shalt have my worship: this was the impious tower of stone she built up to scale Heaven. (bk. I, ch. 5)

Mrs. Clennam's Lord, we see, is created in her own image.

Eventually we discover that, like Lady Dedlock, Mrs. Clennam carries the guilty burden of having "murder[ed] in her breast" the warm human emotions of love and forgiveness. When she learned many years ago, soon after her marriage, of the illicit love affair between Arthur's father and the young girl who had borne him a son, Mrs. Clennam set out on a path of "justice" modeled on her idea of God. Convinced of the sinfulness of the affair, she closed her heart to her husband, subjected his sweetheart to cruel punishment, and reared their son, Arthur, under the stern religion supposed to protect him—as it had protected her—against evil. Her righteousness turned into self-righteousness; self-righteousness, into rage; and rage, into vengeance.

Now, these many years later, as she and Arthur confront one another, she remains in frozen bondage to her religious convictions. She stoically accepts her infirmities and afflictions as the just and righteous outcome of her own wrongdoing, whatever that may be. She still hides from herself, however, the possibility that her motives were anything but good, or that what she imposed on her husband, his sweetheart, his child, and herself as "justice" could be wrong.

She therefore responds with explosive anger to Arthur's suggestion that his father might have suffered from some "kind of secret remembrance which caused him trouble of mind—remorse?" Arthur, fearing that the wealth of the House may rightfully belong to someone else, urges upon her the idea of "reparation": "'Someone may have been grievously deceived, injured, ruined,'" he surmises. "'If reparation can be made to any one, let us know it and make it.'"

In a fury, Mrs. Clennam accosts her son. She finds it outrageous that he should spurn as "plunder" an inheritance of valuables "'which we have painfully got together early and late,'" and that "'he asks to whom they shall be given up, as reparation!'"

> "Reparation!" said she. "Yes truly! it is easy for him to talk of reparation, fresh from journeying and junketting in foreign lands, and living a life of vanity and pleasure. But let him look at me, in prison, and in bonds here. I endure without murmuring, because it is appointed that I shall so make reparation for my sins. Reparation! Is

> there none in this room? Has there been none here this fifteen years?" (bk. I, ch. 5)

Mrs. Clennam has twisted Arthur's notion of reparation as some kind of repayment or compensation to an injured party into conformity with her own rigid beliefs: reparation to her means paying in suffering for one's sins. Since she genuinely believes what she says, she is like other marsh dwellers, both perpetrator and victim of her marsh world.

Toward the end of the novel, in the "Closing In," "Closed" chapters (like the "Closing In" of Tulkinghorn on Lady Dedlock), a remarkable change occurs. As Mrs. Clennam perceives that the whole story, which she has concealed for years, is about to come out, she is transformed. "'It is closing in, Flintwinch'" (bk. II, ch. 30), she says to her servant. To Rigaud she explains, "'I am a resolved woman.'" Rigaud, agreeing, describes her resolve in interestingly selected terms: "'a resolved lady, a stern lady, a lady who has a will that can break the weak to powder: a lady without pity, without love, implacable, revengeful, cold as the stone, but raging as the fire.'"

Her resolve is finally to make full reparation for the wrong she has done to her husband, his sweetheart, and their child. We realize now that her kindnesses to Little Dorrit have been her feeble efforts to assuage the twinges of conscience she could not completely suppress. In her new resolve, the bonds of paralysis begin to fall away "with [a] new freedom in the use of her hand of which she showed no consciousness whatever." Learning that Little Dorrit has the papers that will accomplish her "reparation," Mrs. Clennam springs to her feet ("almost as if a dead woman had risen") and takes off through the early evening.

> The sun had set, and the streets were dim in the dusty twilight, when the figure so long unused to them hurried on its way. In the immediate neighbourhood of the old house, it attracted little attention for there were only a few straggling people to notice it; but, ascending from the river, by the crooked ways that led to London Bridge, and passing into the great main road, it became surrounded by astonishment.
>
> Resolute and wild of look, rapid of foot, and yet weak and uncertain, conspicuously dressed in its black garments and with its hurried head-covering, gaunt and of an unearthly paleness, it pressed forward, taking no more heed of the throng than a sleep-walker. More remarkable by being so removed from the crowd it was among, than if it had been lifted on a pedestal to be seen, the figure attracted all

> eyes. Saunterers pricked up their attention to observe it; busy people, crossing it, slackened their pace and turned their heads; companions pausing and standing aside, whispered one another to look at this spectral woman who was coming by; and the sweep of the figure as it passed seemed to create a vortex, drawing the most idle and most curious after it. (bk. II, ch. 31)

The details here invite comparison with Rogue Riderhood. As with him, the "very fashion of humanity had departed from [her] feet." Reduced to a "figure," an "it," she shares with him the implacable, unswerving purpose of a primitive creature. But, in contrast to Riderhood, her resolution to accomplish a benevolent rather than a sinister purpose indicates a singularly complex marsh monster.

As Mrs. Clennam relates to Little Dorrit the entire history of what she has done, it becomes apparent that her action has at least temporarily released her emotions from their paralysis. This woman who has herself been so unforgiving throws herself on the mercy of Little Dorrit, begging her not to reveal the story to Arthur, at least not until after Mrs. Clennam's death. "'Will you promise to spare me until I am dead?'" she asks. When Little Dorrit responds affirmatively, she says simply, "'GOD bless you!'" As she does so: "she stood in the shadow so that she was only a veiled form to Little Dorrit in the light; but, the sound of her voice, in saying those three grateful words, was at once fervent and broken. Broken by emotion as unfamiliar to her frozen eyes as action to her frozen limbs" (bk. II, ch. 31).

Mrs. Clennam explains that while she can face Little Dorrit as a relative of the young girl who wronged her and to whom she administered "justice," she can find no such justification for her treatment of the innocent child, Arthur. In final analysis, then, she must remain a permanent victim of the marsh, for she cannot free herself from belief in justice as the fundamental good. She still must defend her motives as justification for her actions. "'If this house was blazing from the roof to the ground,'" she has said, "'I would stay in it to justify myself, against my righteous motives being classed with those of stabbers and thieves'" (bk. II, ch. 30).

Even with regard to Arthur, Mrs. Clennam explains to Little Dorrit, what she did was "'for his good. Not for the satisfaction of my injury.'"

> "What was I, and what was the worth of that, before the curse of Heaven! I have seen that child grow up; not to be pious in a chosen way (his mother's offence lay too heavy on him for that), but still to be

> just and upright, and to be submissive to me. He never loved me, as I once half-hoped he might—so frail we are, and so do the corrupt affections of the flesh war with our trusts and tasks; but, he always respected me, and ordered himself dutifully to me." (bk. II, ch. 31)

In the conflict within her between the gods of the Old and the New Testaments, the Old Testament god prevails. "'I have done,' said Mrs. Clennam, 'what it was given to me to do. I have set myself against evil; not against good.'"

Mrs. Clennam returns home to witness the final collapse of the old house, fated not to "burn," but rather to fall into dusty rubble as a result of its weakened foundation and structure.

> There, Mrs. Clennam dropped upon the stones; and she never from that hour moved so much as a finger again, or had the power to speak one word. For upwards of three years she reclined in her wheeled chair, looking attentively at those about her, and appearing to understand what they said; but, the rigid silence she had so long held was evermore enforced upon her, and, except that she could move her eyes and faintly express a negative and affirmative with her head, she lived and died a statue. (bk. II, ch. 31)

Thus Mrs. Clennam ends her days in the deadly monotony that has characterized most of her life.

The message is that a monotonous existence cannot be imposed upon human beings by either their environment or their own doing without catastrophic consequences. The life forces that characterize human beings—their warm-blooded emotions—may be temporarily "frozen" or controlled, but sooner or later will assert themselves, if necessary in devastating ways. The "Hands" in Coketown, for example, will explode into destructive rebellion. The narrator of *Hard Times,* turning from the poor factory workers to the rich Gradgrind children subjected to the "Hard Facts" school of education, is mildly astonished to note a possible parallel between their lives. "Is it possible, I wonder, that there was any analogy between the cases of the Coketown population and the case of the little Gradgrinds?" (*HT,* bk. I, ch. 5). Could it be that there was any "Fancy" in them "demanding to be brought into healthy existence instead of struggling on in convulsion: That exactly in the ratio as they worked long and monotonously, the craving grew within them for some physical relief . . . which craving must and would be satisfied aright, or must and would inevitably go wrong until the laws of Creation were repealed"? Monotony, Dickens asserts repeatedly and in many ways, is antithetical to life. Its existence creates a human craving for "physical" relief. If that relief does not come in creative and life-sustaining ways—"be satisfied aright"—it must and will "inevitably go wrong." This is a warning to be sounded often in the chapters yet to come.

Sometimes the monotony of existence breeds its own marsh monsters. Coketown has lured into itself such a monster from London, James Harthouse: bored, weary, completely indifferent, frozen against all human feeling. Superficially like Lady Dedlock, unlike her he is a destructive monster far more dangerous than even a Bill Sikes. He appears on the scene playing with his watch-chain "wearily," with "all imaginable coolness," and with a "certain air of exhaustion upon him." According to the narrator: "It was to be seen with half an eye that he was a thorough gentleman, made to the model of the time—weary of everything, and putting no more faith in anything than Lucifer" (bk. II, ch. 1).

We quickly learn that this gentleman has "tried life as a Cornet of Dragoons, and found it a bore," has "strolled to Jerusalem and got bored there," and has finally "gone yachting about the world, and got bored everywhere" (bk. II, ch. 2). A gentleman eminently equipped to meet the approval of the Hard Fact Fellows. As he explains to Louisa Gradgrind:

> "I have not so much as the slightest predilection left. I assure you I attach not the least importance to any opinions. The result of the varieties of boredom I have undergone is a conviction (unless conviction is too industrious a word for the lazy sentiment I entertain on the subject) that any set of ideas will do just as much good as any other set, and just as much harm as any other set." (bk. II, ch. 2)

To him, ideas of good and evil are meaningless. The world of values is as undifferentiated and monotonous as everything else. He is committed to nothing.

Even after the machinations of Harthouse are well advanced and their outcome in human grief is evident, his motives could not be said to be *committedly* evil: "he had not, even now, any earnest wickedness of purpose in him." But this fact does not soften the excoriations of his creator:

> Publicly and privately, it were much better for the age in which he lived that he and the legion of whom he was one were designedly bad than indifferent and purposeless. It is the drifting icebergs, setting with any current anywhere, that wreck the ships.

> When the Devil goeth about like a roaring lion, he goeth about in a shape by which few but savages and hunters are attracted. But when he is trimmed, smoothed, and varnished, according to the mode; when he is aweary of vice, and aweary of virtue, used up as to brimstone, and used up as to bliss; then, whether he take to the serving out of red tape or to the kindling of red fire, he is the very Devil. (bk. II, ch. 8)

This demonic wrecker of ships, this "drifting iceberg" devoid of human feeling, understands very well that boredom and indifference are his elemental qualities. He senses at once, for instance, when Tom will be willing to help in the scheme against his sister. "'Tom is misanthropical today,'" says Harthouse, "'as all bored people are now and then'" (bk. II, ch. 7).

Harthouse, then, is seen to be a type of monster related to the marsh—cold, rigid, and monotonous. He is a relatively uncomplicated ancestor of John Jasper, the complex and guilt-ridden character who dominates *The Mystery of Edwin Drood.*

Without any preparation, Dickens plunges the reader directly into the consciousness of John Jasper in the brilliant associational paragraph that introduces the novel. This paragraph describes an opium dreamer's slow return to consciousness:

> An ancient English Cathedral Town? How can the ancient English Cathedral Town be here! The well-known massive grey square tower of its old Cathedral? How can that be here![11] There is no spike of rusty iron in the air, between the eye and it, from any point of the real prospect. What IS the spike that intervenes, and who has set it up? Maybe it is set up by the Sultan's orders for the impaling of a horde of Turkish robbers, one by one. It is so, for cymbals clash, and the Sultan goes by to his palace in long procession. Ten thousand scimitars flash in the sunlight, and thrice ten thousand dancing-girls strew flowers. Then, follow white elephants caparisoned in countless gorgeous colours, and infinite in number and attendants. Still the Cathedral Tower rises in the background, where it cannot be, and still no writhing figure is on the grim spike. Stay! Is the spike so low a thing as the rusty spike on the top of a post of an old bedstead that has tumbled all awry? Some vague period of drowsy laughter must be devoted to the consideration of this possibility. (*MED,* ch. 1)

An unoriented reader groping for footing in this confusion must struggle along with the disoriented consciousness of the dreamer to find some semblance of reality in the images flashing past apparently chaotically, though actually in a pattern of beautifully synthesized dream logic. Bedpost, tower (spire), spike, and scimitar merge together without quite coalescing. Why has the bedpost become the spike? Why does the spike with the suggestion of an impaled human figure hover before the Cathedral tower? They are all drawn together by the ambiguous guilt within the dreamer. The images interplay from three different levels of experience. In the immediate situation, Jasper is aware that he has perverted his capacity to dream into the guilty journey of the opium dream, whose "Eastern" attraction is yet so powerful that he cannot resist it. In the larger world of Cloisterham, he knows he conducts a hypocritical and guilty relationship to the Cathedral, which should lead to salvation but for him leads only to the graveyard. And in between, the glamorous, guilty Sultan flashes past in resplendent colors at once alluring and repellent.[12] Thus, in its interpretation of experience, the dream consciousness has hooked external reality together with two configurations—the marsh and the fairy tale—on the point of a shared image. The ironic, drowsy laughter acknowledges the power of the mind to construct so much from the rusty spike on the old bedstead—as Proust would later marvel at the conjuring powers in a bit of madeleine and a cup of tea.

With returning consciousness, the man moves about the opium den, while the reader moves outside to observe him. The dream world is much on the man's mind as he unsteadily contemplates the sleeping Chinaman, the Lascar, and the haggard woman, who has lapsed again into unconsciousness after performing her duties as hostess. "'What visions can *she* have,'" he muses. She mutters; he listens. "'Unintelligible,'" he comments. When the Chinaman and the Lascar also give indications of some kind of internal activity, he regards them with equal bafflement and the repeated observation: "Unintelligible." He thus reassures himself with the reminder that nobody can penetrate the dream world of another to violate his privacy: a source of "gloomy" satisfaction in this guilt-ridden world of perverted opium dreams. The reader, too, feels the exclusion, not only from them, but, more importantly, from Jasper.

Now, at the end of the chapter, comes a break in the printed page before the last paragraph. This break emphasizes the withdrawal from the personal view of John Jasper to the distant perspective of the narrator, whose interpretation coincides with and legitimizes that of the character.

> That same afternoon, the massive grey square tower of an old cathedral rises before the sight of a jaded traveller. The bells are going for daily vesper service, and he must needs attend it, one would say, from

> his haste to reach the open cathedral door. The choir are getting on their sullied white robes, in a hurry, when he arrives among them, gets on his own robe, and falls into the procession filing in to service. Then, the Sacristan locks the iron-barred gates that divide the sanctuary from the chancel, and all of the procession having scuttled into their places, hide their faces; and then the intoned words, "WHEN THE WICKED MAN—" rise among groins of arches and beams of roof, awakening muttered thunder. (ch. 1)

For the observer, too, the tower of the old cathedral is ominous as, without suggest of sanctuary, it receives the "jaded traveller" returning from the London opium den. The service is one he "must needs attend" as he hastens to join the choir (with its rhyming echo of spire)[13] getting on their "sullied" white robes "in a hurry," like prisoners falling tardily into a procession "filing" into service, while the Sacristan "locks the iron-barred gates" behind them. The jaded traveller, among the other figures of guilt, like them hides his face while the accusing words echo through the threatening arches.

Within the course of the three pages of chapter 1, the point of view has moved progressively away from the anonymous man whose view we are experiencing, from the completely subjective to the completely objective. In the first paragraph, we peer out through this man's eyes; in the last paragraph, we have moved far out to become detached and unacquainted observers—strangers to the man through whose consciousness we entered the world of the novel. In between, we hover intimately over this man to observe closely his every move, but without the power to enter again the secret recesses of his consciousness.

This process invests John Jasper with deep mystery because the reader remembers his complex and enigmatic internal world and is now excluded from it. The total effect of this introductory chapter enlarges the meaning of the mysterious man, whose anonymity is preserved throughout, to include others as well. John Jasper therefore becomes an allegorical figure projecting the reader into a world where one must attempt self-reconciliation. Whatever the individual guilt of John Jasper, it looks basically to be the guilt of Everyman, torn between the unlimited dream and the circumscribed reality, and with a propensity to corrupt both.

As Jasper hurries from the sordid episode in the London opium den to the evening service in Cloisterham cathedral, he begins to shift ambiguously between good and evil, the angelic and the demonic. While he is master of the choir, he dons a "sullied robe."

Some of the characters, like his nephew Edwin, greatly respect him; others, like Rosa, are terrified of him. In an early scene, Edwin speaks admiringly of the place of honor his uncle has earned for himself by his good work in the church. He finds his uncle's response bewildering: "'I hate it. The cramped monotony of my existence grinds me away by the grain.'" The service, which to Edwin sounds "quite celestial," to Jasper seems "devilish." He explains:

> "I am so weary of it. The echoes of my own voice among the arches seem to mock me with my daily drudging round. No wretched monk who droned his life away in that gloomy place, before me, can have been more tired of it than I am. He could take for relief (and did take) to carving demons out of the stalls and seats and desks. What shall I do? Must I take to carving them out of my heart?" (ch. 2)

In Jasper, as in the Coketown population, the craving grows for "some physical relief—which craving must and would be satisfied aright, or must and would inevitably go wrong." Asking his nephew to "'take it as a warning,'" Jasper explains that "even a poor monotonous chorister and grinder of music—in his niche—may be troubled with some stray sort of ambition, aspiration, restlessness, dissatisfaction, what shall we call it?'" Here are the forewarnings of the potential explosive outlet.

His association with the stonemason Durdles identifies Jasper more specifically with the criminal-martyr of the marsh. More than a hint of analogy glances between the name of the one and the occupation of the other. What could a stonemason have to do with "Jasper," except perhaps in a carving way? Around the person of Durdles, Dickens has assembled a fantastic array of stone images and associations. He is chiefly "in the gravestone, tomb, and monument way, and wholly of their colour from head to foot."

> He is an old bachelor, and he lives in a little antiquated hole of a house that was never finished:[14] supposed to be built, so far, of stones stolen from the city wall. To this abode there is an approach, ankle-deep in stone chips, resembling a petrified grove of tombstones, urns, draperies, and broken columns, in all stages of sculpture. Herein two journeymen incessantly chip, while other two journeymen, who face each other, incessantly saw stone; dipping as regularly in and out of their sheltering sentry-boxes, as if they were mechanical figures emblematical of Time and Death. (ch. 4)

Durdles, known among the urchins of the town as "Stony," has hired one of them for the unusual occupation of stoning Durdles home on any occasion the urchin catches him out "arter ten." Jasper is curious enough about the significance of his friend's nickname to drag the question into a conversation quite gratuitously. "'There was a discussion the other day among the Choir,'" he observes, "'whether Stony stood for Tony; . . . or whether Stony stood for Stephen; . . . or whether the name comes from your trade. How stands the fact?'" (ch. 4). Although he gets no answer from his uncommunicative and apparently unhearing companion, the various possibilties have been suggested, prominent among them the name of the stoned martyr. Lest the point be missed, however, Dickens labors it further a short time later when Jasper and Durdles are accosted by a group of stone-throwing urchins.

> "Stop, you young brutes," cried Jasper angrily, "and let us go by!"
>
> This remonstrance being received with yells and flying stones, according to a custom of late years comfortably established among police regulations of our English communities, where Christians are stoned on all sides, as if the days of Saint Stephen were revived, Durdles remarks of the young savages, with some point, that "they haven't got an object," and leads the way down the Lane. (ch. 5)

Jasper, like Quilp with the amphibious boy, feels a kind of kinship with "The Stony One," a feeling given some objectivity in this shared stoning. He recognizes that both live a "curious existence" inasmuch as their "lot is cast in the same old earthy, chilly, never-changing place," though he considers that Durdles has a much more mysterious and interesting connection with the Cathedral than his own. On the midnight excursion made into the crypt by the pair, Durdles falls unaccountably asleep after imbibing from his companion's wicker bottle, while Jasper himself comes and goes shadowily through the night on some undisclosed business. In Dickens's total depiction, Durdles remains enigmatic, but he seems to be a figure of allegory, partly identifying Jasper ever more unmistakably with the criminal-martyr of the marsh, partly personifying some kind of nemesis operant in Jasper's life.

Soon after the midnight excursion comes Christmas Eve—the night Edwin Drood is to disappear. Three men are to meet in the gatehouse/lighthouse on this night: Jasper, Neville, and Edwin. During his preparations for this occasion, John Jasper begins to emerge clearly as a marsh monster with marked similarity to Rogue Riderhood. It has been a good day for the singing master. He has never sung better; his time is perfect. "These results are probably attained through a grand composure of the spirits. The mere mechanism of his throat is a little tender,[15] for he wears, both with his singing-robe and with his ordinary dress, a large black scarf of strong close-woven silk, slung loosely round his neck" (ch. 14). Jasper has been out on chores of hospitality. Now he hurries to get home before his guests arrive, singing delicately in a low voice as he goes. "It still seems as if a false note were not within his power tonight, and as if nothing could hurry or retard him. Arriving thus under the arched entrance of his dwelling, he pauses for an instant in the shelter to pull off that great black scarf, and hang it in a loop upon his arm." Like Riderhood, this man pursues some unswerving and cataclysmic course. Looking "as if nothing could hurry or retard him," he too might be compared to an ugly fate, or be described as impervious to implacable weather. Attention is drawn to the scarf to reenforce its analogy as he hangs it "in a loop upon his arm."

As Jasper approaches the postern stair, he meets Mr. Crisparkle, the Minor Canon, who has been concerned of late about the choir master's "black humours." Jasper is unaccountably buoyant and cheerful. He tells Crisparkle that he plans to burn his diary at year's end because he has been "out of sorts, gloomy, bilious, brain-oppressed, whatever it may be." As he explains: "A man leading a monotonous life . . . and getting his nerves, or his stomach, out of order, dwells upon an idea until it loses its proportions." Crisparkle expresses his pleased surprise at the improvement in his colleague. As *David Copperfield*'s Martha drew attention to her similarity to the river, Jasper explains himself to Crisparkle in a related analogy: "'Why, naturally,'" he returns. "'You had but little reason to hope that I should become more like yourself. You are always training yourself to be, mind and body, as clear as crystal, and you always are, and never change; whereas I am a muddy, solitary, moping weed.'" Despite Jasper's apparent recovery of spirits, his self-description reminds us of his "muddy" nature on this stormy and destructive night when "nothing is steady but the red light" in the gatehouse. His metaphorical comment also foreshadows his physical condition as he later searches through the muddy land around the river for signs of the vanished Edwin.

On one night when Jasper returns home from this search, Mr. Grewgious, Rosa's guardian, is waiting for him. Jasper has arrived exhausted, looking rather like Magwitch or Gaffer Hexam: "Unkempt and disordered, bedaubed with mud that had dried upon him, and with much of his clothing torn to rags" (ch. 15). Grewgious tells Jasper that Rosa and Edwin are not in fact engaged to be married. Although Grewgious does not know it, this is crucial information for Jasper. In the case against him that Dickens is building in the mind of the reader, Jasper has presumably disposed of Edwin as his rival for the affections of Rosa. Now, as Grewgious fulfills his errand by delivering a message that renders this act meaningless, a startling transformation takes place: "Mr. Grewgious heard a terrible shriek, and saw no ghastly figure, sitting or standing; saw nothing but a heap of torn and miry clothes upon the floor." Thus has Jasper, the "muddy weed," by steps been reduced into a heap of muddy residue, his human character fallen completely away from him. And here the unfinished novel leaves John Jasper.

It is tempting to try to solve at least one part of the mystery of Edwin Drood by extrapolating from an analysis of Jasper's depiction as a marsh monster: what would have been the truth ultimately revealed about John Jasper? Actually, there could be no important truth not already inherent in his portrayal. Whether he was guilty of the death of his nephew is almost incidental, like the fate of Browning's duchess. He has made it clear that he feels driven by the boring monotony of his existence to any kind of relieving action. Does his desire for Rosa follow or precede his weariness and boredom? In either event, it is a guilty desire, as was Lady Dedlock's wish for Tulkinghorn's death. It seems most probable that his guilty desire for his nephew's fiancée helped turn his life into the "cramped monotony" from which he must seek relief. Under similar circumstances, Lady Dedlock seeks relief in flight. Where can he seek it? In the wish-fulfillment dreams of the opium den? ("Take it as a warning," he has said to Edwin.) A similarly wretched ancient monk, he says, could have found relief "carving demons out of the stalls and seats and desks. What shall I do? Must I take to carving them out of my heart?" Where Lady Dedlock becomes frozenly dehumanized, Jasper becomes a savage monster. And yet not a monster like Sikes or Riderhood, nor a savage like Gaffer, nor even quite a suave devil like James Harthouse. Though savage, he is capable of human thought and feeling; though bored, he is not indifferent.

After Edwin's disappearance, Jasper once more makes his way to the London opium den after a long absence. The haggard woman who supplies him with his pipe suspects him of some villainous act and prods him to reveal his secret to her. As the opium takes effect, he becomes confidential while she intermittently furnishes sympathetic encouragement. "'Look here,'" he says,

> "Suppose you had something you were going to do. . . . But had not quite determined to. . . . Might or might not do, you understand. . . . Should you do it in your fancy, when you were lying here doing this?"
>
> She nods her head. "Over and over again."
>
> "Just like me! I did it over and over again. I have done it hundreds of thousands of times in this room."
>
> "It's to be hoped it was pleasant to do, deary."
>
> "It *was* pleasant to do!" (ch. 23)

The savage air with which he makes the final comment demonstrates that the wish-fulfilling power of the opium dream obviously satisfies the craving for physical relief. In fact, strangely enough, it was once better than the actuality has proven to be: "'I did it so often, and through such vast expanses of time, that when it was really done, it seemed not worth the doing, it was done so soon.'" The implication is clearly that Jasper is guilty of finally making in actuality the journey so often taken in dream; but the implication is almost too clear. Dickens is not to be trusted here: for Jasper to say "when it was really done" is not quite equivalent to saying "when I did it." One is reminded of the vague false suspicion cast upon Gaffer, of the trick played on good Mr. Boffin by the alligator in Venus's specialty shop, or of the elaborate circumstantial case built against Lady Dedlock only to be exploded.[16]

The same scene in the opium den that implies guilt prepares equally well for the opposite conclusion—that he is innocent of the deed. The haggard woman is priming the pump for further revelations.

> "I see now. You come o' purpose to take the journey. Why, I might have known it, through its standing by you so."
>
> He answers first with a laugh, and then with a passionate setting of the teeth: "Yes, I came on purpose. When I could not bear my life, I came to get the relief, and I got it. It WAS one! It WAS one!" This repetition with extraordinary vehemence, and the snarl of a wolf. (ch. 23)

The present journey he is taking, however, is less than relieving. It is slow in coming ("'Is it as potent as it used to be?'" he asks regarding the pipe). In addition, the event of which he dreams has presumably now taken place in reality, and "when it comes to be real at last, it is so short that it seems unreal for the first time." Furthermore, the reality somehow does not equal the dream, being disappointing and unsatisfying by comparison. And, finally, now that "it" is real, the relief of the dream is needed at least as much as it was. Jasper laments:

> "It has been too short and easy. I must have a better vision than this; this is the poorest of all. No struggle, no consciousness of peril, no entreaty—and yet I never saw *that* before." With a start.
>
> "Saw what, deary?"
>
> "Look at it! Loók what a poor, mean, miserable thing it is! That must be real. It's over." (ch. 23)

The meaning of "that" and "it" remains shrouded in ambiguity,[17] but it clearly has not finally brought relief to Jasper: it also prevents his achieving relief in the formerly totally satisfying way. The wicked desire for Edwin's death, like the wicked relief felt by Lady Dedlock, becomes additional cause for Jasper to carve demons out of his heart: "What was his death but the key-stone of a gloomy arch removed?" Although it is of course possible—perhaps probable—that Jasper could have proved to be a murderer, yet I believe it more consistent with Dickens's practice that he would have been found guilty only as Lady Dedlock was guilty of the murder of Mr. Tulkinghorn: in will, but not in deed. The difference, however, is negligible for the difference made in the effect upon him. Whether he did the deed or not, he is self-condemned by guilt.

With the creation of John Jasper, the last of the monsters to be summoned forth by Dickens, the warning of the marsh necessarily receives its final iteration. He is a subtle monster. Into his nature enter the refinement and sophistication that make of the "drifting icebergs" like James Harthouse a "very Devil," much more fearful and dangerous than the "roaring lions by which few but savages and hunters are attracted." He, however, is not protected by indifference: rather, like Pip and Lady Dedlock, he is capable of a sensitive internal torment much subtler than that primitively manifested by Gaffer and Sikes in their fearful looks over their shoulders. Despite their differences from one another, each of the marsh creatures[18] sounds the death-in-life warning: People who think or feel like these creatures, who will or act like them, might as well live in the marsh, for they bring the marsh with them wherever they go. They may live and die as amphibians, as unawakened human beings; tramp mud through the drawing rooms of London; fly into the marsh miasma even while fleeing in boredom from it; or transform a counting/gatehouse into an ugly lighthouse. Subhuman or dehumanized, victims or perpetrators, they are living reminders that there are many kinds of self-imposed death. People may turn both themselves and those they touch into monsters through forgetting their humane links with others.

The double guilt felt by Pip can be echoed in the heart of any sensitive person. Every marsh monster to be encountered in human affairs reminds us that "All about this was quite familiar knowledge down in the slime, ages ago." Of what account is our great myth of human progress if we still permit our fellows to remain subhuman or cause them to be dehumanized, or if we ourselves can revert so readily to the monster? This, or something very like it, is the warning of the marsh, allegorically represented in the two journeymen of Stony Durdles, incessantly sawing stone in a petrified grove of tombstones "as if they were mechanical figures emblematical of Time and Death."

# IV

## *A Struggle in Time*

WITH THE RIVER and marsh world in the background with all its intimations of human mortality, the remaining chapters of this study contemplate the world of life, which was Dickens's real concern. It will be recalled that the death-related features of the marsh share three basic qualities: monotony, coldness, and rigidity. Life, conversely, is characterized by diversity, warmth, and flexibility. Its values are positive rather than negative. Unlike the timeless, featureless, unchanging marsh world, perpetually in gray darkness, this world of life is diversified with natural sunshine and shadow, a riot of colors, an abundance of things, a constantly changing order of events, complex people with passions and dreams—and the ticking of a clock.

Moving into the image patterns that assert the positive values making life-in-time meaningful, one turns away from the death configurations but can never leave them behind, for full attachment to life requires continual awareness of human mortality. No one can permanently ignore that life is a private, individual affair rushing through time to its dissolution. How, then, is it possible to avoid the pessimism that would seem the only intelligent response to this fate?

The egocentric view of life need not in itself be pessimistic, of course, if one is prepared to reach out boldly beyond death to assert some kind of afterlife, or if one can rest comfortably in an established faith. The journey of Everyman, for instance, never questions whether anything could be more absorbingly meaningful than the private search for salvation. Nor is it pessimistic if one is capable of achieving some kind of tragic stance. Oedipus rises to lonely greatness through his private voyage of discovery. Dickens, however, gives no evidence of being prepared for either a religious or a tragic escape from pessimism; his characters must look elsewhere for meaning.

It is notable, however, that in Dickens's creation of river and marsh, the egocentric view of life is presented as in itself defective. Lower river and marsh are always threatening and life-destroying. Their denizens are not just alone, a condition of all people at times: rather, they are all terribly isolated and alienated. Their journey of life is a journey of death, sterile and joyless, through a wasteland world. Guilt and corruption rise like the fog from both river and marsh. In addition to underscoring the inescapable fact of personal death, Dickens insistently warns his readers that they risk losing their one chance at life if they cannot or will not escape bondage to the egocentric view.

To perceive Dickens's total mode of experience, then, we must postulate, in addition to the linear private view of life, a circular public one visible from the perspective of society rather than of the individual. Whereas the linear view inevitably leads one to the terminal fact of personal death, the public and social view has no terminus but keeps leading past death back into life again. The individual may die, but human life itself goes on undiminished. The escape from pessimism according to Dickens, then, will be seen to be a social escape relating the individual to the remainder of humanity. Though every person lives but once briefly, individual life takes on extended meaning to the degree that each person can identify with the ongoing life of society.

Some sensitive Dickens characters, like Lizzie Hexam, seem always to have understood this secret. But more representative human beings, like Pip, must struggle painfully to outgrow the destructive demands of the ego. Not even Meredith had a more lively perception than Dickens that the most life-destroying force of all is the monster Ego. In the ensuing chapters, the antagonist will always be incarnated in one of the Protean shapes assumed by egotism.

The world of life is before all else a world where time matters, where people with a strong attachment to life also possess a strong sense of the meaning of time. One of their dependable characteristics is their recognition and continued awareness of their own mortality, which leads them not only to wish to "make much of time" in the small period allotted them out of eternity, but also to view time warmly as a friend. Sometimes people previously detached or withdrawn from life, such as Scrooge or the Haunted Man, can be brought to this realization by being shown a vision of themselves dead, whereupon time takes on urgent meaning for them and they are drawn back into the stream of life with a feeling of rebirth. A proper sensitivity to time, then, helps define the person who will struggle to find a meaning in life that will prevent it from falling into the vast wasteland of Lady Dedlock and John Jasper.

One of the Christmas stories, an allegory clearly setting forth how meaning is given to life through a right relationship to time, illustrates explicitly the difference between the "one-way" and the "round-trip" ticket. The central character in "Mugby Junction" (Christmas story for 1866) is an anonymous man known first only as Barbox Brothers—"so to call the traveller on the warranty of his luggage." Landing at Mugby Junction "at past three o'clock of a tempestuous morning," he pulls up "the woollen muffler round his throat with both hands" and looks about him.

> A place replete with shadowy shapes, this Mugby Junction in the black hours of the four-and-twenty. Mysterious goods trains, covered with palls and gliding on like vast weird funerals, conveying themselves guiltily away from the presence of the few lighted lamps, as if their freight had come to a secret and unlawful end. Half-miles of coal pursuing in a Detective manner, following when they lead, stopping when they stop, backing when they back. Red-hot embers showering out upon the ground, down this dark avenue, and down the other, as if torturing fires were being raked clear; concurrently, shrieks and groans and grinds invading the ear, as if the tortured were at the height of their suffering. . . . An earthquake, accompanied with thunder and lightning, going up express to London. Now, all quiet, all rusty, wind and rain, in possession, lamps extinguished, Mugby Junction dead and indistinct, with its robe drawn over its head, like Caesar. (MJ, ch. 1)

Surrounded by ominous images of the marsh and of violent death calling for a pursuing detective, this traveller seems himself marked for death. Mugby Junction, like Lizzie Hexam in a similarly apprehensive situation (see ch. II), draws its robe over its head.

The journey of this traveller, like that of Lady Dedlock, is an analogy for his futile attempts to fly from his own meaningless life. The mysterious goods train rushes through the night to London, but the traveller has stopped off at this obscure station because, as the natives shrewdly detect, he is really "the gentleman for Nowhere," flying from something but towards nothing. Now,

> as the belated traveller plodded up and down, a shadowy train went by him in the gloom which was no other than the train of a life. From whatever intangible deep cutting or dark tunnel it emerged, here it came, unsummoned and unannounced, stealing upon him, and passing away into obscurity. . . . Attendant, with many a clank and wrench, were lumbering cares, dark meditations, huge dim disappointments, monotonous years, a long jarring line of the discords of a solitary and unhappy existence. (ch. 1)

The reader soon learns that the gentleman for Nowhere is flying from that "penitential anniversary . . . called a birthday." At Mugby Junction, however, he falls into the hands of Phoebe, a young invalid whose happy view of life begins to infect his thinking as he realizes that she apparently has even less cause for personal happiness than he does.

One day he once more boards the train, for "the great ingenious city," but for the first time he has purchased a round-trip ticket. He returns with a miniature piano for the little invalid to whom, as her father says, "everything is music." Now the traveller decides to try each of the seven roads leading out of Mugby Junction, each time coming back to report to Phoebe what he has found. This occupation is time-consuming. What with loitering so long about the Junction, it is suddenly two days before his birthday. It is more than time for him to set out—not, however, for the vague wild country of "misty mountains, swollen streams, rain, cold, a wild seashore, and rugged roads," which had previously been his intention; instead, "at last the gentleman for Nowhere took a ticket for Somewhere, and his destination was the great ingenious town."[1] Here he begins to suspect that:

> Mugby Junction was a Junction of many branches, invisible as well as visible, and had joined him to an endless number of byeways. For, whereas he would, but a little while ago, have walked these streets blindly brooding, he now had eyes and thoughts for a new external world. . . . "I too am but a little part of a great whole," he began to think; "and to be serviceable to myself and others, or to be happy, I must cast my interest into, and draw it out of, the common stock." (ch. 2)

In the city, he does indeed cast his interest into the common stock of people, so much so that his birthday hits him as a shocking surprise "when he heard the town clocks striking, and, referring to his watch, found the evening to have so slipped away, that they were striking twelve." He regards himself in the chimney-glass.

> "Why, it's your birthday already," he said smiling. "You are looking very well. I wish you many happy returns of the day."
>
> He had never before bestowed that wish upon himself. "By Jupiter!" he discovered, "it alters the whole case of running away from one's birthday! It's a thing to explain to Phoebe. Besides, here is quite a long story to tell her, that has sprung out of the road with no story. I'll go back, instead of going on." (ch. 2)

And so he does go back, to stay permanently in Mugby Junction, "a convenient place to live in, for being joined at will to all sorts of agreeable places and persons"—a place of "many happy returns."

The traveller, who has been running away from time itself in trying to escape his birthday, now can wave it a friendly greeting as *it* flies past him each year as the anniversary of his rebirth into life. What was previously for him a linear flight through time to death has now become a circular journey where other lives pull him back into the stream of human life.

Two basic ideas keep recurring in the image clusters of time perception: first, living in time subjects human beings to a relentless process of progressive change (the mutability theme); and second, living in time requires continual effort and painful struggle. Though the ticking of a clock may be monotonously regulated, the time it ticks off is fraught with changing meaning for every person from the moment of birth to the moment of death. In the individual life, time will always have the last word. This is what Pip realizes on the day he becomes simultaneously aware of his birth and death—when he finds out "for sure" what the graveyard means; thus this day of his spiritual birth marks the onset of his spiritual struggles.

A natural tension relates these two ideas of human subjection to time and struggle for existence; for the line of least resistance, the path of comfort, is *not* to struggle, but to relax in actual death or into the death-in-life possible through withdrawal into a remote state of mind, making one day very like another—or through concealing the truth from oneself with the delusion that one is really the master of time and can make it do one's bidding. The marshy borderland between life and death is inhabited by many people who manage in one of these fashions to rub up against most of life without being painfully affected by it.

Sir Leicester Dedlock, for instance, has little sympathy with the limiting concept of time, which leads only to foolish practices of hurrying and to dangerous "leveling" ideas of change and progress. At the "dreary place" in Lincolnshire, Sir Leicester, in contrast to Lady Dedlock, is unaffected by the marshy conditions. In fact, he seems placidly at home there.

> He is at his place in Lincolnshire; but the waters are out again on the low-lying grounds, and the cold and damp steal into Chesney Wold, though well-defended, and eke into Sir Leicester's bones. The blazing fires of faggot and coal—Dedlock timber and antediluvian forest—that blaze upon the broad wide hearths, and wink in the twilight on the frowning woods, sullen to see how trees are sacrificed, do not exclude the enemy. (*BH*, ch. 28)

This is not the first, nor will it be the last time trees and human beings imaginatively fuse together in the Dickens imagery. The reader may recall, for instance, that Lizzie Hexam, viewing a red sunrise and filled with thoughts of death, was reminded at once of a forest fire and a pool of blood. Here the frowning woods react quite humanly to the "sacrifice" of their fellows on the altar of Sir Leicester's comfort. He, of course, is oblivious to the wisp of warning, for Sir Leicester considers himself to be in complete command of time and resents any challenge to his position. His visitor, the busy and prosperous ironmaster Rouncewell, represents an intrusion by time and is therefore a personal affront to Sir Leicester: living proof that the Lincolnshire flood waters have their analogues in human affairs: "The floodgates of society are burst open, and the waters have—a—obliterated the landmarks of the framework of cohesion by which things are held together" (ch. 40).

Although the upstart Rouncewell seems insensitive to the Dedlock position, Sir Leicester asserts his continued repose:

> Sir Leicester is content enough that the ironmaster should feel that there is no hurry there; there, in that ancient house, rooted in that quiet park, where the ivy and the moss have had time to mature, and the gnarled and warted elms, and the umbrageous oaks, stand deep in the fern and leaves of a hundred years; and where the sun-dial on the terrace has dumbly recorded for centuries that Time, which was as much the property of every Dedlock—while he lasted—as the house and lands. Sir Leicester sits down in an easy-chair, opposing his repose and that of Chesney Wold to the restless flights of ironmasters. (ch. 28)

As Sir Leicester sits impervious and immovable he looks like a ponderous anachronism from a primitive world patiently enduring such ephemeral encroachments on his domain in the complacent expectation that these too will pass. He merges into the protective coloration of the middle and ancient past before his fire of "faggot and coal—Dedlock timber and antediluvian forest" in the ancient house standing "deep in the fern and leaves of a hundred years." It is thus made clear that Sir Leicester inhabits the borderland to the marsh and shares its characteristics.

The same insularity of mind that incapsulates an individual against time also seems to instill a provincial idea of space. The monotonous world of Mr. Podsnap, for example, is "not a very large world, morally; no, nor even geographically; seeing that although his business was sustained upon commerce with other countries, he considered other countries, with that important reservation, a mistake, and of their manners and customs would conclusively observe, 'Not English!' when PRESTO! with a flourish of the arm, and a flush of the face, they were swept away" (*OMF,* bk. I, ch. 11). Podsnap remains comfortable in his position as a result of his happy faculty of settling "that whatever he put behind him he put out of existence." The small world of Sir Leicester likewise dominates the universe: "The fashionable world—tremendous orb, nearly five miles round—is in full swing, and the solar system works respectfully at its appointed distances" (*BH,* ch. 48). Thus do the monuments of egocentricity put both time and space into their respectful places.

Elsewhere in *Bleak House,* Harold Skimpole, the parasite, carelessly parades *his* indifference to time. John Jarndyce has asked him to pause a moment, as he wishes to say a word to him. "'My dear Jarndyce,' he cheerfully replied, going back to his sofa, 'as many moments as you please. Time is no object here. We never know what o'clock it is, and we never care. Not the way to get on in life, you'll tell me? Certainly. But we *don't* get on in life. We don't pretend to do it'" (ch. 43). When, a short time after this declaration, Sir Leicester is announced in the Jarndyce town-house drawing room where Skimpole is a guest, it is hardly surprising to learn that Sir Leicester is highly impressed by that gentleman and hopes "he might have the good fortune to be at Chesney Wold when Mr. Skimpole next came into Lincolnshire." He recognizes a kindred spirit in a world oblivious to time.

Lesser people than the Sir Leicester Dedlocks and the Harold Skimpoles also have opinions on the subject of time. For example,

Mr. Snagsby, the law-stationer of Cook's Court, somewhat restively awaits the arrival of guests. Mrs. Snagsby, a follower of the unctuous minister, Chadband, has invited the Chadbands to tea. The table is spread with mouthwatering delicacies assembled in recognition of Chadband's being "rather a consuming vessel . . . [who] can wield such weapons of the flesh as a knife and fork remarkably well" (ch. 19). Despite his appreciation of this world's infinite variety of good things, Chadband seems to be somewhat loosely attached to life, for the Chadbands, as Snagsby remarks "in a mild and casual way," are late. Mrs. Snagsby retorts reproachfully that perhaps he wishes to begin without them.

> Mr. Snagsby does look as if he would like it very much, but he says, with his cough of mildness, "No, my dear, no. I merely named the time."
>
> "What's time," says Mrs. Snagsby, "to eternity?"
>
> "Very true, my dear," says Mr. Snagsby. "Only when a person lays in victuals for tea, a person does it with a view—perhaps—more to time. And when a time is named for having tea, it's better to come up to it." (ch. 19)

Common sense, of course, is the great leveler of pretension and delusion. Quite true: Time is *nothing* to eternity. But Snagsby might well have added that time is the individual's stake in eternity—the only part of it one has. Although indifference to time permits one to relax, life demands a more precise view that enables one, when a time is named for having tea, to "come up to it."

This cold eye of common sense always quickly reduces to figures of ridicule those who act as if all eternity is theirs. The narrator of the first chapter of *Dombey and Son* views his subject through such an eye. The result is a masterpiece of irony as Dombey's whole relationship to time is explored, while his name tolls its way through the whole book like an old church-bell—or like the gong on some old clock: Dombey, Dombey, Dombey.

The moment at which the reader meets Dombey is one of triumph, for his wife has just presented him with his first child (the earlier girl being not worth mentioning). Dombey and Son present interesting points of comparison and contrast:

> Dombey was about eight-and-forty years of age. Son about eight-and-forty minutes. Dombey was rather bald, rather red, and though a handsome well-made man, too stern and pompous in appearance to be prepossessing. Son was very bald, and very red, and though (of course) an undeniably fine infant, somewhat crushed and spotty in

> his general effect, as yet. On the brow of Dombey, Time and his brother Care had set some marks, as on a tree that was to come down in good time—remorseless twins they are for striking through their human forests, notching as they go—while the countenance of Son was crossed and recrossed with a thousand little creases, which the same deceitful Time would take delight in smoothing out and wearing away with the flat part of his scythe, as a preparation of the surface for his deeper operation. (*DS,* ch. 1)

Imagining this scene, one might easily fall into the illusion that the same person is being viewed at different times on the same continuum. Inherent in every birth there is a funeral. The infant delicately foreshadows the condition to which life will bring the adult; Dombey is further along on that common road to eternity than Son, but each is already marked to "come down in good time." Time is a "wearing" operation, first wearing away the infantile baldness, redness, and wrinkles later to wear away the man.

For Sir Leicester Dedlock is in one respect right. Inherent in the idea of time is that of change—the decay and death of all created things as well as their growth and progress are the advancing products of time. Dickens reminds the reader that an individual's stake in eternity is precisely measured out with the analogy of the forest and the woodman: "On the brow of Dombey, Time and his brother Care had set some marks, as on a tree that was to come down in good time—remorseless twins they are for striding through their human forests, notching as they go." Once again the fates of tree and human being merge sympathetically together.

This analogy takes on an additional convergence-of-the-twain meaning in the beginning of *A Tale of Two Cities* as Dickens reviews some of the cruelties that over many years would lead to the French Revolution:

> It is likely enough that, rooted in the woods of France and Norway, there were growing trees when that sufferer [a youth tortured to death because "he had not kneeled down in the rain to do honour to a dirty procession of monks"] was put to death, already marked by the Woodman, Fate, to come down and be sawn into boards, to make a certain movable framework with a sack and a knife in it, terrible in history. It is likely enough that in the rough outhouses of some tillers of the heavy lands adjacent to Paris, there were sheltered from the weather that very day, rude carts, bespattered with rustic mire, snuffed about by pigs, and roosted in by poultry, which the Farmer, Death, had already set apart to be his tumbrils of the Revolution. But

> that Woodman and that Farmer, though they work unceasingly, work silently, and no one heard them as they went about with muffled tread: the rather, forasmuch as to entertain any suspicion that they were awake, was to be atheistical and traitorous. (*T2C,* ch. 1)

Jostling together here elbow to elbow in ironic relationship are four different woodmen: The Woodman Fate who marks the fatal tree(s), the human woodman who cuts down the literal tree, the Woodman Time who brings together in fearful convergence the felled tree and the about-to-be-felled man, and finally the hooded woodman (the Farmer, Death) who wields the axe of the guillotine. All four of these merge in some sense with the transcendent "woodman," Time itself, which moves both people and trees along the life/death continuum.

Here the woodman's axe foretells actual death, but Dickens also finds the analogy useful for other purposes. In *Our Mutual Friend,* for example, following the night John Harmon is almost murdered, he confusedly remembers his experience:

> I saw a figure like myself lying dressed in my clothes on a bed. What might have been, for anything I know, a silence of days, weeks, months, years, was broken by a violent wrestling of men all over the room. The figure like myself was assailed and my valise was in its hand. I was trodden upon and fallen over. I heard a noise of blows and thought it was a wood-cutter cutting down a tree. I could not have said that my name was John Harmon—I could not have thought it—I didn't know it—but when I heard the blows, I thought of the woodcutter and his axe, and had some dead idea that I was lying in a forest. (*OMF,* bk. II, ch. 13)

The reader's inclination in making sense out of this blurred yet vivid recollection is to attach the adjective to the more sensible substantive: I had "some idea that *I* was lying *dead.*" Thus with the summoning of the associational image, Dickens manages not only to suggest the imminence of death, but also to recreate the hazy, apparently irrational vagaries of semiconsciousness with all the subjective logic such wanderings usually possess. Although the woodcutter who seems to be chopping down John Harmon turns out on this occasion to be after someone else, our mutual friend, like Dombey, is already marked "to come down in good time."

The woodman's axe may also sound in the background when other than physical kinds of death threaten. Muffled by the wet weather at Sir Leicester Dedlock's Lincolnshire place, "the soft loppings and prunings of the woodman's axe can make no crash or crackle as they fall" (*BH,* ch. 2)—the sound certainly can't reach the ears of Sir Leicester any more than he observes "the frowning woods, sullen to see how trees are sacrificed" as he interviews the ironmaster Rouncewell before his blazing fire of "Dedlock timber and antediluvian forest." The felling of these ancient giants has no meaning except comfort for the unperturbed Sir Leicester, though he himself may be the next to go.

People with a capacity for life, on the other hand, are quick to detect that trees and human beings share an identical relationship to time. In *Hard Times* young Louisa Gradgrind, engaged in her favorite occupation of looking to the fire and watching "the red sparks dropping out of the fire, and whitening and dying," is made to think "'after all, how short my life would be . . .'" (*HT,* bk. I, ch. 8). Aware of her own mortality, Louisa is likewise acutely conscious of the inexorable working of "The Great Manufacturer": "Time," who "with his innumerable horse-power, worked away, not minding what anybody said" (bk. I, ch. 14) on all the people in their various stages of being woven into the human fabric.

In this inexorable process, Louisa passes from a blighted childhood[2] to womanhood, to marriage with Mr. Bounderby, to the frozen state of indifference (a monotonous existence) that seems to make her vulnerable to the machinations of the drifting iceberg, James Harthouse. The time has come for him to attempt the seduction. "It was not by any wonderful accident that he found her, the time of day being that at which she was always alone, and the place being her favourite resort. It was an opening in a dark wood, where some felled trees lay, and where she would sit watching the fallen leaves of last year, as she had watched the falling ashes at home" (bk. II, ch. 7). This grove with its images of felled trees, fallen leaves, and falling ashes is wonderfully adapted to convey the mortal danger confronting Louisa's blighted soul.

Harthouse has ascertained that the only penetrable spot in Louisa's defense is her love for her brother Tom. He therefore affects a desire to aid the "Whelp" in overcoming his dissipation, and declares to her his sympathetic awareness of her brother's ingratitude. As he speaks, the "wood floated before her" through the unaccustomed tears rising "from a deep well, long concealed." Now appears that brother, "yonder among the trees," and the signal appropriateness of his coming "idly beating the branches as he lounged along, or . . . stoop[ing] viciously to rip the moss from the trees with his stick," betrays his violent indifference to garden life and foreshadows his implication in the action threatening the tree. Later, as Harthouse talks to the young man, Tom sits "plucking buds and picking them to pieces" or "biting the rosebuds now, and tearing them away from his teeth with a hand that trembled like an infirm old man's," a destructive monster of fearful threat to tender growth.[3]

Even though in these later passages from *Hard Times* Dickens picks up and extends the analogy in scenes viewed from the distant perspective of the narrator, Louisa herself first clearly perceives the similarity between her own mortality and that of trees.

Dombey, however, on the occasion of the birth of his son, is ironically oblivious to the wearing operations of the woodman Time as he sits complacently "wearing" time in the shape of a loudly ticking watch: "Dombey, exulting in the long-looked-for event, jingled and jingled the heavy gold watch-chain that depended from below his trim blue coat, whereof the buttons sparkled phosphorescently in the feeble rays of the distant fire" (*DS*, ch. 1).[4] Dombey, like Sir Leicester, clearly considers himself in command here in this darkened room: he is master of the ship, a sea captain with his "trim blue coat" and his buttons sparkling "phosphorescently." For Dombey also has his related illusions about space: for him, where he happens to be is the center of the universe, just as time exists for his well-being:

> The earth was made for Dombey and Son to trade in, and the sun and moon were made to give them light. Rivers and seas were formed to float their ships; rainbows gave them promise of fair weather; winds blew for or against their enterprises; stars and planets circled in their orbits, to preserve inviolate a system of which they were the centre. Common abbreviations took new meanings in his eyes, and had sole reference to them. A. D. had no concern with anno Domini, but stood for anno Dombei—and Son. (ch. 1)

Thus Dickens ironically establishes Dombey's absurd blindness to his sublunary condition at a time that brings his son to birth and takes away his wife. The chapter moves faster and faster to the accompaniment of Dombey's watch, ostensibly engaged in a race with Dr. Parker Peps's watch, but actually reminding us that Time itself is racing all the figures already on the human continuum inexorably toward death. "Mr. Dombey sat jingling and jingling his heavy gold watch-chain in the great arm-chair by the side of the bed. . . .

The child glanced keenly at the blue coat and stiff white cravat, which, with a pair of creaking boots and a very loud ticking watch, embodied her idea of a father. . . . There was no sound in answer but the loud ticking of Mr. Dombey's watch and Dr. Parker Peps's watch, which seemed in the silence to be running a race. . . . No word or sound in answer. Mr. Dombey's watch and Dr. Parker Peps's watch seemed to be racing faster. . . . The race in the ensuing pause was fierce and furious. The watches seemed to jostle, and to trip each other up" (ch. 1).

As the tempo increases, time runs out for the mother, who holds to her single frail support—the negligible small daughter—until "clinging fast to that slight spar within her arms, the mother drifted out upon the dark and unknown sea that rolls round all the world." Meanwhile, the captain of the ship stands awkwardly apart in the shadows, looking slightly ridiculous in his commanding costume.

Many Dickens characters with or without an attachment to life are constantly reminding the reader of the passage of time, though they are not always alert to the significance of what they say. In *David Copperfield,* for example, time's inexorable passing is a continual thematic note struck consciously by David, but also echoed by other characters, whether tossed off as a cliché by Mr. Micawber: "But punch, my dear Copperfield, like time and tide, waits for no man" (*DC,* ch. 28); as a flight of suitable rhetoric from the pen of J. M., writing to D. C. regarding his love problems: "Must not D. C. confide himself to the broad pinions of Time?" (ch. 38); or the commonplace observation of Agnes: "How the time goes!" (ch. 35). David himself in his "Retrospect" chapters repeatedly throws his life into the perspective of passing time and plays the *ubi sunt* theme. Chapter 18 looks back aross his school-days: "My school-days! the silent gliding on of my existence—the unseen, unfelt progress of my life—from childhood up to youth! Let me think, as I look back upon that flowing water, now a dry channel overgrown with leaves, whether there are any marks along its course, by which I can remember how it ran."

For "time has stolen on unobserved." David has progressed from the lowest boy to the head boy: "That little fellow seems to be no part of me; I remember him as something left behind upon the road of life—as something I have passed, rather than have actually been—and almost think of him as someone else." As in *Dombey and Son,* the basic configuration is a picture showing human figures in various stages of life appearing, progressing along, and vanishing from the moving road of time. Whereas Dombey and Son imaginatively fuse into one, the single entity David Copperfield proliferates into a series of such shadow figures, all with their own persisting, though transitory, reality.

On the eve of his marriage to Dora at twenty-one, David once more pauses to look back over his life.

> Let me stand aside, to see the phantoms of those days go by me, accompanying the shadow of myself, in dim procession.
>
> Weeks, months, seasons, pass along. They seem little more than a summer day and a winter evening. Now, the Common where I walk with Dora is all in bloom, a field of bright gold; and now the unseen heather lies in mounds and bunches underneath a covering of snow. In a breath, the river that flows through our Sunday walks is sparkling in the summer sun, is ruffled by the winter wind, or thickened with drifting heaps of ice. Faster than ever river ran towards the sea, it flashes, darkens, and rolls away. (ch. 43)

David has the ability to back far enough away from his own life to put it into perspective as a progress through time, with a definite beginning and ending marking out his own little stake in eternity. As Pip comes to a simultaneous recognition of birth and death, as the birth of little Dombey both creates his own death and brings the death of his mother, David thinks of the two boundaries of existence together. Looking back on his infancy when "I lay in my basket, and my mother lay in her bed," he again cannot refrain from a glance in the direction of death as well: "The land of dreams and shadows, the tremendous region whence I had so lately travelled; and the light upon the window of our room shone out upon the earthly bourne of all such travellers, and the mound above the ashes and dust that once was he, without whom I had never been" (ch. 1). Once more comes the flash of insight as the child's creation and his demise merge in the person of his parent.

Birth and death are equally solemn occasions for the thoughtful, for here the struggle is especially crucial: by very definition failure here sends one forever into the "land of dreams and shadows" that David apprehends. When that small "item of mortality" who comes to be known as Oliver Twist is born, "there was considerable difficulty in inducing Oliver to take upon himself the office of respiration,—a troublesome practice, but one which custom has rendered necessary to our easy existence: and for some time he lay gasping on a little flock mattress, rather unequally poised between this world and the next: the balance being decidedly in favour of the latter" (*OT*, ch. 1). Oliver and nature "fought out the point between them," and—again—even as the child accepts the challenge of the struggle for existence, his mother gives it up as not worth the effort. Similarly, Dombey, Son, comes into the world "with his little fists curled up and clenched," seeming, "in his feeble way, to be squaring at existence for having come upon him so unexpectedly" (*DS*, ch. 1). In another part of the house Mrs. Chick is earnestly remonstrating with her dying sister-in-law. "'Now, really Fanny my dear,'" she chides: "'I shall have to be quite cross with you, if you don't rouse yourself. It's necessary for you to make an effort, and perhaps a very great and painful effort which you are not disposed to make; but this is a world of effort you know, Fanny, and we must never yield, when so much depends upon us. Come! Try! I must really scold you if you don't!'" Dickens seems to enjoy making unlikely characters his mouthpieces. Distasteful as Chick may be with her complacent clucking of her little formula for life, what she says is irritatingly true—too true for poor Fanny, who proves unable or unwilling to come up to it.

The power of inertia in these boundary experiences always sends the balance in favor of death; living requires the vigorous assertion of a vital power combining strength and will. John Harmon, confronted with such an extremity in *Our Mutual Friend*, marshals enough of both to survive. He later recalls his confused impression of hearing a woodman's axe before being dropped unconscious into the river.

> It was only after a downward slide through something like a tube, and then a great noise and a sparkling and a crackling as of fires, that the consciousness came upon me, "This is John Harmon drowning! [not a tree falling!] John Harmon, struggle for your life. John Harmon, call on Heaven and save yourself!" I think I cried it out aloud in a great agony, and then a heavy horrid unintelligible something vanished, and it was I who was struggling there alone in the water. (*OMF*, bk. II, ch. 13)

The struggle for existence here, seen through the eyes of John Harmon, is experienced as the reader's own.

Elsewhere in *Our Mutual Friend* the point of view shifts. Here another river victim hovers between life and death while the reader hovers over him, an absorbed spectator with unsettling questions rising to mind.

> If you are not gone for good, Mr. Riderhood, it would be something to know where you are hiding at present. This flabby lump of mortality that we work so hard at with such patient perseverance, yields no sign of you. If you are gone for good, Rogue, it is very solemn, and if you are coming back, it is hardly less so. Nay, in the suspense and mystery of the latter question, involving that of where you may be now, there is a solemnity even added to that of death, making us who are in attendance alike afraid to look on you and to look off you, and making those below start at the least sound of a creaking plank in the floor. (bk. III, ch. 3)

Did an eyelid tremble? A nostril twitch? The chest flutter faintly? "Over and over again No, No. But try over and over again, nevertheless." Finally comes an unmistakable sign of life, a spark that may "smoulder and go out, or it may glow and expand, but see!" The spectators shed tears: "Neither Riderhood in this world, nor Riderhood in the other, could draw tears from them; but a striving human soul between the two can do it easily." Breathlessly the onlookers follow this fundamental human battle as the man struggles: "Now he is almost here, now he is far away again. Now he is struggling harder to get back. And yet—like us all, when we swoon—like us all, every day of our lives when we wake—he is instinctively unwilling to be restored to the consciousness of this existence, and would be left dormant, if he could."

It is now apparent that Rogue is returning from one of the analogues of death, for unconsciousness is a "little death" that, in sleep, daily reenacts the boundary struggle for existence. Riderhood is "instinctively unwilling to be restored to the consciousness of this existence"—"like us all," says Dickens, interestingly, "every day of our lives." In a few moments, as the "low, bad, unimpressible face" comes up unmistakably from the depths, the spectators will fall away indifferently. But their rapt attention has demonstrated their awareness that, whatever the character of the individual in the daily business of living, any return from death is a pure triumph of the human body and spirit over their own inertia.

The first such triumph, then, is birth itself. Once safely past that hazardous struggle, the infant has already demonstrated a certain toughness of body and spirit—can now be expected, like baby Dombey, "to accomplish a destiny. A destiny, little fellow!" (*DS*, ch. 1).

# V

## *The Ideal Childhood*

IT CANNOT BE effectively denied that Dickens dealt sentimentally with children; yet to dwell too much upon those instances when he pulled out the stops on a melodramatic theme is to blind oneself to the allegorical significance of children in the Dickens view. Children in their sunny innocence far upriver presumably live in an Eden lost long ago by humankind and more recently by every individual adult. Nonetheless, the belief that as long as humanity endures, children will never cease to inhabit the springtime garden repeatedly sends a breath of renewed hope into people who recall as a distant dream their own childhood, however flawed, when anything seemed possible. The tears for a lost Dombey or Jo or Little Nell thus have universal wellsprings much deeper than the sentimental pathos attendant upon propaganda or a cheap play on the emotions.

In addition, childhood itself has for Dickens a special meaning related to a configuration already asserted in this study: When David looks back across his memory to observe a boy, a little fellow who "seems to be no part of me; I remember him as something I have passed, rather than have actually been," he is calling forth an interpretation of the human consciousness so natural to his creator that its reflection is met everywhere in his works. This is the con-

Four main sources will be used to put together the composite picture of childhood depicted in this chapter: three Christmas stories—"The Child's Story" (CS), "A Christmas Tree" (CT), and "The Haunted House" (HH); and one novel—*David Copperfield* (*DC*).

figuration of the person as a composite of successive figures, one of whom exists physically at a given time, but the remainder of whom live intact in memory. The condition of each successive existence depends upon what has been the fate of its predecessor. Many "blighted" characters turn out to include in their processions a "child with no childhood"—or to lack the child entirely. Our friend who finds himself in Mugby Junction (see ch. IV), for instance watches go by him on "the train of a life" a "child who had never had a childhood or known a parent." Mr. Grewgious, talking with his ward, Miss Rosa Bud, in *The Mystery of Edwin Drood,* attributes his "dry" nature to a similar situation:

> "I mean," he explained, "that young ways were never my ways. I was the only offspring of parents far advanced in life, and I half believe I was born advanced in life myself. No personality is intended towards the name you will so soon change, when I remark that while the general growth of people seem to have come into existence, buds, I seem to have come into existence a chip. I was a chip—and a very dry one—when I first became aware of myself." (*MED,* ch. 9)

"Given the deficiencies in the nature of this human being," these comments seem to reason, "one can only infer that he was deprived of the childhood which would have furnished him with what he lacks." This reasoning in turn rests upon well-developed and firm assumptions regarding the pattern of an ideal, natural childhood, a pattern which can readily be reconstructed from Dickens's direct statements on the subject.

In order to illuminate ensuing configurations, this chapter will temporarily suspend the method of analysis used elsewhere in the study. Instead, it will tell the running story of the ideal childhood, describing its surroundings and narrating its events, for among the phenomena of this childhood will be encountered the elements that will return, often grotesquely distorted and perverted, in many subsequent configurations to test and criticize society, or to evaluate individuals.

Dickens's actual tracing of the permanent imprint made on a child's mind as a result of associating certain images with certain affective attitudes is a record comparable in a number of ways to Wordsworth's *Prelude.* At first, the natural condition of childhood, as allegorically pictured in "The Child's Story," is idyllic and innocent. Life in the garden of childhood is beneficent and carefree, and the business of life is only "playing." A traveller setting out on the journey of life comes first upon a beautiful child in this garden who says: "I am always at play. Come and play with me." A little later the traveller loses the child, but meets a boy who says to him: "I am always learning. Come and learn with me." And yet a little beyond, he loses the boy likewise but comes upon a youth who says: "I am always in love. Come and love with me" (CS).

These three, the child, the boy,[1] and the youth, all live in the idyllic garden where they develop the emotional responses that will equip them for life, because the sensitive young human soul must be protected and well prepared if it is to develop to accomplish a destiny. "Fair seedtime had my soul," Wordsworth wrote of a similar idyllic garden where a child also matured through three stages, "and I grew up / Fostered alike by beauty and by fear" (*The Prelude,* Bk. I, ll. 305–6). Dickens's idealization of childhood bears a marked resemblance to that of Wordsworth, for he too sees it as a "seedtime"[2] indispensable for the natural development of the soul, which is "fostered alike by beauty and by fear." Although it is doubtful that Dickens would have echoed the Wordsworthian sentiment that his soul had had such a "fair seedtime" (if, indeed, he thought any child knew it in its totality), nonetheless, like Wordsworth, he found rushing out upon him from childhood certain epiphanal experiences with elemental forces, which would remain with him throughout life as types or emblems of those forces.

The traveller, then, responds in turn to the child, the boy, and the youth. In the idyllic garden of the child

> he played with that child, the whole day long, and they were very merry. The sky was so blue, the sun was so bright, the water was so sparkling, the leaves were so green, the flowers were so lovely, and they heard such singing-birds and saw so many butterflies, that everything was beautiful. This was in fine weather. When it rained, they loved to watch the falling drops, and to smell the fresh scents. When it blew, it was delightful to listen to the wind, and fancy what it said, as it came rushing from its home—where was that, they wondered!—whistling and howling, driving the clouds before it, bending the trees, rumbling in the chimneys, shaking the house, and making the sea roar in fury. But, when it snowed, that was best of all; for, they liked nothing so well as to look up at the white flakes falling fast and thick, like down from the breasts of millions of white birds; and to see how smooth and deep the drift was; and to listen to the hush upon the paths and roads.
>
> They had plenty of the finest toys in the world, and the most

> astonishing picture-books: all about scimitars and slippers and turbans, and dwarfs and giants and genii and fairies, and blue-beards and bean-stalks and riches and caverns and forests and Valentines and Orsons: and all new and all true. (CS)

All of the forces of life play benevolently about the trusting child as he plays: whether sun, rain, wind, or snow betokens the changing seasons, "everything was beautiful." The child in the garden is also surrounded by human creations: "the finest toys in the world" and "the most astonishing picture-books"—"all new and all true." Sun, rain, wind, snow, dwarfs and giants and genii and fairies: all the "bran-new" objects of experience impinging on his consciousness have equal integrity: there is nothing to choose among them for truth or goodness or beauty.

With the help of the objects of experience about him, the developing boy begins to discriminate among the separate forces in the outside world, to learn that they are not all merely a sympathetic extension of himself. These objects are more clearly seen in another Christmas story, "A Christmas Tree," where Dickens hangs upon the Christmas trees of childhood memory the specific toys and books glancingly referred to in "The Child's Story." "All toys at first, I find": the Tumbler, the Jack-in-the-box, the cardboard dancing lady and the cardboard man on a string, the mask, the Doll's house, and the toy theatre. All in their turn acquire special meanings to be permanently etched on the boy's memory. First the toys in the form of human figures, the puppets and dolls, whose superficial resemblance to real people but fundamental difference from them would fuse in the child's imagination, provide many a later analogy helping to interpret life for his successors in the procession, such as the Tumbler who wouldn't lie down, but "persisted in rolling his fat body about, until he rolled himself still, and brought those lobster eyes of his to bear upon me—when I affected to laugh very much, but in my heart of hearts was extremely doubtful of him." The "infernal snuff-box" from which sprang "a demoniacal Counsellor in a black gown, with an obnoxious head of hair, and a red cloth mouth, wide open" developed a scary habit of flying "out of Mammoth Snuff-boxes in dreams, when least expected" and "in a highly magnified state." The cardboard lady who "stood up against the candlestick to dance" was beautiful, but the larger cardboard man had "a sinister expression in that nose of his."

What was awakening in the child soul was the sense of wonder, a compound of beauty and fear—an apprehension of "unknown modes of being" latent even in the inanimate objects one could touch and feel in everyday experience.

But no other of the toys held the possibilities for terror that resided in the "dreadful Mask":

> When did that dreadful Mask first look at me? Who put it on, and why was I so frightened that the sight of it is an era in my life? It is not a hideous visage in itself; it is even meant to be droll; why then were its stolid features so intolerable? Surely not because it hid the wearer's face. An apron would have done as much; and though I should have preferred even the apron away, it would not have been absolutely insupportable, like the mask. Was it the immovability of the mask? The doll's face was immovable, but I was not afraid of her. Perhaps that fixed and set change coming over a real face, infused into my quickened heart some remote suggestion and dread of the universal change that is to come on every face, and make it still? Nothing reconciled me to it. . . . Nor was it any satisfaction to be shown the Mask, and see that it was made of paper, or to have it locked up and be assured that no one wore it. The mere recollection of that fixed face, the mere knowledge of its existence anywhere, was sufficient to awake me in the night all perspiration and horror, with "O I know it's coming! O the Mask!" (CT)

The ramifications of the fearful mask reach out later through many a death-related analogy. The early memories of the gentleman for Nowhere, for instance, are filled with fearful masks. In a dreamlike vision, a parade of the adults who played a part in shaping his lost soul passes before him, each asking of him: "What am I like, Young Jackson?" First he responds to a woman, who is "like a blight all through the year to me. You hard-lined, thin-lipped, repressive, changeless woman with a wax mask on. You are like the Devil to me; most of all when you teach me religious things, for you make me abhor them" (MJ, ch. 1).[3] Later he answers a man—"like my father, I sometimes think. You are hard enough and cold enough so to have brought up an acknowledged son. I see your scanty figure, your close brown suit, and your tight brown wig; but you, too, wear a wax mask to your death. You never by chance remove it—it never by chance falls off—and I know no more of you."

The result of subjection to these masked figures is another memory, of a child held prisoner behind "that horrible mask" and fated to eat and drink "in silence and constraint with the mask before me, every day." The deathlike mask is indeed a fearful apparition. But the difference between the experience of the child in the garden and the blighted child, such as the gentleman for Nowhere, is that the former has time to assimilate the *idea* of the mask (as of other threatening forces) before he must encounter it in reality.

Then, in contrast to the mask with its presentiments of death: "Ah! The Doll's house!" with its wonderful miniature furniture "perched among the boughs as if in preparation for some fairy housekeeping."

> I don't admire the Houses of Parliament half so much as that stone-fronted mansion with real glass windows, and door-steps, and a real balcony—greener than I ever see now except at watering places; and even they afford but a poor imitation. . . . Could all the Temperance Societies of these later days, united, give me such a tea-drinking as I have had through the means of yonder little set of blue crockery, which really would hold liquid (it ran out of the small wooden cask, I recollect, and tasted of matches), and which made tea, nectar. (CT)

The affective values of the abundantly fitted-out Doll's house become inseparably associated with it: its warmth and safety and delicious pleasures epitomize a snug security magically provided long after the traveller has left both child and boy behind.[4]

And now, on the Christmas tree, "How thick the books begin to hang"—"What fat black letters to begin with!" as the boy learns that "'A was an archer, and shot at a frog'" (CT). The whole panorama of the human imagination spreads before him. Everything in the books pulsates with imagined life, from the alphabet on. "To this day," David Copperfield recalls, "when I look upon the fat black letters in the primer, the puzzling novelty of their shapes, and the easy good nature of O and Q and S, seem to present themselves again before me as they used to do" (*DC,* ch. 4).

With the appearance of the books, the mysterious forces of beauty and fear, of good and evil, begin to open before the boy with increasing complexity and ambiguity. "Jack and the Beanstalk" fires his imagination with dreams of heroic exploits against those "dreadfully interesting, double-headed giants" (CT). He falls in love with Little Red Riding-Hood, and gains understanding of "the cruelty and treachery of that dissembling Wolf who ate her grandmother." He travels to far lands with Sinbad the Sailor, and lives in the fairy-tale land of wish fulfillment where giants always fall and Jack lives happily ever after—the only land the boy will ever know where, with the help of a fairy godmother and one's own "sword of sharpness, and . . . shoes of swiftness" (CT), one's dreams and great expectations all come true.

Now vague presentiments of a threatened paradise are gradually succeeded by the disturbing certainty that not all the new things are equally true—at least not all true in the same way. "I seem to have walked along a path of flowers," writes David, for whom the realization comes as an abupt shock, "as far as the crocodile book" (*DC,* ch. 4).[5] Ogres and giants are sometimes overpowering, and even Jack may tumble from his beanstalk country in the sky.

But within his books imagination can still run free, and the boy can redress many a grievance against hard reality by (writes David) "impersonating my favourite characters in them—as I did—and by putting Mr. and Miss Murdstone into all the bad ones." David recalls with gratitude the books from his father's library: "From that blessed little room, Roderick Random, Peregrine Pickle, Humphrey Clinker, Tom Jones, the Vicar of Wakefield, Don Quixote, Gil Blas, and Robinson Crusoe, came out, a glorious host, to keep me company. They kept alive my fancy, and my hope of something beyond that place and time,—they and the Arabian Nights, and the Tales of the Genii,—and did me no harm."

For now comes "the setting-in of the bright Arabian Nights" (CT). In the fancy of the boy, the hero Jack gives way to a glamorous "Eastern King with a glittering scimitar and turban. . . . Oh, now all common things become uncommon and enchanted to me. All lamps are wonderful; all rings are talismans. . . . Any iron ring let into stone is the entrance to a cave which only waits for the magician, and the little fire, and the necromancy, that will make the earth shake."

The boy discovers that the land of the imagination is a seductive Eastern land. He proposes to "another creature like myself, also with the smoothest of faces and the shortest of legs" an astounding thing: that they form with their schoolmates a forbidden sweet thing called "a Seraglio" (HH, ch. 2). He becomes the "Sultan Haroun Alraschid" and basks "in the smiles of eight of the fairest of the daughters of men." Miss Bule, a young lady "whom I judge to have attained the ripe age of eight or nine," becomes the "Favourite." He maintains his position not without some objection from the other creature, who "had already fallen into the second male place in the State, and was set apart for Grand Vizier. He afterwards resisted this disposal of events, but had his hair pulled until he yielded."[6]

The seraglio must be kept secret from Miss Griffin, the mistress of the school, who was "a model of propriety" and must never know when "she paraded us down the Hampstead-Road two and two, that she was walking with a stately step at the head of Polygamy and Mohamedanism." The boy also waits breathlessly with Dinerzade and Scheherazade as they cleverly lead the tyrannical Sultan into granting one more day of life, after which grace "we all three breathe again" (CT). Part of the time the boy parades proudly in the secret splendor of the Sultan, while at other times he resists or cowers before his tyrannical power.

Significantly, at about this time the boy begins to see "a prodigious nightmare" crouching indistinctly among the leaves of the Christmas tree—like the mask: "I don't know why it's frightful—but I know it is." It advances and recedes before his eyes:

> When it comes closest, it is worse. In connexion with it I descry remembrances of winter nights incredibly long; of being sent early to bed, as a punishment for some small offence, and waking in two hours, with a sensation of having been asleep two nights; of the laden hopelessness of morning ever dawning; and the oppression of a weight of remorse. (CT)

David has similar impressions of the terrible five days of imprisonment by Mr. Murdstone when, ridden by guilt, he wondered fearfully whether prison or hanging was to be his fate—of "The length of those five days I can convey no idea to anyone. They occupy the place of years in my remembrance." He recalls "the uncertain pace of the hours, especially at night, when I would wake thinking it was morning, and find that the family were not yet gone to bed, and that all the length of night had yet to come—the depressed dreams and nightmares I had." And all of this remembrance surrounded by an atmosphere of "gloom, and fear, and remorse" (*DC,* ch. 4).

Somewhere along the way, it seems, the reality of malevolent and evil forces, long suspected and increasingly corroborated by experience, has increased its personal threat by moving inside the boy himself. The glittering Sultan with his cruelty and his harem is am ambiguous figure of enticing guilt.[7] The well-preserved secret of the seraglio is a "mysterious and terrible joy" until the awful moment one Sunday morning in church "when the description of Solomon in his domestic glory happened to be read" and "conscience whispered me, 'Thou, too, Haroun'":

> The officiating minister had a cast in his eye, and it assisted conscience by giving him the appearance of reading personally at me. A crimson blush, attended by a fearful perspiration, suffused my fea-

> tures. The Grand Vizier became more dead than alive, and the whole Seraglio reddened as if the sunset of Bagdad shone direct upon their lovely faces. At this portentous time the awful Griffin rose, and balefully surveyed the children of Islam. My own impression was, that Church and State had entered into a conspiracy with Miss Griffin to expose us, and that we should all be put into white sheets, and exhibited in the centre aisle. But, so Westerly—if I may be allowed the expression as opposite to Eastern associations—was Miss Griffin's sense of rectitude, that she merely suspected Apples, and we were saved. (HH)

John Jarndyce would detect a strong "East" wind as the boy finds himself guiltily poised between the Eastern Sultan and the Western "Apples" on the very borderland of the prelapsarian garden and about to be expelled from it, for whether green apples or apples of Eden, their consumption brings disastrous consequences. Certainly one with such growing knowledge of good and evil cannot long continue in the garden of innocence.

"And now it was, at the height of enjoyment of my bliss, that I became heavily troubled." Reality interposes to assert the impracticality of taking the harem home to mother at Midsummer. Then one day, doubly oppressed by guilt and anxiety, the boy sees a strange man talking with Miss Griffin. "Supposing him to be a minion of the law, and that my hour was come, I instantly ran away, with the general purpose of making for Egypt." But the man has really come to tell the boy the stark fact that "'Your pa's dead!'"[8] At these words, "Haroun Alraschid took to flight . . . ; the Seraglio vanished; from that moment, I never again saw one of the eight of the fairest of the daughters of men." Now comes debt at home as well as death, and for him a great cruel school "where the boys knew all about the sale, before I got there, and asked me what I had fetched, and who had bought me, and hooted at me, 'Going, going, gone!' I never whispered in that wretched place that I had been Haroun, or had had a Seraglio." The world of fact and the world of dream are coming to seem less and less satisfactorily related: while nightmare slides in and out of life in a frightening fashion, the wonderful dream seems more and more reserved for a world apart.

But, in compensation, as the traveller is about to leave the boy behind him, a most fair thing appears under the Christmas tree:

> I see a wonderful row of little lights rise smoothly out of the ground, before a vast green curtain. Now, a bell rings—a magic bell, which still sounds in my ears unlike all other bells—and music plays, amidst

> a buzz of voices, and a fragrant smell of orange-peel and oil. Anon, the magic bell commands the music to cease, and the great green curtain rolls itself up majestically, and The Play begins. (CT)

Remembering the days when he could forget hard reality by "impersonating," the boy discovers that in the pantomime and the toy theatre he can still live with the old freedom as he weeps for Jane Shore or George Barnwell,[9] or marvels at Harlequin, Pantaloon, and the Clown. In the theatre:

> Everything is capable, with the greatest of ease, of being changed into Anything; and "Nothing is, but thinking makes it so." Now, too, I perceive my first experience of the dreary sensation—often to return in after-life—of being unable, next day, to get back to the dull, settled world; of wanting to live for ever in the bright atmosphere I have quitted; of doting on the little Fairy, with the wand like a celestial Barber's Pole, and pining for a Fairy immortality along with her. (CT)

The boy—and later the man—delights in the experience of restoration for the time to a world where "nothing is but thinking makes it so": where distasteful "realities" can simply be made to disappear. He has also begun to sense, however, the danger attached to the seductive allure of withdrawing permanently into a fantasy world: it can become a boundary experience between life and death where the return to this "world of effort" would seem to be not worth it. Nonetheless, so magical is the bell of the toy theatre that its memory will always surround with charm the "dark, dirty, real Theatres in the day-time, adorned with these associations as with the freshest garlands of the rarest flowers."

And now the traveller comes upon the youth, "always in love," for whom the "everlastingly green garden" revives once more as the whole world becomes transformed with the freshest garlands of the rarest flowers. David captures most poignantly the dazed rapture of this enchanted time as he tells of falling in love with Dora. David has just been articled to Spenlow and Jorkins. Now he has been invited to the home of Mr. Spenlow, of whose private life David knows only that he is a widower with one daughter. He walks into Spenlow's house quite his own man; even though rather shaken by recent worldly experiences, he is feeling a rather confident young man of the world, with a coolly appraising if appreciative eye for his surroundings:

> There was a lovely garden to Mr. Spenlow's house; and though that was not the best time of the year for seeing a garden, it was so beau-

> tifully kept, that I was quite enchanted. There was a charming lawn, there were clusters of trees, and there were perspective walks that I could just distinguish in the dark, arched over with trellis-work, on which shrubs and flowers grew in the growing-season. "Here Miss Spenlow walks by herself," I thought. "Dear me!" (*DC*, ch. 26)

In an instant, however, he has met Dora ("What a beautiful name!") and "All was over in a moment. I had fulfilled my destiny. I was a captive and a slave." Dora is "a Fairy, a Sylph, I don't know what she was—anything that no one ever saw, and everything that everybody ever wanted." In a daze he tries to make appropriate responses to other guests, noting without alarm the intrusion of Miss Murdstone into the "garden," though as a child he had described the influence of the Murdstones upon him as "the fascination of two snakes on a wretched young bird" (ch. 4). David tries to listen to an amiable gentleman with a polished head who is, appropriately, telling him a long story "which I think was about gardening. I think I heard him say, 'my gardener,' several times. I seemed to pay the deepest attention to him, but I was wandering in a garden of Eden all the while, with Dora" (ch. 26). Looking back on this time from the perspective of years, David says: "There is no doubt whatever that I was a lackadaisical young spooney; but there was a purity of heart in all this, that prevents my having quite a contemptuous recollection of it, let me laugh as I may." This is something of a rueful acknowledgment that youthful love is the last of the experiences in the fair seedtime of the soul before the everlastingly green garden is "left for everlasting, unregainable, and far away." The soul must now put on its maturity.

But it is ready. In the idyllic garden it has been prepared to survive the hard facts of life. In a protected world it has been able to "play" at life before it must take part in the real struggle for existence. It has come to apprehend its own mortality and to envision evil before it has to cope with it; and gradually it has been hardened to reality so that it may leave the garden and proceed upon its journey. In the garden it has expanded to wonder, to know beauty and fear, to imagine, to dream, and to love. The traveller who has accompanied the child, the boy, and the youth through the garden carries inside him a world against which to evaluate and measure the world outside. He will not again fully know the happiness of the garden, for he will never feel quite at home in the world as it is, though it might be "that every object I looked at reminded me of the happy old home, which was like a dream I could never dream again" (*DC*, ch. 8) [cf. note 4]). Neither will he again have the freedom from responsibility and from awareness of time that through childhood surrounded him like a protective cocoon. Nonetheless he has memories, which tell him that the objects of the imagination are as precious and real as the objects of external experience; with such resources he is equipped to become a complete human being. The child who has been deprived of this leisurely fair seedtime, however, has a blight upon him from which he may well never recover.

In coming to its radically different conclusion, the Dickensian idealization of childhood is seen to have veered sharply away from that of Wordsworth. It is true that the last item to be hung on the Dickens Christmas tree is the star, tacked on insecurely at the top with suitable and sincere encomiums to the Christ whose teachings Dickens constantly reiterated. Christian concepts, however, belong to Dickens's discursive equipment rather than to his mode of experience, and we shall not meet Christian images among the tapestried associations and analogies. Nor did he, as Wordsworth did, find other transcendental meaning: instead of intimations of immortality, Dickens received from his recollections of childhood those intimations of an earthly paradise that would make of him a humanist and a humanitarian. The very images that would help him interpret life would be embodied, not in clouds and lakes and mountains, but in surrogate human figures, from the snuff-box to the Sultan; not in objects of nature, but in objects of human creation. Furthermore, for Dickens, childhood is not a time or condition to look back upon with nostalgia or to retreat into as an escape from life. One can visualize with some amusement the horror with which Dickens must have regarded the Wordsworthian prayer for the Cottage child:

> that this fair creature, checked
> By special privilege of Nature's love,
> Should in his childhood be detained for ever!
> (*Prelude,* Bk. 7, ll. 374–76)

The nearest approach to such an idea in the Dickens imagery is that bobbing preserved monster in Mr. Venus's specialty shop, "a Hindoo baby in a bottle, curved up with his big head under him, as though he would instantly throw a summersault if the bottle were large enough" (*OMF,* ch. 7).

For Dickens, the most tragic spectacle was that of a child prevented from growing through a free childhood into maturity, while one of the most despicable of human creatures was the particular kind of egoist who tried to remain in the idyllic garden after the time had come to put away childish things. In the next chapters, the scene will be filled with such blighted and warped human beings, all caught somehow in configurations naturally appropriate to childhood, but which grow monstrously grotesque and perverted when unnaturally tampered with and invaded by adults.

# VI

## *The Blighted Child and a Sense of Justice*

AND NOW, as Dickens might have written, comes the crowding in of the dreadful masks—the ogres and giants, the tyrannical Sultans, the dolls and the puppets with their collapsing legs. For the child must now confront all of the fearful or pathetic figures ever encountered in story book or dream—all disguised as adults encountered in life. Far from enjoying the ideal childhood, in reality all children must thread a precarious way through a crowd of dangerous adults in a position to control their lives. Milling about in the scene as object lessons are also other half-adults, permanently crippled as a result of their own blighted childhood or from having no childhood at all.

These are the actors in the scenario to unfold in this chapter: the defective adults, the hapless children, and their adult oppressors. The story that develops through their interactions points to a deeply felt conviction of Dickens: adults may not exploit childhood without releasing powerful forces of revenge, for some power in the world will not permit the violation to take place without imposing just consequences. Although Dickens may sometimes even go so far in discursive explanation as to deliver this warning in an oratorical statement reminiscent of Thomas Carlyle, it is also tellingly conveyed as his other messages are: directly through the images and patterns in which he embodies his felt thought.

### 1

We have already encountered several adults *manqué* in Scrooge, the gentleman for Nowhere, Grewgious, and Tulkinghorn. The last of these, however, is somewhat different from the other three, each of whom has a soul, however crippled. If Tulkinghorn ever had one, it long ago atrophied and died. Tulkinghorn is quite openly an object lesson in the totally destructive effects of childhood blight, for he actually lives beneath a "painted ceiling, with foreshortened Allegory staring down at his intrusion" and pointing a vague finger into the room. Tulkinghorn's deprivation, we are told, seems principally to be that he is "an Oyster of the old school, whom nobody can open."

This marsh creature lives in an apartment as withdrawing as he is. Even "the titles on the backs of his books have retired into the binding; everything that can have a lock has got one; no key is visible" (*BH*, ch. 10). Tulkinghorn is the tight-lipped depository for all the secrets of the great ones of the earth. What a comfort to them to know that he is an "Oyster" whom nobody can open! But he is likewise an oyster in a much more significant sense, for nobody can open him to any kind of emotion or sentiment. Although he would certainly resist Lady Dedlock's attempts to soften him, the narrator marvels, he *surely* might have been expected to feel something like triumph after he had succeeded in publicly revealing to her, in a slightly veiled version, his knowledge of her story? Not even this feeling, however, is available to him: "To say of a man so severely and strictly self-repressed that he is triumphant, would be to do him as great an injustice as to suppose him troubled with love or sentiment, or any romantic weakness" (ch. 41).

With his customary fanciful inventiveness, Dickens has found the striking controlling metaphor for Tulkinghorn's nature, rigidly closed to all human feeling. He is likewise a closed oyster to the reader; if he possesses an inner life, it is not revealed. Although little sympathy is engendered in *Bleak House* for this man, the description of him as "of what is called the old school—a phrase generally meaning any school that seems never to have been young" is a glancing acknowledgment of the deprivation that has destroyed his humanity.

Mr. Tulkinghorn is a projection into adulthood of the child born old and (therefore) somehow soulless. He has his child counterparts in the allegorical monster children of A Christmas Carol and The Haunted Man. These are the children revealed to the shrinking gaze of Scrooge by the Ghost of Christmas Present, brought forth from the foldings of its robe after Scrooge has seen something not quite clear—is it a foot or a claw?:

> two children; wretched, abject, frightful, hideous, miserable. They knelt down at its feet, and clung upon the outside of its garment. . . . They were a boy and a girl. Yellow, meagre, ragged, scowling, wolfish; but prostrate, too, in their humility. Where graceful youth should have filled their features out, and touched them with its freshest tints, a stale and shrivelled hand, like that of age, had pinched, and twisted them, and pulled them into shreds. Where angels might have sat enthroned, devils lurked, and glared out menacing. No change, no degradation, no perversion of humanity, in any grade, through all the mysteries of wonderful creation, has monsters half so horrible and dread. (CC, stave III)

A similar apparition materializes before the chemist Redlaw, the "haunted man": a "something" rushing past him to crouch in a corner; "a baby savage, a young monster, a child who had never been a child, a creature who might live to take the outward form of man, but who, within, would live and perish a mere beast" (HM, ch. 2).

The very existence of these children, who will live to prey on mankind as monster adults, sounds a dark note of foreboding. They are obviously not intended to be real children. Rather, they are Dickens's emblems for an abhorrent condition of society in the most abhorrent analogy he can conceive: that of the child turned into an aged monster as a result of "blight" by the indifference and neglect of society.

Other victims of the same social conditions are less able to avenge themselves; for example, the blighted children bred like maggots in the dilapidated street described here: "These tumbling tenements contain, by night, a swarm of misery. As, on the ruined human wretch, vermin parasites appear, so, these ruined shelters have bred a crowd of foul existence that crawls in and out of gaps in walls and boards; and coils itself to sleep, in maggot numbers, where the rain drips in; and comes and goes, fetching and carrying fever" (*BH,* ch. 16). This is Tom-All-Alone's: home of "Name, Jo. Nothing else that he knows on. Don't know that everybody has two names. Never heard of sich a think. . . . No father, no mother, no friends. Never been to school. What's home?" (ch. 11). This anonymous child of ignorance and want is likewise a walking allegory with his constant "moving-on" past the indifferent stream of society, befriended only by another nameless outcast: "'Nemo!' repeats Mr. Tulkinghorn [lest we miss it]. 'Nemo is Latin for no one'" (ch. 10).

Many of the other blighted children in *Bleak House* are the victims, not of an anonymous society, but of specific individual adults who are careless or neglectful. While these individuals usually represent societal types, they are also the particular adults—parents—who might be expected to be careful and attentive to the needs of children. Their peccadillos and families have received adequate attention elsewhere, and need only to be mentioned here: the Jellybys, the Pardiggles, the Coavinses, the Skimpoles. The source of such neglect is either parental preoccupation, such as that of Mrs. Jellyby with a distant "good cause" that blinds her to the reality around her; or absorption in their own selfish desires, which makes them callous, as with Harold Skimpole (to be discussed in ch. VII).

In addition to such children of neglect, other people have been denied their childhood by design. One such child who must be shaped "to accomplish a destiny" is little Paul Dombey who, seemingly knowing what was in store for him, came into the world, as already seen, with his fists clenched as if "squaring at existence for having come upon him so unexpectedly." Says Mr. Dombey: "'There is nothing of chance or doubt in the course before my son. His way in life was clear and prepared, and marked out before he existed'" (*DS*, ch. 11). As a result, Paul, apparently aware that his destiny could never afford the luxury of a leisurely childhood, looks and talks "like one of those terrible little beings in the fairy tales, who, at a hundred and fifty or two hundred years of age, fantastically represent the children for whom they have substituted" (ch. 8). Paul, as we are frequently reminded, is "old-fashioned."

Other people denied their childhood by design are all the members of the Smallweed family in *Bleak House*. The first member of this family to appear is Bart, already "an old limb of the law" at something under fifteen. Indeed, whether he "was ever a boy, is much doubted in Lincoln's Inn":

> He is a weird changeling, to whom years are nothing. He stands precociously possessed of centuries of owlish wisdom. If he ever lay in a cradle, it seems as if he must have lain there in a tail-coat. He has an old, old eye, has Smallweed: and he drinks and smokes, in a monkeyish way; and his neck is stiff in his collar; and he is never to be taken in; and he knows all about it, whatever it is. In short, in his bringing up, he has been so nursed by Law and Equity that he has become a kind of fossil imp. (*BH*, ch. 20)

Bart is the scion of a most unusual family: "There has been only one child in the Smallweed family for several generations. Little old men and women there have been, but no child, until Mr. Smallweed's grandmother, now living, became weak in her intellect, and fell (for the first time) into a childish state" (ch. 21). As already suggested in Bart's being nursed "by Law and Equity," it was not neglect but plan that turned the younger Smallweeds into little old men and women, committed by their elders to the pattern of life they must follow.

Responsibility for monstrous children falls always and totally on the adults—the gardeners—controlling their world. When, instead of nurturing and protecting the childhood garden, adults invade and manipulate it for reasons of their own, the children whose lives they touch stand in grave danger: as tender plants, the growth of the garden, children are readily susceptible to blight.

Every one of these children "without a childhood" is deficient in precisely those qualities dependent for their development on the conditions of the childhood garden: imagination and fancy, the sense of wonder and fear, love and sentiment. All are qualities rooted in the "child's heart" and related to the inner life whose reality is asserted in that Edenic world sheltered from time and responsibility.

Edith Granger (to become Edith Dombey) was brought up on a system whose tenets denied the childhood conditions for developing the soul. As an adult, Edith is well aware that a designing mother, Mrs. Skewton, denied her a protected childhood. Edith is provoked into retaliation when her mother insists upon calling her daughter her "darling child":

> "A child!" said Edith, looking at her, "when was I a child! What childhood did you ever leave to me? I was a woman—artful, designing, mercenary, laying snares for men—before I knew myself, or you, or even understood the base and wretched aim of every new display I learnt. You gave birth to a woman. Look upon her. She is in her pride tonight. . . . Look at me," she said, "who have never known what it is to have an honest heart, and love. Look at me, taught to scheme and plot when children play; and married in my youth—an old age of design—to one for whom I had no feeling but indifference." (*DS*, ch. 27)

Five little Gradgrinds also were brought up on a system obstructing the development of the soul. Like Edith, Louisa as a young woman is aware that she was never truly a child. Now she confronts her father with the knowledge:

Lous

> "The baby-preference that even I have heard of as common among children, has never had its innocent resting-place in my breast. You have been so careful of me that I never had a child's heart. You have trained me so well that I never dreamed a child's dream. You have dealt so wisely with me, Father, from my cradle to this hour, that I never had a child's belief or a child's fear." (*HT,* bk. I, ch. 15)

Louisa Gradgrind also understands exactly both the nature and the source of her deprivation: "'What do I know, Father,' said Louisa in her quiet manner, 'of tastes and fancies; of aspirations and affections; of all that part of my nature in which such light things might have been nourished? What escape have I had from problems that could be demonstrated, and realities that could be grasped?'" Louisa knows that her unfitness for identification with humanity, despite her instincts of kindness and compassion, is traceable to the "stony" home to which she physically returns on the occasion of her mother's death. Otherwise, "she had no inducements to go back and had rarely gone":

> Neither, as she approached her old home now, did any of the best influences of old home descend upon her. The dreams of childhood—its airy fables, its graceful, beautiful, humane, impossible adornments of the world beyond: so good to be believed in once, so good to be remembered when outgrown, for then the least among them rises to the stature of a great Charity in the heart, suffering little children to come into the midst of it, and to keep with their pure hands a garden in the stony ways of this world, wherein it were better for all the children of Adam that they should oftener sun themselves, simple and trustful, and not worldly-wise—what had she to do with these? (bk. II, ch. 9)

The "airy fables" denied Louisa are emblems, as everywhere in Dickens, of the stimulus and nourishment the imagined story provides the soul.

Although adults *manqué* like Tulkinghorn, who totally lack awareness or understanding of their deficiencies, appear to be without souls, both Edith and Louisa, who have the inner capacity to understand their situation and to comment upon it, show evidence of a soul struggling for survival. Paul Dombey, as a matter of fact, suffers from a soul too large for his body. Mrs. Chick early points out Paul's problem to his father. "'The fact is,'" she says, "'that his mind is too much for him. His soul is a great deal too large for his frame'" (*DS,* ch. 8). Nonetheless, Dombey, intent only upon his design for his son, remains exultant as his six-year-old changeling enrolls in Dr. Blimber's educational establishment. "'You are almost a man already,'" he assures Paul; "'Almost,'" returns the child (ch. 11). "'Shall we make a man of him?'" says the Doctor; "'I had rather be a child,'" Paul replies, "with a curious expression of suppressed emotion in his face."

Paul's dreams for the future are of being able to "'go away into the country with my darling Florence, have a beautiful garden, fields, and woods, and live there with her all my life'"—in a touching reversal of the natural order of life—"'if I grow up'" (ch. 14). The childhood garden and the suppressed emotions live wistfully together in his dreams.

Dombey's rigid design for Paul is typical of the parental meddling in the maturing process of children that prevents their natural growth. The father's enslavement to some idea according to which he controls his child's "education" has ruled out the childhood influences that nourish the soul.

In most instances of parental meddling, the "idleness" of reading fairy tales or of "playing" must be rigidly weeded out of children for their own good. In *Bleak House,* the Smallweed achievement of a complete family of adults has resulted from rigid avoidance of such stimulus and nourishment:

> During the whole time consumed in the slow growth of this family tree, the house of Smallweed, always early to go out and late to marry, has strengthened itself in its practical character, has discarded all amusements, discountenanced all story-books, fairy tales, fictions and fables, and banished all levities whatsoever. Hence the gratifying fact, that it has had no child born to it, and that the complete little men and women whom it has produced, have been observed to bear a likeness to old monkeys with something depressing on their minds. (*BH,* ch. 21)

The "Hard Facts" school of *Hard Times* has built the same discipline into an educational system. Fact one, as expounded to Mr. M'Choakumchild's class by the gentlemen who was a government officer, "'You must discard the word Fancy altogether'":

> "You have nothing to do with it. You are not to have, in any object of use or ornament, what would be a contradiction in fact. You don't walk upon flowers in fact; you cannot be allowed to walk upon flowers in carpets. You don't find that foreign birds and butterflies come and perch upon your crockery; you cannot be permitted to paint foreign birds and butterflies upon your crockery. You never meet with quadrupeds going up and down walls; you must not have

> quadrupeds represented upon walls. . . . This is the new discovery. This is fact. This is taste." (*HT,* bk. I, ch. 1)[1]

Fancy, as Mr. Gradgrind later explains, includes "'anything fanciful, fantastic, or (I am using synonymous terms) sentimental'" (bk. I, ch. 15). Fact Two, as propounded by Mr. Bounderby: "'An idle imagination, Gradgrind, [is] a very bad thing for anybody'" (bk. I, ch. 4). Fact Three, communicated as a reproof to Louisa Gradgrind, overheard saying to her brother, "'Tom, I wonder'": "'Louisa, never wonder'" (bk. I, ch. 8). Fact Four, remarked upon when Sissy Jupe irrationally expects to get a letter from her vanished father: "'If Jupe had been properly trained from an early age she would have demonstrated to herself on sound principles the baselessness of these fantastic hopes'" (bk. I, ch. 9). All of these facts upon which the system is based can be reduced to one principle: always reject and deny the world of dreams—of fancy, imagination, wonder, and hopes—in which the soul finds its true home. Any children so unfortunate as to fall into this bondage are doomed to a blighted childhood.

When it becomes clear that something has gone wrong in the disciplined development of Louisa, Gradgrind is confronted with discovering and eliminating the cause. Bounderby is sure the problem is an idle imagination, "'a cursed bad thing for a girl like Louisa.'" Wherever can it have come from?

> "Whether," said Gradgrind, pondering with his hands in his pockets, and his cavernous eyes on the fire, "whether any instructor or servant can have suggested anything? Whether, in spite of all precautions, any idle storybook can have got into the house? Because, in minds that have been so practically formed by rule and line, from the cradle upwards, this is so curious, so incomprehensible." (bk. I, ch. 4)

Bounderby (erroneously) identifies Sissy Jupe as the culprit: Sissy, who has already shown herself possessed of a disrupting fancy; who lives in the free and fantastic atmosphere of Sleary's Circus; and who, he will soon discover, has a disreputable father who encourages her to read him stories "'About the Fairies, sir, and the Dwarf, and the Hunchback, and the Genies'"—clearly a "case for rigid training" (bk. I, ch. 7).

Gradgrind prattles his theories oblivious, however, to the most basic "fact" of all: that only in the fantastic fairy tale can an analogue be found adequate to describe him. Five little Gradgrinds are held captive by this "monster in a lecturing castle"—"not that they knew, by name or nature, anything about an ogre." Like "a dry Ogre chalking ghastly white figures" on the blackboard, Gradgrind, "taking childhood captive, and dragging it into statistical dens by the hair" (bk. I, ch. 3), grinds into the bones of his children the hard facts of life.

In fact, the Gradgrind children live in a world of giants and ogres.[2] Both Louisa and Tom exist in the shadow of the "Giant Bounderby" of "the red brick castle" (bk. II, ch. 4). For Louisa, still a third giant later stalks the world in the form of Mrs. Sparsit, who erects in her mind for the girl "a mighty Staircase, with a dark pit of shame and ruin at the bottom; and down those stairs, from day to day and hour to hour, she saw Louisa coming" (bk. II, ch. 10). The "black eyes wide open with no touch of pity, with no touch of compunction" watch Louisa drifting into the Harthouse plot, descending "this new Giant's Staircase," steadily "verging, like a weight in deep water, to the black gulf at the bottom."

The Dickens fancy dips into a different type of airy fable to depict the blight of childhood brought about by the guilty sultan of the Eastern Arabian Nights. Paul Dombey was born into the empire of such a sultan: a rich, tyrannical "Tartar."

> Though the offices of Dombey and Son were within the liberties of the City of London, and within hearing of Bow Bells, when their clashing voices were not drowned by the uproar in the streets, yet were there hints of adventurous and romantic story to be observed in some of the adjacent objects. . . . Just round the corner stood the rich East India house, teeming with suggestions of precious stuffs and stones, tigers, elephants, howdahs, hookahs, umbrellas, palm trees, palanquins, and gorgeous princes of a brown complexion sitting on carpets [magic?], with their slippers very much turned up at the toes. (*DS*, ch. 4)

If Dombey and Son is not itself an East India House, it is close to one. Perch, the messenger, hurries about willingly to anticipate Dombey's every wish and to contribute to his slightest comfort: "so little objection had Perch to doing deferential in the last degree, that if he might have laid himself at Mr. Dombey's feet, or might have called him by some such title as used to be bestowed upon the Caliph Haroun Alraschid, he would have been all the better pleased" (ch. 13). Dombey, now established as the "Sultan," occupies the inner room, and next to him as second in degree of descent is the tigerish manager, Mr. Carker, the "Grand Vizier." This empire of an Eastern potentate, like the den of the ogre, is a threatening world for a child yearning for love and approval from the stern ruler even while breathlessly waiting for the decree that will mean life or death for him: a child such as Paul.

Though not an ogre himself, Dombey easily finds one to aid him in developing Paul to fulfill his destiny. "'Dear me,'" says Dombey, sitting in the parlour of her "Castle" with that "ogress and child-queller" (ch. 8), Mrs. Pipchin, "'six will be changed to sixteen, before we have time to look about us'" (ch. 11). Although Pipchin croaks unsympathetically that ten years is a long time, Dombey is unperturbed. "'It depends,'" he observes coolly, "'on circumstances.'" Between them, as it turns out, the Sultan and the Ogress will see that the right circumstances prevail to reduce the time.

As Mr. Gradgrind dragged childhood itself captive to his statistical den, so are any children who wander into the Dombey empire in danger of imprisonment. As Rob, Charitable Grinder one hundred and forty-seven, swims before his mother's eyes "with his very small legs" rigidly encased in "red worsted stockings; and very strong leather small-clothes" (ch. 5), she half foresees the threat to his "blessed legs": that he will become, as Paul will, "her own poor blighted child" as a result of Dombey's patronage. The childhood of Dombey's ignored other child, Flo, is indeed externally blighted, like that of Oliver Twist, but like him she survives internally with a kind of magical immunity to the effects of the blight—probably at first because, as Mrs. Chick has said, "'She will never, never, never be a Dombey . . . she is so very unlike a Dombey . . . the child, you see, has poor Fanny's nature'" (ch. 5); and also because so far Dombey has considered her too inconsequential to arrange a destiny for her.

In the course of things, however, Florence too is eventually threatened, for the time has come for Dombey to take a second wife. Unfortunately for him, it is also time for the insubordinate Grand Vizier to assert himself. Mr. Carker, like that "other creature," the Grand Vizier of "The Haunted House" (see ch. V), has long resisted the disposal of events that has put him into "the second male place in the State" and sees a way to advance and avenge himself through undoing the new "Favourite." Mr. Carker has already seen, "in his fancy, a crowd of people slumbering on the ground at his feet, like the poor native at his master's door: who picked his way among them: looking down, maliciously enough: but trod upon no upturned face—as yet" (ch. 26).

Unfortunately for both Sultan and Grand Vizier, the intended victim is another blighted child grown to desperate maturity: proud and handsome Edith Granger. The Sultan finds an eager accomplice in her mother, Mrs. Skewton, another Eastern ruler. This aged "Cleopatra" finds: "'There is such an obvious destiny in it, that really one might almost be induced to cross one's arms upon one's frock, and say, like those wicked Turks, there is no What's-his-name but Thingummy, and What-you-may-call-it is his prophet!'" (ch. 27). Her readiness thus to convert to Muslimism helps establish her complicity.

As the two conspire to effect a marriage between her and Dombey, Edith responds with bitter understanding. Just as she comprehended her childhood deprivation, she also has an exact perspective on her current situation: she is once again being offered in the slave market and she is about to be purchased by the tyrannical Sultan.

> "There is no slave in a market; there is no horse in a fair: so shown and offered and examined and paraded, mother, as I have been, for ten shameful years," cried Edith, with a burning brow, and the same bitter emphasis on the one word. . . . "Who takes me, refuse that I am, and as I well deserve to be . . . shall take me, as this man does, with no art of mine put forth to lure him. He sees me at the auction, and he thinks it well to buy me. Let him! When he came to view me—perhaps to bid—he required to see the roll of my accomplishments. I gave it to him. When he would have me show one of them, to justify his purchase to his men, I require of him to say which he demands, and I will exhibit it. I will do no more. He makes the purchase of his own will, and with his own sense of its worth, and the power of his money; and I hope it may never disappoint him." (ch. 27)

The underlying threat in her words promises that it will not be a happy marriage. Indeed, by the time the Dombeys have been two years married, his disappointment with his purchase approaches desperation.

By now, the haughty Sultan with "his cold and easy arrogance" has encountered an unexpected problem with the second Mrs. Dombey. With his first wife, he had no such trouble:

> He had asserted his greatness during their whole married life, and she had meekly recognised it. He had kept his distant seat of state on the top of his throne, and she her humble station on its lowest step; and much good it had done him so to live in solitary bondage to his

> own idea! He had imagined that the proud character of his second wife would have added to his own—would have merged into it, and exalted his greatness. He had pictured himself haughtier than ever, with Edith's haughtiness subservient to his. He had never entertained the possibility of its arraying itself against him. (ch. 40)

But it has arrayed itself against him. He must therefore remind her of their respective roles as master and slave. Only now, as the weapon against his unruly wife, has Flo become important enough to her father for him to arrange a destiny for her. He therefore sends a message to Edith that her attentions to his daughter displease him and must cease. He has no way of knowing that in making Carker his messenger he has provided his subordinate with the opportunity to advance and avenge himself against the Sultan, for both Sultan and Grand Vizier, each in his own way, expect with this errand to enhance their own respective positions as her lord and master.

Some of the children whose souls stand in peril from the controlling adults around them manage to escape at least some of the consequences of childhood blight. Rob the Grinder is fortunate in having a careful mother who encased his legs in "very strong leather small-clothes." Other children find within themselves both the strength and the will to survive or even to triumph over the circumstances of their lives. These are often children like Louisa and Edith, whose "largeness of soul" enables them to see and evaluate their oppressors and thus to acquire a power soon to be demonstrated.

For a blighted child in *Bleak House,* Esther Summerson, it takes many years of patient endurance and outside nurturing influences before her life acquires something like a natural equilibrium. Brought up by an aunt enslaved to the notion that the child must pay for the sins of her parents, Esther is taught to flee (like the gentleman for Nowhere) the very thought of her own birthday, to see it as the anniversary of a tragedy for herself and everyone else involved. During these childhood years, Esther's only companion and comfort is her "dear faithful Dolly," whom she loves and clings to as a real person: "How often I repeated to the doll the story of my birthday, and confided to her that I would try, as hard as ever I could, to repair the fault I was born with . . . and would strive as I grew up to be industrious, contented, and kind-hearted, and to do some good to some one, and win some love to myself if I could" (*BH*, ch. 3). After her aunt's death (her "godmother," though far from a fairy one), Esther "wrapped the dear old doll in her own shawl, and quietly laid her—I am half ashamed to tell it—in the garden-earth." She is about to set out into a new phase of her life.

The last blighted child in the Dickens gallery, Miss Jenny Wren, shares with Paul Dombey both the large soul and the crippled legs. The schoomaster, Bradley Headstone, along with Charley Hexam, is the first person in *Our Mutual Friend* to meet this eccentric figure. In response to Charley's knock on the door:

> the door promptly opened with a spring and a click. A parlour door within a small entry stood open, and disclosed a child—a dwarf—a girl—a something—sitting on a little low old-fashioned arm-chair, which had a kind of little working bench before it.
>
> "I can't get up," said the child, "because my back's bad, and my legs are queer. But I'm the person of the house." (*OMF,* bk. II, ch. 1)

This child/"person of the house" explains her "trade" to Headstone and Charley. She works, she says, for a clientele of "Fine Ladies," who are, it turns out, "'Dolls. I'm a Doll's Dressmaker.'" These fine ladies are not an easy group to work for. They pay her poorly and are inconsiderate.

> "I had a doll married, last week, and was obliged to work all night. And it's not good for me, on account of my back being so bad and my legs so queer. . . . And they take no care of their clothes, and they never keep to the same fashions a month. I work for a doll with three daughters. Bless you, she's enough to ruin her husband!" The person of the house gave a weird little laugh here, and gave them another look out of the corners of her eyes. (bk. II, ch. 1)

Headstone asks Jenny whether she is always alone: "Don't any of the neighbouring children—?"

> "Ah, lud!" cried the person of the house, with a little scream, as if the word had pricked her. "Don't talk of children. I can't bear children. *I* know their tricks and their manners." She said this with an angry little shake of her right fist close before her eyes.
>
> Perhaps it scarcely required the teacher-habit, to perceive that the doll's dressmaker was inclined to be bitter on the difference between herself and other children. But both master and pupil understood it so. (bk. II, ch. 1)

Jenny continues with an account of how children tease her, mocking her bad back, and leading her to concoct plans to get even with them. Her conclusion is firm.

> "No, no, no. No children for me. Give me grown-ups."
>
> It was difficult to guess the age of this strange creature, for her poor figure furnished no clue to it, and her face was at once so young and so old. Twelve, or at the most thirteen, might be near the mark.
>
> "I always did like grown-ups," she went on, "and always kept company with them. . . . And I mean always to keep among none but grown-ups till I marry. I suppose I must make up my mind to marry, one of these days." (bk. II, ch. 1)

Despite her afflictions, Jenny is hopeful about her future and will indeed continue with nothing but grownups, for she considers and treats as dolls all those adults in her environment who still function as children. Prematurely catapulted into responsibility, Jenny has surrounded herself with a society that, like David's reading, keeps her fancy alive and does her no harm.

All of the fairy-tale oppressors of children are emblems for Dickens of the tyrants who appear in actual life in other guises. Playing out their fairy-tale roles, these adults set about to invade and destroy the childhood garden by various methods, usually by either "forcing" or "cultivating" (though sometimes by "spoiling")[3] the development of the children entrusted to them. Dombey, for instance, finds "forcing" perfectly adapted to his purposes in preparing Paul for his destiny.

Although a condition of the springtime garden is its freedom from the restrictions of time, Dombey's whole concept of time blinds him to the effects of his view on his son. Impatient with the measured movement of time, he sees no reason to give in to its natural processes. Though he loves his son with all the love he has, he does not love him "as an infant or as a boy, but as a grown man—the 'Son' of the Firm." As a consequence,

> He was impatient to advance into the future, and to hurry over the intervening passages of his history. Therefore he had little or no anxiety about them, in spite of his love; feeling as if the boy had a charmed life, and *must* become the man with whom he held such constant communication in his thoughts, and for whom he planned and projected, as for an existing reality, every day. (*DS*, ch. 8)[4]

He sets out, that is, to abolish time. As he has pointed out to Mrs. Pipchin, it is no trouble at all to reduce ten years to nothing, given the circumstances of Dr. Blimber's "forcing" establishment.

> In fact, Dr. Blimber's establishment was a great hot-house, in which there was a forcing apparatus incessantly at work. All the boys blew before their time. Mental green-peas were produced at Christmas

> and intellectual asparagus all the year round. Mathematical gooseberries (very sour ones too) were common at untimely seasons, and from mere sprouts of bushes, under Dr. Blimber's cultivation. Every description of Greek and Latin vegetable was got off the driest twigs of boys, under the frostiest circumstances. Nature was of no consequence at all. No matter what a young gentleman was intended to bear, Doctor Blimber made him bear to pattern, somehow or other. This was all very pleasant and ingenious, but the system of forcing was attended with its usual disadvantages. There was not the right taste about the premature productions, and they didn't keep well. (ch. 11)

Despite Paul's failing health, he submits bravely to the forcing routine of Dr. Blimber, who, "in some partial confusion of his ideas, regarded the young gentlemen as if they were all Doctors, and were born grown up" (ch. 12). Paul's natural cleverness makes his father "more bent than ever on his being forced and crammed." Dr. Blimber is confirmed as usual in his practices: "In short, however high and false the temperature at which the Doctor kept his hot-house, the owners of the plants were always ready to lend a helping hand at the bellows, and to stir the fire." In this fashion, blowing at the bellows and stirring up the fire, Dombey succeeds overnight in turning six into sixteen, but simultaneously reduces a lifetime to a few unnatural years.

Paul himself, meanwhile, has been "forced" into an early realization of his true relationship to time. He is very sensitive to the fact that time and life are inseparable. Paul's best friend during these months in Dr. Blimber's establishment, in addition to his sister Florence, is the great clock in the hall, which he never passes without its inquiring, "'how, is, my, lit, tle, friend? how, is, my, lit, tle, friend?'" "'Very well, I thank you, sir,'" he replies (ch. 11).

Paul soon loses "such spirits as he had" in the new environment, and becomes "even more strange, and old, and thoughtful, than ever before. . . . He loved to be alone; and in those short intervals when he was not occupied with his books, liked nothing so well as wandering about the house by himself, or sitting on the stairs, listening to the great clock in the hall" (ch. 12). As Paul grows so weak that he must spend much time in bed, he discovers one day when he goes downstairs that:

> Lo and behold, there was something the matter with the great clock; and a workman on a pair of steps had taken its face off, and was poking instruments into the works by the light of a candle! This was a great event for Paul, who sat down on the bottom stair, and watched

> the operation attentively; now and then glancing at the clock-face, leaning all askew, against the wall hard by, and feeling a little confused by a suspicion that it was ogling him. (ch. 14)

So Paul looks on "until the clock had quite recovered its familiar aspect, and resumed its sedate inquiry." The clock and he continue to exist in a sympathetic relationship while his time continues to run out.

When Dombey conceives the design to take a hand in his daughter's life, an invasion into the childhood garden of a somewhat different type—"cultivating"—is contemplated, this time with the collusion of "Cleopatra." As soon as they meet, Flo identifies Edith with her own mother, and Edith also sees a mother/child relationship between them, though in a different sense. What Edith was, Florence is now: a warm, loving, human child suffering under a blighted childhood. Behind this concept lies a familiar image pattern: a continuum of life along which people at various stages of development proceed to a shared destination—Edith and Florence on the same continuum. Mrs. Skewton, in pointing out the resemblance between Florence and Edith at the same age, also presents her plan for improving the child as she has improved Edith: Florence, the "flower" of the garden, must be "cultivated": "'I do think that I see a decided resemblance to what you were then, in our extremely fascinating young friend. And it shows,' said Mrs. Skewton, in a lower voice, which conveyed her opinion that Florence was in a very unfinished state, 'what cultivation will do.'" Edith responds sternly: "'It does indeed'" (ch. 30).

In fact, the picture of the cultivation process is so deeply engraved in Edith's mind that her one purpose in life becomes to protect the threatened child's soul. Skewton has conceived the idea of keeping Flo with her during the wedding trip of Dombey and Edith. Dombey would be delighted for this prompt attention to the formation of his child's mind. But they have reckoned without Edith, whose ultimatum is absolute: either the child goes home, or there will be no wedding. The program for Florence's cultivation must therefore be postponed. But now, two years later when the rift comes between Edith and her husband, the message carried by Carker tells her that time on the postponement has run out: the cultivation process will begin.

Although Paul Dombey is literally unable to survive the forcing process to which he is subjected, Edith has survived through withdrawal into a cold condition distancing her from her own troubling emotions.[5] After the humiliating message carried by Carker, she retires completely behind a frozen facade: "Little by little, she receded . . . like the retiring ghost of what she had been" and "became frozen up in the bold, angry hardihood with which she stood, upon the brink of a deep precipice" (ch. 47).

It is not surprising to find Louisa Gradgrind Bounderby similarly frozen. As a young woman married to a man she detests, and keenly aware of her lack of those qualities needed to be a warm and loving human being, Louisa seeks to make her father understand what has happened to her. She turns instinctively to the garden imagery: "'What have you done, oh, Father, what have you done, with the garden that should have bloomed once, in this great wilderness here?'" As she speaks, she strikes herself "with both her hands upon her bosom." Despite his blindness, she cannot believe that he would knowingly have so deprived her.

> "Would you have doomed me, at any time, to the frost and blight that have hardened and spoiled me? Would you have robbed me—for no one's enrichment—only for the greater desolation of this world—of the immaterial part of my life, the spring and summer of my belief, my refuge from what is sordid and bad in the real things around me, my school in which I should have learned to be more humble and more trusting with them, and to hope in my little sphere to make them better?" (*HT*, bk. II, ch. 12)

Both Louisa and Edith demonstrate that the marsh-related frozen condition of adults, despite the fiery passions pent up within them, may result from blight of the springtime garden.

It would seem at first that the giants and ogres, the tyrannical Sultans and other monstrous adults have it all their own way: that a child in the garden is totally powerless against them, whether they fail to protect the garden through indifference or invade it through design.

But this is not the end of the story of the blighted children.

## 2

It is not by chance that Mr. Tulkinghorn lives and dies under the warning finger of Allegory. Even after his death, it continues helplessly to point at him from night to morning, "lying face downward on the floor, shot through the heart" (*BH*, ch. 48). If warning is contained in this finger of Allegory, it is certainly justified in the case of Tulkinghorn. It would be hard to argue that "justice" was not seen by the stern Roman with the implacable finger, no more stern and implacable than the lawyer himself. Yet whatever warning resides in the finger—pointing "with far greater significance than he ever had in Mr. Tulkinghorn's time, and with a deadly meaning'"—could not be intended for the dead man, but rather appears to say to whom it may concern: beware this sad fate of a man who was never nurtured with memories and hopes, or led to wonder, or sensitized to human feelings and dreams.

Like all of the other notes of warning sounded by Dickens, Tulkinghorn's fate reflects an unquestioned assumption of some kind of Nemesis operant in human affairs, a belief in a kind of retributive justice that not only rectifies inequality, but does so in a poetically appropriate way. The operation of this justice is most blatantly evident when Dickens is being frankly the propagandist and social critic, as he is in his allegorical portrayals of monster children: "'This boy is Ignorance,'" warns the Ghost of Christmas Present. "'This girl is Want. Beware them both, and all of their degree but most of all beware this boy, for on his brow I see that written which is Doom, unless the writing be erased'" (CC, stave III). The retribution here will be direct and uncomplex. These monster children will go forth as monster adults to wreak their vengeance upon a society that continues to deny them their humanity.

Even more direct and immediate will be the justice wrought for the children of Tom-All-Alone's. Jo, for instance, urged to "move along," travels other roads than the literal one intended by an indifferent society concerned only with getting rid of him. Like Betty Higden, he travels also that linear road to death on a figurative cart shaking him harder and harder as the road grows rougher. But of most interest in the present context is the road along which he is ironically driven for a rendezvous with all sorts of unlikely people: a rendezvous that will establish all human beings as his brothers and sisters:[6]

> What connexion can there be, between the place in Lincolnshire, the house in town, the Mercury in powder, and the whereabout of Jo the outlaw with the broom, who had that distant ray of light upon him when he swept the churchyard-step? What connexion can there have been between many people in the innumerable histories of this world, who, from opposite sides of great gulfs, have, nevertheless, been very curiously brought together! (*BH*, ch. 16)

Very soon, in the inevitable convergence of the twain, revenge is wrought by Tom-All-Alone's for each of his blighted children, befriended in time by "no one," but pushed on to spread his contagion, of whatever variety, wherever they go:

> [Tom] has his revenge. Even the winds are his messengers, and they serve him in these hours of darkness. There is not a drop of Tom's corrupted blood but propagates infection and contagion somewhere. It shall pollute, this very night, the choice stream (in which chemists on analysis would find the genuine nobility) of a Norman house, and his Grace shall not be able to say Nay to the infamous alliance. There is not an atom of Tom's slime, not a cubic inch of any pestilential gas in which he lives, not one degradation about him, not an ignorance, not a wickedness, not a brutality of his committing, but shall work its retribution, through every order of society, up to the proudest of the proud, and to the highest of the high. Verily, what with tainting, plundering, and spoiling, Tom has his revenge. (*BH*, ch. 46)

This concept of a kind of cosmic justice seems to echo the thunder of the Carlylean belief that "the great soul of the world is just and not unjust": at least it makes a useful weapon to brandish about.

It might be possible to dismiss the concept as a rhetorical tool of social criticism were it not for the manner in which the same idea filters its way into all kinds of situations where it would be curiously Chadbandian to hold anything so imposing as a "great soul" responsible for what happens. Take, for example, the case of Grandfather Smallweed, who has been known to say "with sharp sly triumph," "'No, no. We have never been readers in our family. It don't pay. Stuff. Idleness. Folly. No, no!'" (*BH*, ch. 21). Grandfather, however, is deluded, for he himself is the victim of a sly trick played by the discountenanced inhabitants of idleness and folly to be found in the enchanted world of childhood. As if to point out to him that an adult without childhood has poor underpinnings, he has been reduced to a helpless puppet from the toy theatre, for "he is in a helpless condition as to his lower, and nearly so as to his upper limbs."

Though physically helpless, Grandfather is given to violent expressions of abuse, and "the contrast between those powerful expressions and his powerless figure is suggestive of a baleful old malignant, who would be very wicked if he could": an old sinner who sometimes is capable of "an Ogreish kind of jocularity." Fortunately, "his mind is unimpaired. It holds as well as it ever held, the first four rules of arithmetic, and a certain small collection of the hardest facts. In respect of ideality, reverence, wonder, and other such phrenological attributes, it is no worse off than it used to be."

Unfortunately, Smallweed must play out the roles of the puppet he has become. He is wheeled from place to place by his granddaughter "Judy," who as a child "never owned a doll." Now, however, she has something suspiciously like one as she and her grandfather go about in their own "Punch"-and-Judy show, for he has a habit under duress of sliding down into a bundle of clothes, "a mere clothes-bag with black skull-cap on the top of it,"—"like a broken puppet." He does not become animated again "until he has undergone the two operations at the hands of his grand-daughter, of being shaken up like a great bottle, and poked and punched like a bolster."

In the absence of Judy, Grandfather finds it necessary to call upon Mr. George to "shake me up a little."

> Mr. George . . . takes his venerable acquaintance by the throat on receiving this request, and dragging him upright in his chair as easily as if he were a doll, appears in two minds whether or not to shake him into his grave. Resisting the temptation, but agitating him violently enough to make his head roll like a harlequin's, he puts him smartly down in his chair again, and adjusts his skull-cap with such a rub, that the old man winks with both eyes for a minute afterwards. (ch. 21)

Judy has acquired her doll too late to do her any good.

Jenny Wren, on the other hand, well knows what she is doing when she gives her drunken father the name of "Mr. Dolls" and treats him as her "bad child." "'A muddling and a swipey old child,' said Miss Wren, rating him with great severity, 'fit for nothing but to be preserved in the liquor that destroys him, and put in a great glass bottle as a sight for other swipey children of his own pattern,—if he has no consideration for his liver, has he none for his mother?'" (*OMF,* bk. III, ch. 10). The answer, of course, is "No." Like the Hindoo baby, Mr. Dolls is a monstrously preserved child who is frequently in a "worse than swinish state (for swine at least fatten on their guzzling, and make themselves good to eat)." Jenny threatens him with a fate similar to that of Grandfather Smallweed: "'You wicked old boy,' Miss Wren would say to him, with a menacing forefinger, 'you'll force me to run away from you, after all, you will; and then you'll shake to bits, and there'll be nobody to pick up the pieces!'" (bk. IV, ch. 8). Nonetheless, Jenny takes good care of her wayward child and when he dies pronounces fair judgment on him: "'If my poor boy,' she would say, 'had been brought up better, he might have done better. Not that I reproach myself. I hope I have no cause for that'" (bk. IV, ch. 9).

Jenny also has the last word on the "real" fine ladies, those "dolls" whom she forces to serve *her* in her role as Doll's Dressmaker. "The fun is," she says, "how I make the great ladies try my dresses on."

> "When I see a great lady very suitable for my business, I say 'You'll do, my dear!' and I take particular notice of her, and run home and cut her out and baste her. Then another day, I come scudding back again to try on, and then I take particular notice of her again . . . saying to myself, 'I must hollow out a bit here; I must slope away there;' and I am making a perfect slave of her, with making her try on my doll's dress." (bk. III, ch. 2)

Once again like David, she has managed to reduce her oppressors to figures from childhood where nothing is but thinking makes it so.

Such is another case of selective vengeance based on something like poetic justice, but the spirit behind it resembles more that malign sprite with his oblique light and his volleys of silvery laughter—a comic spirit rather than a cosmic soul, which reduces its targets to their ridiculous and pitiable size.

So long as the stories of childhood rising up to avenge its blighted children remain on the comic level, the tone remains relatively light. When the story is seen through the eyes of suffering children, however, the vision darkens and the retribution becomes more terrible.

Little Paul Dombey is one of those who must pay for the sins of their fathers. "Fulfilling a destiny," it seems, is a very tiring business. Sitting before the fire warming his hands and "looking in between the bars of the grate, as if some ghostly puppet-show were performing there," Paul says wearily: "'I am so tired some times . . . and my bones ache so (Mrs. Wickam says it's my bones), that I don't know what to do'" (*DS,* ch. 8). Mr. Dombey is irritated. Why on earth should anyone have been discussing his son's bones? "'He is not a living skeleton, I suppose.'" Mrs. Chick murmurs "'Very far from it,'" but "with an unspeakable expression": "'If the dear child,' pursues Mrs. Chick, ' . . . has some temporary weakness in his system, and does occasionally seem about to lose, for the moment, the use of his—'" Considering Dombey's objection to "bones," Mrs. Chick is a little afraid to venture "limbs"; but after some assistance from Miss Tox she decides to be quite direct about it: "'I say, if our dear Paul should lose, for the moment, the use of his legs, these are casualties common to many children at his time of life, and not to be prevented by any care or caution. The sooner you understand that . . . and admit that, the better.'"

As a matter of fact, Paul is the star of the "ghostly puppet-show" he discerns in the fire, suffering pathetically from the same ailment that makes Grandfather Smallweed with his collapsing legs a figure of ridicule. Grandfather Smallweed is a comic type of figure to be laughed—however bitterly—out of the structure of society, while Paul is seen tragically as an individual who has lost his one chance at life. Like the puppets in the toy theatre, they both seem like normal people until they try to stand up.

*Dombey and Son* and *Hard Times* are of special interest in examining the total view of the blighted child and the sense of justice, which imaginatively control both novels. The one may be read as a tale from the Arabian Nights; the other, as a fairy tale. In both, as already illustrated, the besieged children must suffer under the domination of giant, ogre, or tyrannical sultan invading the childhood garden, and in both, as will now be shown, the elements of the denied child world rise up triumphantly to avenge or rescue its children.

The weapon of vengeance in *Dombey and Son* has for a long time lain hidden within the bosom of Edith Dombey. On the occasion of a picnic to Warwick Castle prior to the Dombey marriage, this weapon flashes for a brief moment in a private clash between Edith and her mother. The observant Carker knows how to pick up the threads of glance and innuendo to weave a plan for the undoing of the Sultan. But within the chatter of polite conversation, he misses the significance of this verbal interchange, though it is charged with eventual meaning for himself. Edith has just assured Mr. Dombey that, in spite of her previous visits to Warwick Castle, she will be "not at all" bored with the present excursion:

> "We are all enthusiastic, are we not, mamma?" said Edith with a cold smile.
>
> "Too much so, for our peace, perhaps, my dear," returned her mother; "but we won't complain. Our own emotions are our recompense. If, as your cousin Feenix says, the sword wears out that what's-its-name—"
>
> "The scabbard, perhaps," said Edith.
>
> "Exactly—a little too fast, it is because it is bright and glowing, you know, my dearest love."
>
> Mrs. Skewton heaved a gentle sigh, supposed to cast a shadow on the surface of that dagger of lath, whereof her susceptible bosom was the sheath: and leaning her head on one side, in the Cleopatra manner, looked with pensive affection on her darling child. (*DS*, ch. 27)

The significance of this interchange is completely ironic in its foreshadowing. First of all, it is obvious that the "emotions" of Cleopatra are nonexistent. The callousness with which she has destroyed her daughter's emotional life is clear evidence that she possesses no normal human feelings. If, as she says, "our emotions are our recompense," hers is a sterile—though just—compensation. Whatever resides in her bosom can be only a "dagger of lath." Edith, on the other hand, has a strong emotional nature, which has been suppressed and denied. A Grand Vizier from the Eastern land of scimitars and bright daggers might have caught the warning that within the cold, smooth scabbard of Mrs. Granger's breast might gleam the sharpest of blades—no "dagger of lath," but the "bright and glowing pent-up emotions of a life-time waiting to dart out and destroy." Neither the Sultan nor the Grand Vizier, however, accurately measures the passion of their victim or anticipates the effect of their strategy.

And now there is a party on the eve of the second anniversary. After dinner, Mr. Dombey informs Mrs. Dombey that he is planning another small dinner party for the next evening: "'I do not dine at home,'" says Edith (ch. 47). Dombey's insistence, his demand for subservience, makes the outcome of the clash inevitable: "'I will do nothing that you ask,'" she says, adding: "'I will hold no place in your house to-morrow, or on any recurrence of to-morrow. I will be exhibited to no one, as the refractory slave you purchased at such a time. If I kept my marriage-day, I would keep it as a day of shame. Self-respect! appearances before the world! what are these to me? You have done all you can to make them nothing to me, and they *are* nothing.'"

The Sultan's authority has been defied. But he still has one means of control. Give her her freedom? "'No, madam. There is no possibility of separation between you and me.'" He has apparently not heard that the opinion of the world is nothing to his wife or that she is willing to commemorate her wedding day as "a day of shame." When he manages the next morning to force his way into her room, he finds a letter saying that "she had fled, upon her shameful wedding-day, with the man whom he had chosen for her humiliation."

The triumph of the Grand Vizier is short-lived, however. Even as he advances complacently toward his "queen" in the delusion that "'in the idlest and easiest part of the world, my soul, we'll both seek compensation for old slavery,'" he confronts the knife she has caught up from the table. Cowed in spite of himself, he sits in the chair as she commands. "She put the knife down upon the table, and touching her bosom with her hand, said—'I have something lying here that is no love trinket; and sooner than endure your touch once more, I would use it on you—and you know it, while I speak—with less reluctance than I would on any other creeping thing that lives'" (ch. 54). At this moment both the literal and the figurative daggers, fusing together, have been drawn against her oppressors, and especially against the tyrannical Sultan. As she reveals to Carker the depth of her contempt for both him and her husband, she is being simultaneously revenged on them both for the greatest humiliation in a life of humiliation. Will he go out and boast of his conquest over her? He well may—but both she and he know the boast will be a falsehood:

> "In every vaunt you make," she said, "I have my triumph. I single out in you the meanest man I know, the parasite and tool of the proud tyrant, that his wound may go the deeper and may rankle more. Boast, and revenge me on him! You know how you stand cowering there; you see yourself in colours quite as despicable, if not as odious, as those in which I see you. Boast then, and revenge me on yourself." (ch. 54)

But in addition to achieving her own vengeance, Edith "Granger" has succeeded in sheltering the threatened child in the garden, Florence. Also, as a blighted child herself, she has likewise been the instrument of the child world to avenge little Paul and all the other victims of the Dombey empire.

In the metaphor of the sword that wears out its scabbard, Dickens has once more found a contextually appropriate figure to embody one of his recurrent insights: the world of the emotions and inner life can be suppressed and contained, but they cannot be permanently denied. A related insight is caught by Louisa Gradgrind in another contextually chosen analogy, though it is missed by her father, who does not see "the application of the remark." In the fire that she is so fond of watching,[7] Louisa observes a significant phenomenon: fire inwardly contained and allowed to smoulder without free access to the air might suddenly flare into life. In the Coketown chimneys "'there seems to be nothing . . . but languid and monotonous smoke. Yet when the night comes, Fire bursts out'" (*HT*, bk. I, ch. 15).

Like Edith Dombey, Louisa conceals the intensity of her inner feelings behind a frozen façade. While she herself clearly perceives the probable explosion consequent to such suppression, Harthouse, the bored and misanthropic "drifting iceberg" is understandably misled. He is very quickly drawn to frozen Louisa. As Carker believes their shared "slavery" makes a real bond between him and Edith, so Harthouse believes that their shared indifference makes a real bond between him and Louisa: "'The only difference,'" he explains to her, "'between us and the professors of virtue or benevolence, or philanthropy—never mind the name—is that we know it is all meaningless, and say so, while they know it equally and will never say so'" (bk. II, ch. 7).

As Carker misreads Edith, however, Harthouse likewise misreads Louisa. Her indifference stems not from belief that "it is all meaningless," but rather from conviction that she cannot relate to a meaningful world of values that she believes in and yearns for. In her passive state she sees no reason to protest Harthouse's analysis. The narrator asks: "Why should she be shocked or warned? . . . What was there in her soul for James Harthouse to destroy which Thomas Gradgrind had nurtured there in its state of innocence?" Nonetheless, in the final outcome the stifled soul of Louisa gathers enough explosive force to reject Harthouse. At the very moment when he thinks he has seduced Louisa into eloping with him (and when the ogress, Mrs. Sparsit, believes Louisa has finally fallen off the "Giant Staircase" built for her), Louisa confounds them both by returning to her father's home to confront him directly with the results of his educational system. As Edith undoes both the tyrannical Sultan and his Grand Vizier, Louisa brings down both the monster in a lecturing castle and the drifting iceberg.

This, then, is still another view of childhood rising up to avenge its blighted children. The very forces whose denial blighted the child burst forth in an uncontrollable way, violent and destructive instead of life-giving. Tom's fate demonstrates the same rebellion by the same unruly forces in a young gentleman who had never had the freedom necessary to learn to guide and control them—unaccountable, says a sarcastic narrator, "that a young gentleman whose imagination had been strangled in his cradle should be still inconvenienced by its ghost in the form of grovelling sensualities—but such a monster, beyond all doubt, was Tom" (bk. II, ch. 3).

Although in *Hard Times* Dickens the propagandist rides his theme hard for its topical value as social criticism, Dickens the artist constructs the fairy-tale framework to contain a truth much more universal. This truth is the recognition that the creative-destructive Dionysiac forces within a human being will not brook denial. In the

Dickens view, childhood is the crucial time for learning how both to cope and to create with these forces, which are neither good nor bad in themselves. The freedom from responsibility that characterizes the ideal childhood is a license for irresponsibility, for exploring without restraint the dark reaches of the human consciousness, for allowing the forces within and without a chance for free play in the imagination and fancy. Only by coming to know and channel these forces can a person hope to discipline and control them through enlightened rationality.

The perfectly designed Gradgrind/Hard Facts/M'Choakumchild school can in the long run never expect to compete with "Sleary's Horse-riding" as an educational institution. In forbidding his children to go near the Circus, to which they are irresistibly drawn, Gradgrind shows his awareness of the threat it poses to his rigid training: the uncontrollable elements Gradgrind seeks to stamp out and deny are embraced with joyous gusto by the disreputable circus people. Plato's concept of the soul as "a winged charioteer driving a team of winged horses"—the spirited horses of the passions and appetites guided and reined by Reason—powerfully informs and energizes the description of Sleary's Horse-riding.[8] The circus people stay at a public house called the "Pegasus's Arms," whose name is inscribed in Roman letters "underneath the winged horse upon the sign-board," while "Framed and glazed upon the wall behind the dingy little bar, was another Pegasus—a theatrical one—with real gauze let in for his wings, golden stars stuck on all over him, and his ethereal harness made of red silk" (bk. I, ch. 6).

Sissy Jupe gets into her first difficulty at M'Choakumchild's school through her inability properly to define a horse, whereas the colorless boy Bitzer has plenty of "facts" at his disposal to put both the horse and Sissy in their places. This difficulty of hers is all the more remarkable since her father is an employee of Sleary's Horse-riding. Later, defending himself against Sissy's charge that he has been chasing her, Bitzer accuses her: "'You wouldn't have thought of saying such mischief if you hadn't been a horse-rider,'" because: "'The horse-riders never mind what they say, sir; they're famous for it. You know the horse-riders are famous for never minding what they say,'" addressing Sissy. "'It's as well known in the town as—please, sir, as the multiplication table isn't known to the horse-riders'" (bk. I, ch. 5).

This world of the circus is a wonderful combination of unbridled freedom and amazing feats of control achieved by people "not very tidy in their private dresses" and "not at all orderly in their domestic arrangements." A remarkable description of their activities captures their essence:

> There were two or three handsome young women among them, with their two or three husbands, and their two or three mothers, and their eight or nine children, who did the fairy business when required. The father of one of the families was in the habit of balancing the father of another of the families on the top of a great pole; the father of a third family often made a pyramid of both those fathers, with Master Kidderminster for the apex, and himself for the base; all the fathers could dance upon rolling casks, stand upon bottles, catch knives and balls, twirl hand-basins, ride upon anything, jump over everything, and stick at nothing. All the mothers could—and did—dance upon the slack-wire and the tight-rope, and perform rapid acts on bare-backed steeds; none of them were at all particular in respect of showing their legs; and one of them, alone in a Greek chariot, drove six-in-hand into every town they came to. (bk. I, ch. 6)

A general concept emerges gradually from this particular-to-particular description of the "Horse-riding" way of life: real stability and security must be gained through daring dexterity and the ability to maintain balance amid the precarious and hazardous elements that characterize living. "Horse-riding" itself (especially on "bare-backed steeds") emblematizes all such activities, and the "Greek chariot" driven by "one of them alone" into every town they come to glancingly alludes to Plato's Myth of the Soul.[9] Since for Dickens the development of the soul is the great achievement of the child "always learning," Sleary's Circus provides a perfect environment for the educational process.

It is further fitting that in this despised world of the circus the ogre Gradgrind should find himself not only humbled by, but finally actually indebted to the fanciful world he has forbidden to his children. As an ogre recently returned to human form (having made himself "a party to sentimental humbug"), Gradgrind has appeared on the grounds of Sleary's Circus in a desperate effort to rescue his son from arrest and imprisonment. Young Tom, disguised as one of the black servants, has been hidden from his pursuers through being absorbed into a performance of that "'piethe of comic infant bithnith, "Jack the Giant-killer"'" (bk. III, ch. 7). The rescue is almost undone by the proudest product of the Gradgrind system, young Bitzer. Bitzer, with great reasonableness, turns against his former mentor the well-learned tenets of the Hard Facts School.[10] Although Bitzer is determined to return the culprit Tom to his well-deserved punishment, he is no match for Sleary, his dog, and a dancing horse. The despised world of fantasy and fairy tale finally routs the world of fact to send Tom safely off to a new world.

In retrospect, the retributive justice Dickens has brought down upon all these adults who, individually or as a society, have contributed to the blighting of childhood has in no instance been arbitrary or capricious. Upon close examination, it can usually be seen to be inherent in the offense. Thus the pathetic children in the Dickens stories have persistent allegorical referents. The crippling or killing of the child takes place in many more lives than are indicated by the deathbed scenes. Little Paul, with his soul too large for his body, dies when that soul is forced and squeezed out of existence; but Mr. Tulkinghorn lives on like anybody else unless one is acute enough to note the blank spot at the beginning of his procession. Little Paul's collapsing legs signal his approaching total collapse, but Grandfather Smallweed, as well as a host of other Dickens characters, make their way somehow through life, though their helpless limbs reveal the flawed foundation of their childhood. On the one hand, what the child represents cannot be repressed without destroying the essential qualities of a human being and turning what should be full human beings into destructive, sterile, or pathetic half-people. On the other hand, the strong forces of the passions cannot be permanently suppressed and denied, for they will rise up to exact their own revenge in undisciplined violence.

Perhaps Dickens defended the death of Mr. Krook in *Bleak House* on the wrong grounds: what better explanation could be found for apparent spontaneous combustion than the smouldering fires of the denied soul?

# VII

## *Castles in the Air*

Unlike the blighted child, who is always the victim of the adults around him, in the crucial transitional period between childhood and maturity about to be examined, the growing youth must himself take responsibility for the future course of his life. Like the struggle for existence at birth and death, the transition is difficult as, for the second time, the individual is torn from an environment of effortless warmth, support, and comfort. Small wonder if occasionally a potential adult tenaciously assumes the fetal position and makes a career of being a preserved baby in a bottle; for coming out of the childhood garden means that he must acquire a precise sense of time, recognize responsibility and limitations upon personal freedom, and struggle painfully with the implications of his developing understanding. He must likewise accept the conditions of life in the world of hard fact if he is to live at all; he must be both willing and able to make the distinction between dream and actuality, and to acknowledge that whatever may be the relationship between the inner and outer worlds, it is not that of magic wish fulfillment.

For this is the other side of the coin. Although castles in the air are the grand accomplishment of the child imagination and fancy in the protected garden, they are not in fact inhabitable. They emblematize the capacity to see visions and dream dreams—but also portray the soul-destroying consequences of becoming lost in a "groundless" world: of trying to protect the cherished inner world by rejecting the very dubious outer one. For just as the attempt to deny reality to the dream world likewise denies all that gives life real value, so the attempt to deny reality to the world of hard facts is to deny the stuff of life itself.

In childhood, it has been seen, at first the phenomena of both worlds are equally "all new and all true": no gap exists between them, and "great expectations" encompass "great fulfillment" as a matter of course. Now the youth must try to reconcile with his dreams an empirical world that he discovers is quite indifferent to them. In this borderland between child and adult, then, the maturing individual must come to renounce "great expectations." Like all the others, this transitional struggle is crucial, for the person unwilling or unable to relinquish his dreams of magical fulfillment will remain, temporarily or forever, a half-adult fixated at an immature level of development, often hiding as a pseudo-child among the innocents in the garden.

The "great expectations" configuration in Dickens is loosely constructed. The adult builder of air castles is still a child with his easy optimism, irresponsibility, and egocentricity. His character is established by freezing him into the childhood surroundings, either as an adult interloper in the garden or as a bewitched child in a fairy tale. Nothing good may be said for great expectations: they blight or destroy character by encouraging the irresponsible qualities of the "undisciplined heart"; they blind their possessor to the "facts" of life and involve him in a painful readjustment if he is to recover from them. Because of these deadly effects, this configuration overlaps frequently with the marsh images, especially when an adult decides to disguise himself as a child and to remain in the protected garden for his own purposes.

Such an adult is Harold Skimpole, who roams predatorily through the *Bleak House* country as a pseudo-child. Skimpole demonstrates the destructive consequences of air castles, not because they are airy and unrealizable, but rather because he succeeds so well in making them materialize for his selfish purposes. For Harold Skimpole is a professional. As a preserved child he lives a free and easy life quite above the restrictions and limitations that hamper most people. Examination of Skimpole, therefore (and of his foil character, Lawrence Boythorn), will show us the characteristics and consequences of the childhood exploiter in his most efficient and slickly polished form. Skimpole is quite frank about his superiority to a standard of judgment that would condemn his opportunistic betrayal of the child Jo. Says Skimpole: "'I am exactly the man to be placed in a superior position, in such a case as that. I am above the rest of mankind, in such a case as that. I can act with philosophy, in such a case as that. I am not warped by prejudices, as an Italian baby is by bandages. I am as free as the air. I feel myself as far above suspicion as Caesar's wife'" (*BH*, ch. 61). Skimpole might well assert his pride in maintaining himself as a baby without bandages, for it has taken all his endowment of clever resources to preserve himself in that irresponsible state.

Like Grandfather Smallweed, Skimpole has gathered about himself a peculiar family. As he himself observes to Ada Clare and Esther Summerson on the occasion of their visit to his uneven apartment (its elegance fading away from his presence): "'It is pleasant . . . and it is whimsically interesting, to trace peculiarities in families.'" Had he known the Smallweeds, he would have noted with special interest a family peculiarity in direct contrast to his own. "'In this family,'" he adds with simple pride, "'we are all children, and I am the youngest'" (ch. 43). Skimpole the child is his own favorite subject, and Esther observes "the fantastic way in which he took himself under his own protection and argued about that curious person."

John Jarndyce, with his sincere love for all children, also takes this child under his protection, though not without suspicion of an east wind blowing up. "'There's no one here,'" says Jarndyce, "'but the finest creature upon earth—a child. . . . I don't mean literally a child,' pursued Mr. Jarndyce; 'not a child in years. He is grown up—he is at least as old as I am—but in simplicity, and freshness, and enthusiasm, and a fine guileless inaptitude for all worldly affairs, he is a perfect child'" (ch. 6). It would be, suggests this good man, "'the height of childishness . . . to regard him as a man. You can't make *him* responsible.'"

Esther's first impression of this child is that he is "a little bright creature, with a rather large head;[1] but a delicate face, and a sweet voice, and there was a perfect charm about him. All he said was so free from effort and spontaneous, and was said with such a captivating gaiety, that it was fascinating to hear him talk." But Esther has too much common sense to be taken in by this pseudo-child:

> Indeed, [she records] he had more the appearance, in all respects, of a damaged young man, than a well-preserved elderly one. There was an easy negligence in his manner, and even in his dress . . . which I could not separate from the idea of a romantic youth who had undergone some unique process of depreciation. It struck me as being not at all like the manner or appearance of a man who had advanced in life, by the usual road of years, cares, and experiences. (ch. 6)

That other receptacle of common sense, Mr. Bucket, similarly has the number of "'that elderly young gentleman'" (ch. 57). Esther has expressed her view that Skimpole's treachery has passed "the usual bounds of his childish innocence." Bucket quickly gives her a piece of advice respecting the "bounds" of such a person:

> "Bounds, my dear? . . . Bounds? . . . Whenever a person proclaims to you 'In worldly matters I'm a child,' you consider that that person is only a-crying off from being held accountable, and that you have got that person's number, and it's Number One. Now, I am not a poetical man myself, except in a vocal way when it goes round a company, but I'm a practical one, and that's my experience. So's this rule. Fast and loose in one thing, Fast and loose in everything. I never knew it fail. No more will you. Nor no one." (ch. 57)

There never was a man more fast and loose than Harold Skimpole. To acquire freedom, he might have said, looking guileless, one need only demand it—such a simple thing: "'Now, my dear Miss Summerson, and my dear Mr. Richard,' said Mr. Skimpole, gaily, innocently and confidingly, as he looked at his drawing with his head on one side; 'here you see me utterly incapable of helping myself, and entirely in your hands! I only ask to be free. The butterflies are free. Mankind will surely not deny to Harold Skimpole what it concedes to the butterflies!'" (ch. 6). Certainly no bounds constrict the man for whom "time is no object," and who can conceive of the world on no smaller terms than "the universe"[2] with none of the sordid limiting realities of the world of hard facts. He has a delicate sentiment toward Ada, "the child of the universe." Jarndyce advances the opinion that the undifferentiated universe makes "'rather an indifferent parent,'" to which Skimpole replies:

> "Well! . . . you know the world (which in your sense is the universe), and I know nothing of it, so you shall have your way. But if I had mine," glancing at the cousins [Richard and Ada], "there should be no brambles of sordid realities in such a path as that. It should be strewn with roses; it should lie through bowers, where there was no spring, autumn, nor winter, but perpetual summer. Age or change should never wither it. The base word money should never be breathed near it." (ch. 6)

In the world in which Skimpole dwells, this gracious thought is as good as the deed, for he has resolved not to recognize the dismaying gap between the dream and the factual worlds. He therefore plays happily in the idyllic garden of a make-believe world where, as in the toy theatre, nothing is but thinking makes it so. And—dazzlingly—"what with his free hilarious manner, and his engaging candour, and his genial way" he seems to say to all those foolish adults about him, "'I am gay and innocent; forget your worldly arts and play with me!'" in a grotesque imitation of the invitation extended to the traveller by the child in the garden. (see ch. V) His decadent pleasure in the good things of the garden is tagged by his laggard love of fruits out of season. If Dr. Blimber's children were prematurely "forced" to bear flavorless fruit before their time, this man with his parade of "basket(s) of choice hothouse peaches" (ch. 18), his "little plate of hothouse nectarines on the table, and . . . another of grapes" (ch. 43) like them comes to artificial ripeness with a false blush on the cheek. "'Give me my peach, my cup of coffee, and my claret,'" he says, handing about grapes never to be paid for; "'I am content. I don't want them for themselves, but they remind me of the sun'" (ch. 43). The reminder is as good as the actuality—better, for it is never clouded over on a rainy day.

In fact, Skimpole has perfected the art of substituting the thought for the deed, and finds the result personally most satisfactory:

> "I don't regret [he explains] that *I* have not a strong will and an immense power of business-detail, to throw myself into objects with surprising ardour.[3] I can admire [Mrs. Jellyby] without envy. I can sympathise with the objects. I can dream of them. I can lie down on the grass—in fine weather—and float along an African river, embracing all the natives I meet, as sensible of the deep silence, and sketching the dense overhanging tropical growth as accurately, as if I were there." (ch. 6)

With the most engaging and rational of arguments, he cannot understand why the rest of the world fails to accept this eminently sensible position:

> He had been enriching his medical attendant in the most lavish manner. He had always doubled, and sometimes quadrupled, his fees. He had said to the doctor, "Now, my dear doctor, it is quite a delusion on your part to suppose that you attend me for nothing. I am overwhelming you with money—in my expansive intentions—if you only knew it!" And really (he said) he meant it to that degree, that he thought it much the same as doing it. If he had had those bits of metal or thin paper, to which mankind attached so much importance,

> to put in the doctor's hand, he would have put them in the doctor's hand. Not having them, he substituted the will for the deed. Very well! If he really meant it—if his will were genuine and real: which it was—it appeared to him that it was the same as coin, and cancelled the obligation. (ch. 15)

As a matter of strict accuracy, this apparently most frivolous and careless view of life is the most practical of philosophies for the shrewd, willful, and egocentric parasite who declines to accept the pain and suffering that are the real price of commitment to life at this crucial transitional point between childhood and maturity. Although Skimpole smilingly denies that he has the least idea what a "principle" is (ch. 18), he nonetheless has a clear and simple philosophy by which he lives and which he expounds with his usual engaging frankness. Like the Utilitarians, he seeks pleasure and avoids pain. "'When I go anywhere,' he says, 'I go for pleasure. I don't go anywhere for pain, because I was made for pleasure. Pain comes to *me* when it wants me'" (ch. 61). This simple principle quickly removes him from any scene of distress and saves him a great deal of trouble.

"'And he *is* a child. Now, isn't he?'" asks John Jarndyce for reassurance (ch. 6). Well, yes and no. He is a child in form, but the child heart is missing. His innocent benefactor unconsciously recognizes this lack in further observing: "'As to Skimpole . . . a habitable doll's house, with good board, and a few tin people to get into debt with and borrow money of, would set the boy up for life.'" The most that Skimpole dreams of is to endure forever in this hollow existence that will lead Bella Harmon of *Our Mutual Friend* to protest: "I want to be something so much worthier than a doll in a doll's house" (*OMF*, bk. IV, ch. 5). But Skimpole is inconvenienced by no such unsettling ambition.

The curious reader may feel inclined to ask Ada's question: "'Pray, cousin John, . . . what made him such a child?'" Though rubbing his head, a little at a loss, Jarndyce attempts an explanation.

> "Why," he slowly replied, roughening his head more and more, "he is all sentiment, and—susceptibility, and—and sensibility—and—and imagination. And these qualities are not regulated in him, somehow. I suppose the people who admired him for them in his youth, attached too much importance to them, and too little to any training that would have balanced and adjusted them; and so he became what he is. Hey?" (*BH*, ch. 43)

Or, as Bucket might say, nothing has apparently ever put any limiting "bounds" on his studied childish innocence. For what is required to grow up is attaching "sentiment, and—and susceptibility, and—and sensibility—and—and imagination" to living objects rather than freeing them in the imaginary garden for the enhancement of one's own pleasure: to "regulate" and "balance" these qualities of the dream world one must put them to work in the actual world—must transform hypocrisy and sentimentality into honest sentiment. The defining characteristics assigned to Harold Skimpole represented to Dickens a pragmatic failure, and mark the point in the path where he parted company with Wordsworth in his idealization of childhood.

Yet, as if fearful that he might not be understood, Dickens created an antithetical character to help take Skimpole's measure: also "boundless," also childish, also overwhelming—but nonetheless endearing and warm. Lawrence Boythorn, too, may have been a little deficient in "any training that would have balanced and adjusted" his qualities, but who would object when these qualities are an expansive child's heart and a quick, passionate action in response to its promptings? For the child heart, though difficult to maintain, is the one part of the child most precious to preserve.

A gentleman in *Nicholas Nickleby,* telling the story of "The Five Sisters of York," eulogizes the youngest sister, Alice, for her gladsome voice and merry laugh, which infected all around her with witching glee. This gentleman is led to rhapsodize about the measureless worth of the heart from which such joy springs, and to lament the difficulty, if not the impossibility, of maintaining such a heart through the vicissitudes of life.

> "If we all had hearts like those which beat so lightly in the bosoms of the young and beautiful, what a heaven this earth would be! If, while our bodies grow old and withered, our hearts could but retain their early youth and freshness, of what avail would be our sorrows and sufferings! But the faint image of Eden which is stamped upon them in childhood, chafes and rubs in our rough struggles with the world, and soon wears away:[4] too often to leave nothing but a mournful blank remaining." (*NN,* ch. 6)

This child heart of Lawrence Boythorn, through some magic of invulnerability, has survived even a blighted love to make a pathway of some brightness through the world. But the child heart is such an anomaly in the adult world that Boythorn too wears the eccentric look. We repeat, however: who would object to such heart-warming eccentricity?

Yet some do. Harold Skimpole and his admirer, Sir Leicester Dedlock, are less than enthusiastic about Boythorn. It is ironic that a man so unrestrained as Harold Skimpole should be a little reserved about a similar quality in Boythorn. "'Nature forgot to shade him off, I think?' observed Mr. Skimpole . . . 'A little too boisterous—like the sea? A little too vehement—like a bull, who has made up his mind to consider every colour scarlet? But I grant a sledge-hammering sort of merit in him'" (*BH,* ch. 15). Skimpole, of course, is unrestrained in the gratification of his personal desires and appetites, while Boythorn is unrestrained in his right-hearted explosions. Esther, for one, would be surprised if these two thought very highly of each other: "Mr. Boythorn attaching so much importance to many things, and Mr. Skimpole caring so little for anything."[5]

Time, for instance. Boythorn has invited Esther, Ada, and Skimpole for a visit to Lincolnshire. When they arrive, via coach, he is waiting, charged with energy and good-natured impatience.

> "By Heaven!" said he, after giving us a courteous greeting, "this is a most infamous coach. It is the most flagrant example of an abominable public vehicle that ever encumbered the face of the earth. It is twenty-five minutes after its time, this afternoon. The coachman ought to be put to death!"
>
> "*Is* he after his time?" said Mr. Skimpole, to whom he happened to address himself. "You know my infirmity."
>
> "Twenty-five minutes! Twenty-six minutes!" replied Mr. Boythorn, referring to his watch. "With two ladies in the coach, this scoundrel has deliberately delayed his arrival six-and-twenty minutes. Deliberately! It is impossible that it can be accidental!" (ch. 18)

Boythorn's precise sense of time not only sets him at odds with Skimpole, but also points out his vitality. It would seem in the natural order of things, then, that Skimpole and Boythorn should on occasion tangle. If their skirmishes never quite come off, the uneasy peace between them is maintained on the one hand by Skimpole's indisposition ever to take a stand that will bring him into disharmony with his companions of the moment—on the grounds that "everybody's business in the social system is to be agreeable"[6] and on the other hand by Boythorn's high sense of responsible hospitality, which keeps their little dialogues from ending "in some violent explosion on the part of our host."

The Boythorn establishment itself mirrors a man at poles remove from the one who lives provisionally in an untidy apartment spottily supplied with furniture that comes and goes, and who lives on food brought in out of season and never paid for:

> Everything about the place wore an aspect of maturity and abundance. The old lime-tree walk was like green cloisters, the very shadows of the cherry-trees and apple-trees were heavy with fruit, the gooseberry-bushes were so laden that their branches arched and rested on the earth, the strawberries and raspberries grew in like profusion, and the peaches basked by the hundred on the wall. Tumbled about among the spread nets and the glass frames sparkling and winking in the sun, there were such heaps of drooping pods, and marrows, and cucumbers, that every foot of ground appeared a vegetable treasury, while the smell of sweet herbs and all kinds of wholesome growth (to say nothing of the neighbouring meadows where the hay was carrying) made the whole air a great nosegay. Such stillness and composure reigned within the orderly precincts of the old red wall, that even the feathers hung in garlands to scare the birds hardly stirred; and the wall had such a ripening influence that where, here and there high up, a disused nail and scrap of list still clung to it, it was easy to fancy that they had mellowed with the changing seasons, and that they had rusted and decayed according to the common fate. (ch. 18)

This is the home of a man who, with his acceptance of time, has also accepted change and mortality: who is content to mellow into the harvest season of maturity, to grow old and decay along with the rest of the created world. He is a man, that is, in marked contrast to Skimpole, that depreciated and damaged young/old man who has avoided "advancing in life, by the usual road of years, cares and experiences," and whose best wish for his young friends, Richard and Ada, must be that age or change should never wither them.

With the introduction of Richard and Ada, it can be seen that the heart of the difference between Skimpole and Boythorn can be gauged by their attitude and practice toward tender, vulnerable things. Everywhere in Dickens, the really appropriate test for measuring the distance between sentimentality and real sentiment is a child.[7] In *Bleak House,* a parade of children trails through the various plot lines revealing the true nature of the adults around them: Jo, the Smallweeds, the Jellybys, the Pardiggles, the Coavinses—and the hapless brood entrusted to Harold Skimpole.

On the very first occasion when Esther meets Skimpole, John Jarndyce has just prepared his guests for an encounter with "a perfect child." A child, they learn in rapid succession, who knows and admires Mrs. Jellyby (another escapee into a more malleable world) and who is an "Artist"—"an Amateur, but might have been a Professional."[8] And then Esther's guardian ingenuously supplies the other half of the necessary information:

> " . . . he has been unfortunate in his affairs, and unfortunate in his pursuits, and unfortunate in his family; but he don't care—he's a child!"
>
> "Did you imply that he has children of his own, sir?" inquired Richard.
>
> "Yes, Rick! Half-a-dozen. More! Nearer a dozen, I should think. But he has never looked after them. How could he? He wanted somebody to look after *him*. He is a child, you know!" said Mr. Jarndyce.
>
> "And have the children looked after themselves at all, sir?" inquired Richard.
>
> "Why, just as you may suppose," said Mr. Jarndyce: his countenance suddenly falling. "It is said that the children of the very poor are not brought up, but dragged up. Harold Skimpole's children have tumbled up somehow or other.—The wind's getting round again, I am afraid. I feel it rather!" (ch. 6)

For Skimpole long ago, as the youth in the idyllic garden of irresponsibility, having just lost his first position as a medical practitioner, and "having (as he added with delightful gaiety) 'nothing to live upon but love, fell in love, and married, and surrounded himself with rosy cheeks'" (ch. 6). Like the other innocent victims in *Bleak House,* his children too fall under the damaging influence of "adult" irresponsibility. Therefore, he is not only a parasite upon society, but is also a blighter of childhood. His cavalier attitude toward the troubles of the Coavinses children likewise reveals his monstrous callousness as he not only ignores their plight but also pretends to have been their benefactor in giving employment to their father, the debt collector.

> He said, Well, it was really very pleasant to see how things lazily adapted themselves to purposes. . . . He could have dispensed with Coavinses. There had been times when, if he had been a Sultan, and his Grand Vizier had said one morning, "What does the Commander of the Faithful require at the hands of his slave?" he might have even gone so far as to reply, "The head of Coavinses!" But what turned out to be the case? That, all that time, he had been giving employment to a most deserving man; that he had been a benefactor to Coavinses . . . (ch. 15)

Skimpole is again so touchingly affected with sentiment at the thought that his eyes fill with tears and his heart swells magnanimously. Did only Dickens detect the guilty Sultan in this captivating soliloquy—or did he intend to convey that perhaps the shrewd Skimpole was engaged in a furious frenzy of talk to conceal from those about him his own awareness of evaded responsibility? No matter—the guilty Sultan flashes for a glittering moment across the scene.

The truth is that, to Skimpole, children, like other people, are valuable only as convenient props for his own comfort and security, or as marketable commodities to be exploited for their exchange value. Consider the case of Jo. Sick and weary, he has been brought home by the compassionate Esther. Skimpole, a guest at Bleak House, views the wretched boy with fastidious distaste and disposes of him with his customary frivolous logic: "'You had better turn him out,'" says Skimpole. "'If you put him out in the road, you only put him where he was before. He will be no worse off than he was, you know. Even make him better off, if you like. Give him sixpence, or five shillings, or five pound ten—you are arithmeticians, and I am not—and get rid of him!'" (ch. 31). By remarkable coincidence, as Esther long afterwards learns from Mr. Bucket, the callous suggestion only modestly foreshadows what actually happens. For on that very night, Bucket appears at Bleak House on the trail of Jo. "'I made up my mind, that night,'" the detective recalls, "'to come to the door and ask for Toughey [Jo], if that was all.'" Instead, however, he tosses a handful of gravel against a window behind which he sees a shadow moving:

> "As soon as Harold opens it and I have had a look at him, thinks I, you're the man for me. So I smoothed him down a bit, about not wanting to disturb the family after they was gone to bed, and about its being a thing to be regretted that charitable young ladies should harbour vagrants; and then, when I pretty well understood his ways, I said, I should consider a fypunnote well bestowed if I could relieve the premises of Toughey without causing any noise or trouble. Then says he, lifting up his eyebrows in the gayest way, 'it's no use mentioning a fypunnote to me, my friend, because I'm a mere child in such matters, and have no idea of money.' Of course I understood what his taking it so easy meant; and being now quite sure he was the man for me, I wrapped the note round a little stone and threw it up to him. Well! He laughs and beams, and looks as innocent as you like, and says, 'But I don't know the value of these things. What am I to *do* with this?' 'Spend it, sir,' says I. 'But I shall be taken in,' he says, 'they won't

> give me the right change, I shall lose it, it's no use to me.' Lord, you never saw such a face as he carried it with! Of course he told me where to find Toughey, and I found him." (ch. 57)

Thus Jo is put out on the road according to Skimpole's suggestion, but Dickens has slyly slipped the fypunnote from one childish hand to the other.

Skimpole is capable of the most vicious actions against the vulnerable life about him, veiling those actions all the time in tender sentiments of protection and concern. Boythorn, on the contrary, strides thundering onto the scene with a canary riding unconcernedly on his head. Jarndyce tries to prepare his young friends for *this* visitor as he did for Skimpole: "'His language is as sounding as his voice. He is always in extremes; perpetually in the superlative degree. In his condemnation he is all ferocity. You might suppose him to be an Ogre, from what he says; and I believe he has the reputation of one with some people'" (ch. 9). But, as in the case of Skimpole, things are not always what they purport to be, and Boythorn[9] is no blighter of childhood. Though he may be incapable of anything on a limited scale, Boythorn's extremity, as Esther observes accurately, is mostly verbal and his superlatives "'go off like blank cannons and hurt nothing.'" Even as he is "expressing the most implacable and passionate sentiments," his canary is "quietly perched on his forehead"; or, as it "now perched upon his thumb," he softly smooths "its feathers with his forefinger"—to the accompaniment of his booming laughter, for both he and his listeners are in on the joke that his professed violence is a fraud.

Despite the fact that Boythorn has no children of his own, he is sensitively responsive to their presence: his attitude toward them is generous and protective. Jarndyce tells his young friends not to be surprised to observe Boythorn assuming a protective role toward him—"'for he has never forgotten that I was a low boy at school, and that our friendship began in his knocking two of my head tyrant's teeth out (he says six)[10] before breakfast.'" As Esther is recovering from her illness, her guardian appears one day with a letter from Boythorn, "'heart of chivalry, breathing such ferocious vows as never were breathed on paper before, that if you don't go and occupy his whole house, he having already turned out of it expressly for that purpose, by Heaven and by earth he'll pull it down, and not leave one brick standing on another!'" (ch. 35).

Boythorn confounds the Skimpole formula by reversing the relationship of thought and deed, word and action. In him, the tender act neutralizes the violent profession to contrast the hypocritical Skimpole disadvantageously with a man of true sentiment. As usual, Esther's clear eye detects the truth of the matter: it would be most surprising if these two souls *had* thought very highly of one another.

Agreement between Boythorn and Sir Leicester is equally unthinkable as the former storms the gates of Chesney Wold demanding a right-of-way across the marshy place in Lincolnshire with its proscriptions against trespass. While Sir Leicester sits woodenly by his fire of Dedlock timber and antediluvian forest asserting his timeless repose, Lawrence Boythorn, as the force of life (which insists on breaking in with its unsettling changes), joyously sets himself in opposition to the "'most stiff-necked, arrogant, imbecile, pig-headed numskull, ever, by some inexplicable mistake of Nature, born in any station of life but a walking-stick's!'" (ch. 9). Boythorn does battle like a malign and laughing comic spirit, frolicking about with infectious gaiety to undo Sir Leicester's efforts in the sure knowledge that life and time will continue to burst through those boundaries any man is deluded enough to build against them. Boythorn describes their actions and counteractions:

> "The fellow [Sir Leicester] sends a most abandoned villain with one eye, to construct a gateway. I play upon that execrable scoundrel with a fire-engine, until the breath is nearly driven out of his body. The fellow erects a gate in the night. I chop it down and burn it in the morning. He sends his myrmidons to come over the fence, and pass and repass. I catch them in humane man traps, fire split peas at their legs, play upon them with the engine—resolve to free mankind from the insupportable burden of the existence of those lurking ruffians. He brings actions for trespass. I bring actions for trespass. He brings actions for assault and battery; I defend them, and continue to assault and batter. Ha, ha, ha!" (ch. 9)

Though he is firm that there shall be "no closing up of my paths, by any Dedlock," Boythorn bears no malice toward his neighbor, who is himself not malevolent, but simply a rather pathetic anachronism, like the ancient mild reptiles which time passed by. Without a leg to stand on, Sir Leicester yields himself up to the inevitable family complaint, gout.

> And a goodly show he makes, lying in a flush of crimson and gold, in the midst of the great drawing-room, before his favourite picture of my Lady, with broad strips of sunlight shining in, down the long perspective, through the long line of windows, and alternating with soft

> reliefs of shadow. Outside, the stately oaks, rooted for ages in the green ground which has never known ploughshare, but was still a Chase when kings rode to battle with sword and shield, and rode a-hunting with bow and arrow; bear witness to his greatness. Inside, his forefathers, looking on him from the walls, say, "Each of us was a passing reality here, and left this coloured shadow of himself, and melted into remembrance as dreamy as the distant voices of the rooks now lulling you to rest;" and bear their testimony to his greatness, too. And he is very great, this day. And woe to Boythorn, or other daring wight, who shall presumptuously contest an inch with him! (ch. 16)

"'He carries himself,'" observes Boythorn, "'like an eight-day clock at all times; like one of a race of eight-day clocks in gorgeous cases that never go and never went—Ha ha ha!'" (ch. 18)—an interesting simile once more illuminating his perceptiveness of the relationship between life and time.

In the end, Boythorn maintains the pretense of feud and violence against Sir Leicester because his compassionate heart realizes that the broken old relic needs the feud to strike some fire of purpose from an otherwise blasted life: violence once more concealing kindness in the ironic inversion of hypocrisy that constitutes Lawrence Boythorn. The last word to be heard from Harold Skimpole, on the other hand, comes in the diary left at his death five years after coolness developed between him and John Jarndyce following Skimpole's carelessly discarding his depleted young friend, Richard: "'Jarndyce, in common with most other men I have known, is the Incarnation of Selfishness'" (ch. 61). Thus, his last word is the repudiation of the true benefactor, which seems to characterize in general the selfish parasite and in particular the adult dallying in the garden.

In the antithetical characters of Harold Skimpole and Lawrence Boythorn, Dickens develops to its fullest his view of the qualities producing the preserved child. In his perverted or defective relationship to time, responsibility, and worldly affairs; in his attitudes and practices toward the fruits of the garden—children—and benefactors; in his ability to reject the actual world and live in the dream world (substituting the thought for the deed), Harold Skimpole is a frightening monster who embodies the social threat and the individual peril confronting human beings when someone decides to remain a preserved child. He is as grotesque and revolting as the Hindoo baby in a bottle. Lawrence Boythorn not only provides contrast to bring out Skimpole's characteristics even more sharply, but also suggests the delicate balance that needs to be achieved by the mature adult: in putting away childish things, he must strive to keep the child heart, which is closely related to that dream world of childhood. While living in the actual world, he should carry the ideal world within him. As we have already heard the gentleman in *Nicholas Nickleby* observe: "If we all had hearts like those which beat so lightly in the bosoms of the young and beautiful, what a heaven this earth would be!" If Boythorn is an anomaly among men, it is a pity that it should be so.

Although in these two characters the portrait of the adult child is most fully fleshed in, essentially the same picture may be caught in a vignette, or flashing glimpses of it may appear in other characters. Mrs. Matthew Pocket, for example, sits for her miniature in *Great Expectations.* In the same book, Pip successfully makes the transition to maturity, but Dickens does not let the reader forget the alternative possibility, exemplified in the person of this eccentric character permanently frozen in childhood patterns as the cost of maintaining great expectations. Brought up by a father who "had invented for himself a conviction that his deceased father would have been made a Baronet but for somebody's determined opposition arising out of entirely personal motives" (*GE,* ch. 23), and who had firmly planted in his daughter's mind that she was destined for great things, Belinda Pocket comes by her great expectations through both heredity and environment. Even after marriage to Mr. Pocket and the appearance of a bevy of children, she still considers herself as "one who in the nature of things must marry a title, and who was to be guarded from the acquisition of plebeian domestic knowledge." Surrounded by her children, who, like Skimpole's "were not growing up or being brought up, but were tumbling up" (ch. 22), reading her "book of dignities," she lives in serene removal from the world about her. Pip thinks it curiously irrelevant and absentminded of her when she asks him, upon first meeting, "if I liked the taste of orange-flower water." So far as he can see, "the question had no bearing, near or remote, on any foregone or subsequent transactions" (ch. 23). Whether or no, the question establishes at once that taste for exotic fruit (like Skimpole's), which Dickens uses to tag the irresponsible adult dallying in the garden.

Mrs. Pocket's predominant characteristic is her sure method of preserving inviolate a dream world overwhelmingly besieged by the bustling household around her. Pip reports: "[A] neighbouring lady with whom the family were personally unacquainted, wrote in to say that she had seen Millers slapping the baby. This greatly distressed Mrs. Pocket, who burst into tears on receiving the note, and said that it was an extraordinary thing that the neighbours couldn't mind their own business." On another occasion, she sits absorbed in eating an orange steeped in sugar and wine, while the ignored baby in her lap plays happily but dangerously with a pair of nutcrackers. Little Jane jumps to the baby's rescue:

> "Mama dear," lisped the little girl, "baby ood have put hith eyeth out."
>
> "How dare you tell me so!" retorted Mrs. Pocket. "Go and sit down in your chair this moment!" (ch. 23)

With unassailable dignity, she says majestically: "'I will not be interfered with by Jane. . . . I hope I know my poor grandpapa's position.'"

Understandably, Mr. Pocket is in some despair and grief over the conditions in his household:

> "This is a pretty thing, Belinda! . . . Here's the cook lying insensibly drunk on the kitchen floor, with a large bundle of fresh butter made up in the cupboard ready to sell for grease!"
>
> Mrs. Pocket instantly showed much amiable emotion, and said, "This is that odious Sophia's doing!"
>
> "What do you mean, Belinda?" demanded Mr. Pocket.
>
> "Sophia has told you," said Mrs. Pocket. "Did I not see her, with my own eyes, and hear her with my own ears, come into the room just now and ask to speak to you?"
>
> "But has she not taken me downstairs, Belinda," returned Mr. Pocket, "and shown me the woman, and the bundle too?"
>
> "And do you defend her, Matthew," said Mrs. Pocket, "for making mischief?"
>
> Mr. Pocket uttered a dismal groan.
>
> "Am I, grandpapa's granddaughter, to be nothing in the house?" said Mrs. Pocket. "Besides, the cook has always been a very nice respectful woman, and said in the most natural manner when she came to look after the situation, that she felt I was born to be a Duchess." (ch. 23)

The outside world of facts has no way to breach Mrs. Pocket's defenses to assail her dream world, for she accurately sees that the threat to her serenity is not the disturbing fact itself, but the knowledge of that fact. She therefore immediately and unerringly attacks those who presume to be messengers from the outside.[11]

Both Harold Skimpole and Belinda Pocket are grotesque projections of monstrous adults who have voluntarily and even willfully turned their backs on the demanding outside world in order to remain in the effortless world of childhood. These caricatures of life have carefully avoided the test of the critical "struggle in time" necessary to demonstrate their humanity. As a result, they are empty imitations of real people who, as John Jarndyce explains of Skimpole, need no more than "a habitable doll house" to sustain their existence.

Miss Flite, of *Bleak House,* suffers a different fate: she has long ago given up all struggle in her enslavement to great expectations and is permanently suspended in the air-castle world. She represents the long, perspective view on the Court of Chancery. This allegorical figure with her caged birds is both spokesman and oracle for all the Chancery victims from the beginning to the end of the suit. Her memory reaches back to old Tom Jarndyce. She inherits her own expectations from a father, a brother, and a sister, all of whom "expected a Judgment" and who are all "'dead of course, my dear'" (*BH,* ch. 35). She is the first to see the fatal attraction begin in Richard, and the last to give blessing to Gridley, who considers her the one tie he ever had on earth unbroken by Chancery. She perceives the total truth and pronounces judgment with oracular madness and wisdom. It would be wiser of course, she responds to Esther's question, not to expect a judgment that will come only on the Day of Judgment: "'[V]ery wearing to be always in expectation, of what never comes, my dear Fitz-Jarndyce! Wearing, I assure you, to the bone! . . . But, my dear,' she went on, in her mysterious way, 'There's a dreadful attraction to the place. . . . There's a cruel attraction in the place. You *can't* leave it. And you *must* expect.'" Although the comment refers to the Court of Chancery, the judgment might well speak for the "cruel attraction" of all great expectations and castles in the air that make it so difficult to depart from the childhood garden: "You *can't* leave it. And you *must* expect."

The preserved child and the suspended adult, then, have already willfully or involuntarily failed to make the transition that still lies before a parade of characters, central figures in the five great novels extensively exploring this transitional period between child and adult: *Martin Chuzzlewit, David Copperfield, Bleak House, Little Dorrit,* and *Great Expectations.* Martin Chuzzlewit, David Copperfield, Richard Carstone, Arthur Clennam, and Philip Pirrip—"Pip"—are all builders of air castles. They share with Harold Skimpole, Mrs. Pocket, and Miss Flite all or most of the qualities and practices that define their characters.

Within the details of the first of the novels involved, *Martin Chuzzlewit,* the outlines of the familiar scenario quickly begin to take shape. Having been reared with "great expectations" (and therefore in danger of blight by the ideas of his elders), young Martin enters the story as a headstrong young builder of air castles. Having fallen out with his grandfather, Martin is drawn to enroll in a special type of "architectural school" operated by a Mr. Seth Pecksniff—"PECKSNIFF, ARCHITECT," who runs a school for aspiring young air-castle builders, "though of his architectural doings, nothing was clearly known, except that he had never designed or built anything; but it was generally understood that his knowledge of the science was almost awful in its profundity" (*MC,* ch. 2). Once a young man was snared, Pecksniff:

> turned him loose in a spacious room on the two-pair front; where . . . he improved himself, for three or five years, according to his articles, in making elevations of Salisbury Cathedral from every possible point of sight; and in constructing in the air a vast quantity of Castles, Houses of Parliament and other Public Buildings. Perhaps in no place in the world were so many gorgeous edifices of this class erected as under Mr. Pecksniff's auspices . . . (ch. 2)

Young Martin is a gifted pupil in this school.

His entrapment by the air-castle delusion is soon emblematized by a propensity to consider the will as good as the deed. Both he and his friend, Tom Pinch, are much affected when Martin declares that "'If I should turn out a great architect . . . one of the things I'd build [should be] . . . your fortune'" (ch. 12). Like Skimpole, Martin considers his generous professions as good as any coin of the realm.

After an estrangement develops between him and Pecksniff, Martin and his more realistic companion, Mark Tapley, journey to America, where Martin has no doubt his architectural talents will be in great demand. Ominously, from the beginning of the enterprise, Martin's visits to various establishments of the "Golden Balls" variety have driven them hopelessly into debt. This inability to live within one's means (earlier suggested by Skimpole's furniture, which "comes and goes"), is a sure sign of the castle builder. "Poor

Martin!" mourns the narrator. "For ever building castles in the air" (ch. 21).

In *David Copperfield,* the next of the air-castle novels, as David is about to set out from his school days in Canterbury to seek his fortune in London, his head is filled with "misty ideas" of his future. He has no doubt that his dreams will readily materialize. "So powerful were these visionary considerations in my boyish mind," he reports, "that I seem . . . to have left school without natural regret. . . . I know that my juvenile experiences went for little or nothing then; and that life was more like a great fairy story, which I was just about to begin to read, than anything else" (*DC,* ch. 19).

At this critical moment, Aunt Betsey sends him to Yarmouth so that he might think without distraction about his future. Inevitably, he is drawn to make a pilgrimage to "Blunderstone" for the last imperiling blunder of his youth. As he makes his way through the old familiar haunts and lingers by the graves of his parents and brothers, an airy structure arises before him. "My reflections at these times," he recalls, "were always associated with the figure I was to make in life, and the distinguished things I was to do. My echoing footsteps went to no other tune, but were as constant to that as if I had come home to build my castles in the air at a living mother's side" (ch. 22). In the fairy-tale reading of life, castles in the air are quite appropriately built as habitable structures, and David sees no problem arising from their construction.

When, in *Bleak House,* Richard Carstone is introduced to the reader, he is a youth of nineteen on the threshold of maturity. As a ward in Chancery, he has been conditioned from infancy to make no distinction between dream and fact, for the whole world of Chancery is one of great expectations to be magically fulfilled "tomorrow, when the suit is to be settled." It is, then, not surprising that an immature youth should be irresistibly drawn by its magic promise. As John Jarndyce says: "'There are not many grown and matured men too, who, if they were thrown into this same court as suitors, would not be vitally changed and depreciated within three years—within two—within one. How can we stand amazed at poor Rick?'" (*BH,* ch. 35). For despite example and warning, Richard counts on the suit to make his fortune—"'it may, you know!'" he says brightly (ch. 14). Ada confirms her trust in *him* if not in *it:* "So, Richard said there was an end of it,—and immediately began, on no other foundation, to build as many castles in the air as would man the great wall of China. He went away in high spirits."

In *Little Dorrit* a surprising change occurs: unlike the youths who precede him, Arthur Clennam is introduced as a "grave dark man of forty." He does not appear to be a likely candidate for the adolescent crisis.

Clennam first appears in the unnatural marsh world of Marseilles as one of a group of travellers temporarily imprisoned in quarantine. He is returning from twenty years of exile in the East, the "country of the plague" suspected as responsible for the travellers' quarantine in this suspended world. Arthur has fallen in with a small group of fellow travellers that includes the Meagles establishment: Mr. and Mrs. Meagles, their daughter Pet, her young maid, Tattycoram, a Miss Wade, and a Monsieur Rigaud. This group passes the time in social conversation, which soon takes a pointedly personal turn. Arthur shows particular interest in the Meagles family, listening intently as Mr. Meagles begins to clarify his small ménage, with special attention to the pampered daughter, Pet, and to her deceased twin sister, who, in Meagles's mind, continues to live and grow with her sister. The Meagles adore their daughter, whose precarious health has prompted the trip from which they are now returning to England. Pet's tempestuous and angry companion, Tattycoram, we learn, does not share the Meagles's view of things: "'I am younger than she is by two or three years, and yet it's me that looks after her, as if I was old, it's she that's always petted and called Baby!'" (*LD*, bk. I, ch. 2).

Arthur Clennam has shown a gentle sympathy with Meagles's account of his family. Now, when Meagles conversationally inquires: "'Perhaps I may ask you, whether you have yet come to a decision where to go next?,'" Clennam pours out the story of his life.

> "Indeed, no. I am such a waif and stray everywhere, that I am liable to be drifted where any current may set. . . . I have no will. That is to say . . . next to none I can put in action now. Trained by main force; broken, not bent; heavily ironed with an object on which I was never consulted and which was never mine; shipped away to the other end of the world before I was of age, and exiled there until my father's death there, a year ago; always grinding in a mill I always hated; what is to be expected from *me* in middle life? Will, purpose, hope? All those lights were extinguished before I could sound the words."
>
> "Light 'em up again!" said Mr. Meagles.
>
> "Ah! Easily said. I am the son, Mr. Meagles, of a hard father and mother. . . . Austere faces, inexorable discipline, penance in this

> world and terror in the next—nothing graceful or gentle anywhere, and the void in my cowed heart everywhere—this was my childhood, if I may so misuse the word as to apply it to such a beginning of life." (bk. I, ch. 2)

It would appear from this account that Arthur, suspended here "in quarantine" at forty years old, has been a victim of childhood blight. Only when he returns to his old "home" in London does it become clear that such is not the case. When he informs his mother that he renounces his inheritance and plans to leave the House of Clennam, it becomes evident that he is only passing through this house for the last time rather than remaining here in servitude.

But something more important to our immediate purpose emerges from this chapter. After his conversation with his mother on the evening of his return home, Arthur talks with her old servant, Affery, now Mrs. Flintwinch. Arthur asks her about a girl he has seen—Little Dorrit—who, it seems, has been recommended to Mrs. Clennam by his "old sweetheart." Mrs. Flintwinch informs him that the latter is again available as a wealthy widow if he wants her. With this news she has "introduced into the web that his mind was busily weaving, in that old workshop where the loom of his youth had stood, the last thread wanting to the pattern. The airy folly of a boy's love had found its way even into that house, and he had been as wretched under its hopelessness as if the house had been a castle of romance" (bk. I, ch. 3). He recalls that the face of the pretty girl "from whom he had parted with regret" less than a week ago in Marseilles "had had an unusual interest for him, and a tender hold upon him, because of some resemblance, real or imagined to this first face that had soared out of his gloomy life into the bright glories of fancy." And then he begins to dream. "For, it had been the uniform tendency of this man's life—as much was wanting in it to think about, so much that might have been better directed and happier to speculate upon—to make him a dreamer, after all."

At the age of forty, Arthur Clennam is still suspended in the adolescent world of air-castle dreams. This discovery has its humorous aspects, of course,[12] but we must remind ourselves that he has spent twenty years exiled from the society that might have helped him grow up. Only now does any meaning attach to what seemed an isolated incident in the first chapter, "Sun and Shadow." In the literal prison there, two figures, the jailer and his small daughter, are coming "to feed the [imprisoned] birds." He is singing the "revolutionary tune," which will reappear throughout the novel as a leitmotif. One of the lines of this song, "Who passes by this road so late?" seems to be answered. It can only be Arthur Clennam.

As "the last thread wanting to the pattern" was introduced into "the web that [Arthur's] mind was busily weaving," from the memories invoked by his conversation with Mrs. Flintwinch, so has the last necessary thread now been woven into the fabric of the emerging story. The novel can be expected to trace Arthur's path along the road to maturity as he leaves his mother's house and involves himself in the experiences he finds outside in the world of time.

After *Little Dorrit,* Dickens tells the story of one more air-castle builder in *Great Expectations.* Like David Copperfield, Pip relates his own story. Although Pip does not report that his childhood found nourishment in early reading, which David says, "kept alive my fancy," his thinking nonetheless runs along similar lines. His first visit to Miss Havisham sets the fairy-tale dreams going. When his sister and Mr. Pumblechook later cross-examine him about the details of that visit, Pip finds himself inventing a fantastic story about Miss Havisham and the occasion: "'She was sitting . . . in a black velvet coach. . . . And Miss Estella—that's her niece, I think—handed her in cake and wine at the coach-window, on a gold plate. And we all had cake and wine on gold plates. And I got up behind the coach to eat mine, because she told me to'" (*GE,* ch. 9). He rejects as too unbelievable the addition of "four richly caparisoned coursers, which I had had the wild thoughts of harnessing." But he does embellish his account with a description of how "'Estella waved a blue flag, and I waved a red one, and Miss Havisham waved one sprinkled all over with little gold stars, out at the coach-window. And then we all waved our swords and hurrahed.'" Later, Pip miserably confesses to Joe that it was all "lies," and adds: "'I don't know what possessed me, Joe.'" Yet what possessed him is not hard to surmise in light of the Cinderella configuration of images, where Miss Havisham's flag (as her crutch will later do) turns into a sparkling magic wand and the "swords" have a special significance of sharpness to his creator even if their meaning is not quite clear in Pip's mind.

When Mr. Jaggers informs Joe that young Pip is to "'be immediately removed from his present sphere of life and from this place, and be brought up as a gentleman—in a word, as a young fellow of great expectations'" (ch. 18), Pip is quite prepared for the knowledge. "My dream was out; my wild fancy was surpassed by sober reality; Miss Havisham was going to make my fortune on a grand scale." In his eyes, she is nothing less than the magical benefactor of the fairy tale.

> "This is a gay figure, Pip," said she, making her crutch stick play round me, as if she, the fairy godmother who had changed me, were bestowing the finishing gift.
>
> "I have come into such good fortune since I saw you last, Miss Havisham," I murmured. "And I am so grateful for it, Miss Havisham!" (ch. 19)

Thus Pip, too, has built his castles in the air, though he does not give his airy structures that name, being satisfied to refer to them more literally as his "great expectations."

All of our five "youths" are about to be tested by "real life." Their ability to reconcile their dreams with the outer world of stubborn facts will demonstrate whether they possess the strength and will to survive this last borderland struggle for life in the world of time. If they succeed, they will leave the childhood garden and graduate into maturity. If they fail, they will lapse permanently into either literal or figurative death. During their struggle, they will be surrounded by emblematic figures who are involved in, or have already won or lost, the same struggle.

Martin Chuzzlewit and Mark Tapley proceed toward America, the far-off land supposed to bring Martin's dream to reality. Ominously (given the Dickens imagery), their destination in the heart of the American continent is a settlement called the "Valley of Eden," where "'I'm told,' said Mark, 'as there's lots of serpents'" (*MC*, ch. 21).

The two adventurers are temporarily heartened, however, when they are shown a "great plan" of the city of Eden:

> A flourishing city, too! An architectural city! There were banks, churches, cathedrals, market-places, factories, hotels, stores, mansions, wharves; an exchange, a theatre; public buildings of all kinds, down to the office of the Eden Stinger, a daily journal; all faithfully depicted in the view before them. . . .
>
> "But, I am afraid," said Martin, glancing again at the Public Buildings, "that there's nothing left for me to do."
>
> "Well! it ain't all built," replied the agent. "Not quite." (ch. 21)

As a matter of fact, none of it has been erected. It exists only as a foundationless city in the Edenic childhood garden. What they find at journey's end is nothing but "a marsh . . . where even the blessed sun, shining down on festering elements of corruption and disease, became a horror. . . . At Eden too. The waters of the Deluge might have left it but a week before: so choked with slime and matted growth was the hideous swamp which bore that name" (ch. 23). The air-castle and marsh sets of images have merged naturally together in this early novel as they will continue to do in later ones. Here in Eden, the "Bank, and National Credit Office . . . had some feeble props about it" but was "settling down in the mud, past all recovery," like the little shoal-lighthouse in *Great Expectations.*

The groundless nature of Martin's great expectations now becomes clear to him with devastating effect; for "many a man who would have stood within a home dismantled, strong in his passion and design of vengeance, has had the firmness of his nature conquered by the razing of an air-built castle." Despite brave efforts to establish an architectural office, the enterprise is doomed. Martin now must confront squarely the failure of the "real world" to yield and conform to his air-castle specifications.

Martin proves equal to the task, though not without great travail. Presently he falls into a deep illness with the ague and fevers indigenous to the marsh. He hovers for days between life and death in this state of withdrawal into his private inner world.[13] Subsequent events reveal that his illness has provided the catalyst for straightening out his thinking. It has brought him face to face with his own egocentricity and has therefore revolutionized his life: he now cannot vacate "Eden" fast enough.

The profound change in Martin is confirmed by his new relationship with Tom Pinch upon his return home. In the interim, Tom has himself become a success. Says Martin: "'With his advice to guide me, I may do the same. I took Tom under my protection once . . . and promised I would make his fortune. Perhaps Tom will take me under *his* protection now, and teach me how to earn my bread'" (ch. 43). Asked by Tom what his future plans may be, he replies: "'No longer to make your fortune, Tom, . . . but to try to live. . . . I will do anything, Tom; anything; to gain a livelihood by my own exertions. My hopes do not soar above that, now'" (ch. 48). These two conversations between Martin and his friend are like parentheses around the period in Martin's life that constitutes his final testing for manhood.

David Copperfield's confrontation between expectations and hard facts proves to be much more complicated. In the relatively short period of time between his arrival in London, where he is to read the fairy tale of life, and his sobered decision to learn stenography as a practical way to earn a living, David had made four staggering discoveries. First, he has identified his own human fallibility through the famous dinner party when he tumbles down more than one staircase as a result of his drunken state. He has learned the power of evil in the form of Uriah Heep, who has by now accomplished the ruin of Aunt Betsey and Mr. Wickfield. He has experienced the complexity of human love, guilt, and grief in Steerforth's seduction of Little Em'ly. And, finally, he is beginning to identify the impossibility of reconciling love in a doll's house with the demands of the practical world as embodied in the Cookery Book, whose very name prostrates Dora almost beyond recovery. His own sense of responsibility in every one of these areas abolishes the fairy tale with magical swiftness. During this period, he has before him the far from reassuring example of his friends the Micawbers (see note 11).

Now, struggling over the "noble art and mystery of stenography," he finds himself "plunged into a sea of perplexity that brought me, in a few weeks, to the confines of distraction" (*DC,* ch. 38). When he has at length mastered the alphabet, he despairingly comes upon a "procession of new horrors, called arbitrary characters, the most despotic characters I have ever known, who insisted, for instance, that a thing like the beginning of a cobweb, meant expectation, and that a pen-and-ink sky-rocket stood for disadvantageous."[14] The characters were, as he said, purely arbitrary; the "for instance" is not. In it David unconsciously reveals the true nature of his inner struggle through the choice of characters overtly selected to illustrate his outward struggle. The air castles of great expectation, he is perceiving, have more in common with insubstantial cobwebs and fragile skyrockets than they do with houses one can live in. Great expectations, in fact, are positively disadvantageous.

The moment when David truly assimilates this fact marks the turning point in his transition from adolescent to adult. Now ready to assume the responsibilities of maturity, David reports that his assiduous attempts to master shorthand have mirrored "a patient and continuous energy which then began to be matured within me, and which I know to be the strong part of my character" (ch. 42). Without the "companionship of the steady, hard-working qualities," one cannot expect greatly. "There is no such thing as such fulfilment on this earth. Some happy talent, and some fortunate opportunity, may form the two sides of the ladder on which some men mount, but the rounds of that ladder must be made of stuff to stand wear and tear." Thus David quickly gives up his easy great expectations about his career.

Unlike Martin, however, David cannot simply get on a boat and steam away from Eden. Giving up the castle embodied in the doll's house is much too complicated. He becomes plagued with a double vision that causes him to recognize the futile cruelty of trying to change his child wife—the doll in the doll's house—whom he must yet continue to love, protect, and grieve over as an anomaly in life; at the same time he apprehends that a wiser young man would have paid more attention to the foundations of his castle. Although he himself must pay heavily for "the first mistaken impulse of an undisciplined heart" (ch. 48), he must protect Dora against suffering from his mistake. She must not know that "the happiness I had vaguely anticipated, once, was not the happiness I enjoyed, and there was always something wanting."

> What I missed, I still regarded . . . as something that had been a dream of my youthful fancy; that was incapable of realisation; that I was now discovering to be so, with some natural pain, as all men did. But that it would have been better for me if my wife could have helped more, and shared the many thoughts in which I had no partner; and that this might have been; I knew.
>
> Between these two irreconcilable conclusions: the one, that what I felt was general and unavoidable; the other, that it was particular to me, and might have been different: I balanced curiously, with no distinct sense of their opposition to each other. When I thought of the airy dreams of youth that are incapable of realisation, I thought of the better state preceding manhood that I had outgrown. (ch. 48)

These thoughts involve the old solidly based days at Dr. Strong's before the building of the airy dreams.

After the deaths of Steerforth and Dora, David goes abroad to grieve over his lost childhood:

> As a man upon a field of battle will receive a mortal hurt, and scarcely know that he is struck, so I, when I was left alone with my undisciplined heart, had no conception of the wound with which it had to strive.
>
> The desolate feeling with which I went abroad, deepened and wid-

> ened hourly. At first it was a heavy sense of loss and sorrow, wherein I could distinguish little else. By imperceptible degrees, it became a hopeless consciousness of all that I had lost—love, friendship, interest; of all that had been shattered—my first trust, my first affection, the whole airy castle of my life; of all that remained—a ruined blank and waste, lying wide around me, unbroken, to the dark horizon. (ch. 58)

Out of this wasteland, David emerges a man with a "disciplined heart," though he never loses the reluctant notion that the same thing might have been achieved with less travail had the airy castles never been built.

And now Richard Carstone must face *his* ordeal. Richard's fate, however, is already established by the impossible conditions imposed upon him. Although, as John Jarndyce says, if two angels could be concerned in the suit of Jarndyce and Jarndyce it would change their nature, only certain people are susceptible to its blight. Richard is a perfect victim by both timing and character. At nineteen, he stands hopefully at the point of transition. Esther says: "I believe Richard's was as frank and generous a nature as there possibly can be. He was ardent and brave, and, in the midst of all his wild restlessness, was so gentle, that I knew him like a brother in a few weeks" (*BH,* ch. 9). But already the ominous note is sounded by the "wild restlessness": Richard is flighty and up in the air. Even as he laughs at and pities Miss Flite, Esther as usual penetrates to the true facts of the case: "But he never thought—never, my poor, dear, sanguine Richard, capable of so much happiness then, and with such better things before him!—what a fatal link was riveting between his fresh youth and her faded age; between his free hopes and her caged birds, and her hungry garret, and her wandering mind" (ch. 23). Flite, too, sees it: "'Let someone hold him back,'" she warns, "'Or he'll be drawn to ruin'" (ch. 35). Jarndyce has been concerned about the "indecision of character" that Chancery has encouraged in Richard: "'It has engendered or confirmed in him a habit of putting off—and trusting to this, that, and the other chance, without knowing what chance—and dismissing everything as unsettled, uncertain, and confused'" (ch. 13).

Having built his air castles, Richard can live nowhere else. He flits from profession to profession (as Lady Dedlock flits from place to place), and when Esther suggests that he might "settle down," he explains his restlessness in appropriate terms:

"My dear Esther, I am a very unfortunate dog not to be more settled, but how *can* I be more settled? If you lived in an unfinished house, you couldn't settle down in it; if you were condemned to leave everything you undertook, unfinished, you would find it hard to apply yourself to anything; and yet that's my unhappy case. I was born into this unfinished contention with all its chances and changes, and it began to unsettle me before I quite knew the difference between a suit at law and a suit of clothes; and it has gone on unsettling me ever since." (ch. 23)

Like David's doll house, this "bleak house" of Richard's lacks the firm foundation to make it habitable.

All of Richard's fine qualities of the fresh heart and the ardent optimistic spirit gradually lose their natural look as he becomes suspended in the dream world of the child. The real world turns into a monotonous wasteland (see ch. 3); he falls into debt, renounces his true benefactor—and fittingly substitutes Harold Skimpole as confidant and adviser.

These two children are naturally drawn to each other. Richard is laughingly willing to reach into his pocket to relieve Skimpole's financial embarrassment. John Jarndyce is provoked into an unwonted criticism on this occasion: "'But really—'" he exclaims, "'to get hold of you and Esther—and to squeeze you like a couple of tender young Saint Michael's oranges—It'll blow a gale in the middle of the night!'" (ch. 6). As with Skimpole's other hot-house fruit, someone other than he must pay for this delicacy too. But Richard unguardedly finds Skimpole "fresh and green-hearted" (ch. 37); in turn Skimpole appreciates and encourages this "shepherd-youth" who is "full of the brightest visions of the future"—and he continues to squeeze until all the juice is gone.

Everyone around Richard knows from the outset the disadvantageousness of great expectations. Richard closes his ears to the knowledge and, like Mrs. Pocket, rejects any messenger from the world of hard facts. Since Richard is marked to be the sacrificial victim of "Chancery," of "trusting to this, that, and the other chance," he cannot come out of the dream this side of his death.[15] On that occasion:

"It was a troubled dream?" said Richard, clasping both my guardian's hands eagerly.

"Nothing more, Rick; nothing more."

"And you, being a good man, can pass it as such and pity the dreamer, and be lenient and encouraging when he wakes?"

> "Indeed I can. What am I but another dreamer, Rick?"
> "I will begin the world!" said Richard, with a light in his eyes. (ch. 65)

Now, with the recognition that "beginning the world" means coming out of suspension in the dream, Richard has too late shown himself ready for maturity. His death closes the door on his struggle.

As we pick up the story of Arthur Clennam, he has already existed in his suspended world for more years than constitute Richard's entire life. What, exactly, has at this juncture prompted him to resume the interrupted journey of his life—to pass by this road so late? It has something—everything—to do with the young girl from whom he parted less than a week ago and who has stirred within him the same feelings left suspended when Flora Casby foresook him to marry Mr. Finching. He is about to resume his life with a second chance at youthful love.

In the first three chapters of *Little Dorrit,* Dickens embodies the confusing dilemma about to confront Arthur in the persons of the bewildering assortment of women churning around in the web of his mind as he is furnished the last thread needed in the pattern. His success or lack of success in sorting them all out will determine his future: Pet, her dead twin sister, Tattycoram, Miss Wade, his old sweetheart, and Little Dorrit, whom he has just met as a shadowy figure moving through the Clennam household—all represent women in varying states of growth or non-growth. We might well add his mother, frozen in her marshy world, whose influence he has just successfully evaded.

The group of women whom Clennam meets in quarantine are on the surface a puzzling assortment. A little thought about Mr. Meagles's discussion of his family, however, begins to yield clues for conjecture. It seems that this genial and well-intentioned man has reared his daughter in so sheltered an atmosphere that she, like Dora, will never be able to grow up: he has, to be precise, "spoiled"[16] her. His belief that her dead twin sister continues to live and grow with "Pet" confirms rather than challenges the idea that Pet is herself permanently suspended in a deathlike state, for the converse of this notion is that Pet lives and grows no more than her dead twin. Passive and passionless herself, Pet has as companion another young girl who is her exact opposite. In the scene described, tempestuous Tattycoram rages in frustration: "A sullen, passionate girl! Her rich black hair was all about her face, her face was flushed and hot, and as she sobbed and raged, she plucked at her lips with an unsparing hand" (*LD*, bk. I, ch. 2). Miss Wade sits aloof, watching Tattycoram with "a strange attentive smile."

Not until many chapters later when Miss Wade reviews her own past does it become clear that at this moment she sees her youthful self in the sobbing girl. Long frozen at Tattycoram's stage of development, she can recall with passion a time when she was imprisoned in a similar situation. As the fellow travellers are released from quarantine, Mr. Meagles observes: "I bear those monotonous walls no ill-will now. . . . One always begins to forgive a place as soon as it's left behind; I dare say a prisoner begins to relent towards his prison, after he is let out" (bk. I, ch. 2). Miss Wade disagrees: "If I had been shut up in any place to pine and suffer, I should always hate that place and wish to burn it down, or raze it to the ground. I know no more."

Both Pet and Tattycoram fear this solitary, haughty woman: Pet "shrink[ing] childishly in her spoilt way" closer to her father; Tattycoram passionately exclaiming: "'You seem to come like my own anger, my own malice, my own—whatever it is—I don't know what it is.'" Pet and Tattycoram complement each other in a way suggesting that, if their two natures could only be synthesized, they would become a single complete person. Complex in their interrelationships, these women contribute to the web of Arthur's thinking.

As he begins to move through the societal world of London with the fresh and critical perspective of a stranger, he sees, interprets, judges, and acts as one newly engaged in life. Although arrested in his individual development some twenty years back, he has not truly been permanently crippled in his basic nature: "He was a dreamer . . . because he was a man who had, deep-rooted in his nature, a belief in all the gentle and good things his life had been without. Bred in meanness and hard dealing, this had rescued him to be a man of honourable mind and open hand. Bred in coldness and severity, this had rescued him to have a warm and sympathetic heart" (bk. I, ch. 13). "What is to be expected of *me* in middle life," he has asked Meagles, "Will, purpose, hope?" (bk. I, ch. 2). As he becomes engaged in the troubles of those about him, however, both will and purpose have already begun to stir within him.

Hope is another matter. Arthur has just discovered that "his old sweetheart," Flora Finching,[17] was also arrested in her development some twenty years ago. The anomaly of her girlish ways in her matronly figure horrifies him without drawing his attention to the parallel in their lives. He is, as a matter of fact, about to commit the same folly for the second time: falling in love with another child who will never grow up, the child Pet to whom he was first drawn because of her resemblance to Flora.

On this evening of his distressful encounter with Flora, he returns to his lodgings to review his situation. Sitting down before the dying fire, he "turned his gaze back upon the gloomy vista by which he had come to that stage of his existence. So long, so bare, so blank. No childhood; no youth, except for one remembrance that one remembrance proved, only that day, to be a piece of folly" (bk. I, ch. 13). Yet his basic belief "in all the gentle and good things his life had been without" saves him from the weakness and selfishness of "holding that because such a happiness or such a virtue had not come into his little path, or worked well for him, therefore he was not in the great scheme, but was reducible . . . to the basic elements. . . . A disappointed mind he had, but a mind too firm and healthy for such unwholesome air."

As Arthur sits by his dying fire "from which the blaze departed, from which the after-glow subsided, in which the ashes turned grey, from which they dropped to dust," like Louisa Gradgrind he thinks: "'How soon I too shall pass through such changes, and be gone!' To review his life, was like descending a green tree in fruit and flower, and seeing all the branches wither and drop off one by one as he came down towards them."

From the beginning, this man, reared without expectations and suspended in the ruins of his youthful air castle, has expected nothing more to come from this new love than from anything else in his life. He conceals from himself that he is in love by inventing "Nobody" as his surrogate.[18] The course of his infatuation is pursued through the chapters entitled "Nobody's Weakness," "Nobody's Rival," and "Nobody's State of Mind." With "Nobody's Disappearance," the enchantment is gone. Though at his "advanced" age he still has no hope for personal happiness, he is now free to seek it.

The *anima* figure who will guide him to maturity, Little Dorrit,[19] is quite unlike the confused women Arthur is trying to sort out. "This history," observes the narrator, "must sometimes see with Little Dorrit's eyes, and shall begin that course by looking at him" (bk. I, ch. 14). Indeed, although she looks on everything with a clear and free gaze, she looks most of the time "at him" and most of the chapters where he is physically absent are still charged with Arthur's presence.

Little Dorrit, despite her diminutive appearance and despite her peculiar upbringing, has accomplished the miracle of "growing up." Both born and bred in the Marshalsea, she will never need to forgive her "prison," because no prison, physical or mental, has ever had any power over her. Yet her father is the most consummate of air-castle builders. He has fantastically managed a whole lifetime in air castles, converting so unlikely a place as Marshalsea Prison—in the midst of a London slum—into a congenial habitation for the gracious lord of the manor known as the Father of the Marshalsea. In comparison, the later "real" castles where he is for a time granted a fairy-tale wish-fulfillment life seem unreal and ironically diminished, suggesting that air castles flourish best in the dream world. Little Dorrit remains untouched by her father's delusions, which have blighted the lives of her brother and sister. Though about the same age as Pet, Little Dorrit has already long been a mature woman. Ironically, until the end of the novel Arthur imagines her to be a child he must protect.

As Arthur continues along his societal route, he makes a final blunder typical of the castle builder. Inveigled into a speculative investment that leaves both himself and his trusting partner in hopeless debt, Arthur must pass through the debtor's prison before he can be restored to life after the now familiar healing fever.

Finally, Arthur is released from "prison" into a healthy autumn world of abundant harvest. The "Sun and Shadow" of chapter 1 have disappeared. "From the sea-shore the ocean was no longer to be seen lying asleep in the heat, but its thousand sparkling eyes were open, and its whole breadth was in joyful animation" (bk. II, ch. 34). With Arthur's delivery, all the world around him has been restored to a natural state in marked contrast to that earlier scene in Marseilles. Little Dorrit and Arthur are married "with the sun shining on them" in the nurturing church in which Little Dorrit's birth was registered and which has served as her refuge in time of need. After their marriage, "they paused for a moment on the steps of the portico, looking at the fresh perspective of the street in the autumn morning sun's bright rays, and then went down" into life. "Went down," says the narrator, "into a modest life of usefulness and happiness."

Pip, however, is not quite so fortunate. The fairy-tale delusion he falls into as a child subjects him to a more profound blighting influence, from which he will never recover sufficiently to enjoy the happy life available to Arthur.

This suspension in childhood is implied, in fact, by the very conditions laid down by Mr. Jaggers for Pip's being granted his great expectations.

> "Now, Mr. Pip," pursued the lawyer, "I address the rest of what I have to say, to you. You are to understand, first, that it is the request of the person from whom I take my instructions, that you always bear the name of Pip. You will have no objection, I dare say, to your great expectations being encumbered with that easy condition. But if you have any objection, this is the time to mention it." (*GE*, ch. 18)

This condition is laid down with the bland speciousness of Mr. Scratch bargaining for the soul of Jabez Stone in "The Devil and Daniel Webster." One need only recall the first paragraph of Pip's book to catch the implications: "My father's family name being Pirrip, and my Christian name Philip, my infant tongue could make of both names nothing longer or more explicit than Pip. So, I called myself Pip, and came to be called Pip" (ch. 1). Thus the infantile name is the emblem of the child state in which Pip must remain.

The second condition is equally significant: "'Now you are to understand, secondly, Mr. Pip, that the name of the person who is your liberal benefactor remains a profound secret, until the person chooses to reveal it. . . . It is not the least to the purpose what the reasons of this prohibition are. . . . This is not for you to enquire into. The condition is laid down.'" It is important to note here that Pip does in fact have solid expectations, that he does actually have a "liberal benefactor." But in the child world, expectations are magically fulfilled and liberal benefactors are fairy godmothers. The second condition, then, holds Pip as an enchanted child in a fairy-tale world that forbids enquiry into the real facts.[20] As for David, life seems to Pip more like a great fairy tale he is about to read than anything else.

Pip of course cannot permanently hold to either condition: it is precisely his inability to do so that ensures he will grow into maturity. Upon Pip's arrival in London he is conducted by Mr. Wemmick to the rather sordid chambers which he is temporarily to share with Herbert Pocket. Pip is dismayed by all the "dry rot and wet rot and all the silent rots that rot in neglected roof and cellar. . . . So imperfect was this realization of the first of my great expectations," he recalls, with no effort to gloss over the facts, "that I looked in dismay at Mr. Wemmick" (ch. 21). As he and Herbert later get acquainted, Herbert decides to call him "Handel" in preference to any other name. On the occasion of his first trip home, Pip already has reason to be thankful for this decision. He recognizes as a fellow passenger the convict who had brought a message from Magwitch, but who, he hopes, will not recognize him. "'Good bye, Handel!' Herbert called out as we started. I thought what a blessed fortune it was that he had found another name for me than Pip" (ch. 28). Thus quickly has Pip participated in at least token violation of one of the conditions established for his great expectations. As for the other condition, it is easy for Pip to accept it since he is already convinced that he knows the facts: Miss Havisham, his fairy godmother, is his "liberal benefactor."

Pip, though deluded, is not willfully uneducable. One by one his experiences deepen his initial impression that his great expectations are being most imperfectly realized. He and Herbert become members of "the Finches of the Grove," a club dedicated to the life of pleasure: "We spent as much money as we could, and got as little for it as people could make up their minds to give us. We were always more or less miserable, and most of our acquaintance were in the same condition. There was a gay fiction among us that we were constantly enjoying ourselves, and a skeleton truth that we never did" (ch. 34).

But these dissatisfactions become relatively insignificant as Pip begins to realize that the real disadvantage of great expectations is their effect upon their possessor. Somehow they are connected with his increasing feelings of guilt.

> As I had grown accustomed to my expectations, I had insensibly begun to notice their effect upon myself and those around me. Their influence on my own character I disguised from my recognition as much as possible, but I knew very well that it was not all good. I lived in a state of chronic uneasiness respecting my behaviour to Joe. My conscience was not by any means comfortable about Biddy. When I woke up in the night. . . . I used to think, with a weariness on my spirit that I should have been happier and better if I had never seen Miss Havisham's face, and had risen to manhood content to be partners with Joe in the honest old forge. (ch. 34)

Meanwhile, Pip and Herbert live beyond their means.

The parasitical qualities of the adult child are emblematized in Pip's and Herbert's perpetual indebtedness, and their continued receipt of threats of "legal proceedings." Now the two youths are led to that further folly of substituting the thought for the deed. Pip is better at this than Herbert, "who modestly said he had not my administrative genius."

The time has come when the load of debt must be faced. Fortified by a good dinner ceremoniously planned for the occasion, they prepare to set their affairs in order.

> I would then take a sheet of paper, and write across the top of it, in a neat hand, the heading, "Memorandum of Pip's debts;" with Barnard's Inn and the date very carefully added. Herbert would also take a sheet of paper, and write across it with similar formalities, "Memorandum of Herbert's debts."
>
> . . . The sound of our pens going refreshed us exceedingly, insomuch that I sometimes found it difficult to distinguish between this edifying business proceeding and actually paying the money. In point of meritorious character, the two things seemed about equal. (ch. 34)

When the whole memorandum is completed, a further ritual brings affairs to a satisfactory conclusion:

> When I had got all my responsibilities down upon my list, I compared each with the bill, and ticked it off. My self-approval when I ticked an entry was quite a luxurious sensation. When I had no more ticks to make, I folded all my bills up uniformly, docketed each on the back, and tied the whole into a symmetrical bundle. Then I did the same for Herbert . . . and felt that I had brought his affairs into focus for him. (ch. 34)

For the time being, the problem is magically resolved in this world where "thinking makes it so" and anything may be achieved without personal cost.

Immediately ahead of Pip, however, lies the end of the fairy tale. "A great event in my life," he writes, "the turning point of my life, now opens on my view" (ch. 37). With the return of Magwitch thus foreshadowed, Pip discovers what he believes to be the last and most important disadvantage of his great expectations. In his fastidious horror at the reality of his benefactor, so unlike his image of his fairy godmother, he resolves never to take another penny from him. In Pip's view, every penny he has already taken is an unwelcome debt hanging over his head with all the others. "'Think what I owe him already!'" he exclaims to Herbert. "'Then again: I am heavily in debt—very heavily for me, who have now no expectations—and I have been bred to no calling, and I am fit for nothing'" (ch. 41). His expectations, he sees, have actually disqualified him for coping with real life.

Pip is wrong, of course, in thinking he has now learned everything possible regarding his expectations' disadvantages. His great struggle is still ahead as he fights his way out of the irresponsible and egocentric childish world into the responsible and altruistic adult one represented in his changing views toward Magwitch. At the end of this pivotal episode in Pip's life, Magwitch lies on his deathbed. Now Pip has a second chance to make a claim upon the convict's fortune, which he earlier renounced in his effort to rid himself of the loathsome connection with Magwitch. Since he is not related to the convict, it would not come to him without a fight. Jaggers is angry that Pip seems ready to let it slip through his fingers and urges him to make a claim upon it. But Pip is now ready to renounce the fortune for right reasons: "I had no claim, and I finally resolved, and ever afterwards abided by the resolution, that my heart should never be sickened with the hopeless task of attempting to establish one" (ch. 55).

More than that, Pip has now been completely delivered from his enchanted suspension in false values. All of his natural human feelings come flowing back as he develops love and compassion for the benefactor he first found so revolting. After the death of Magwitch, Pip too falls into the fever and delirium that will finally leave him cleansed and restored to life, although he may never find personal happiness. Pip is at peace in realizing that "my great expectations had all dissolved, like our own marsh mists before the sun" (ch. 57).

With *Great Expectations,* Dickens weaves the story of the air-castle builders for the last time. Each reenactment of this final childhood temptation to build one's future on great expectations alone creates the same crisis as a great disparity develops between the wonderful dream and what actually comes to pass. The world outside is indifferent to the world a person has created inside. Anyone who is both willing and able to realize and accept this fact will successfully pass over the border into maturity. Anyone who either can or will not realize and accept it must linger in the childhood garden as a monstrous interloper or a pathetic adult *manqué.*

The final words of John Jarndyce to Richard ("What am I but another dreamer, Rick?") remind us, however, that this discovery does not even yet probe the full story of the relationship between dream and actuality. Paradoxically, Jarndyce, who has warned against building air castles from the beginning, still holds on to dreaming. It remains for the adult to discover the nature of the final reconciliation between the inner and outer worlds of experience.

# VIII

## *The Picture in the Fireplace*

THE IMAGE CLUSTERS in this chapter probe the true relationship between dream and actuality as it is finally revealed to the maturing man or woman through the workings of memory, experience, and hope; that is, through awareness of past, present, and future. In this development, the individual's understanding of time once more emerges during adulthood as the central determinant of the quality of life. Not only does external time bring one to birth and death; not only is the willingness and ability to struggle in that time a condition of real living; but also now, and only now, as time becomes internalized, does it grow clear that individuals possess within themselves what is necessary to put all of life into meaningful perspective.

All of the configurations through which the relationship between dream and actuality is explored contain human beings with an ambiguous or shadowy reality: ghosts, mirrored images, pictures, the successive figures in one's own past. While these insubstantial shadows depend for their existence on a matching reality of some kind and of some time in the physical world, they in turn interpret that reality and evaluate its significance.

The questions they must answer are metaphysical: How real is the past? Is the present experiential world of physical actuality the only reality? How can the unactualized future be considered real? That the first question, "How real is the vanished past?" engaged Dickens's imagination extensively is indicated by the abundance of configurations exploring it.

The first set of such images expresses the idea that the past will not lie down and stay dead, but has a way of asserting itself as a continued palpable force in the present. Sometimes this idea is contained in the image of "the restless graveyard." Out of this graveyard come many ghosts, all with voices reminding those they haunt that past human experience has much to communicate to the present. Everyone now living is surrounded by the shadowy figures of all who have ever lived. Awareness of the restless graveyard, the ability to see and hear ghosts, is a mark of the sensitive human being or of the frozen person about to be humanized. In Eliot's term, it is awareness not of what is dead, but of what is "already living."

On the day Pip meets the convict Magwitch, the churchyard inspires in him a fearful fancy that the dead might momentarily come out of their graves. The child David, too, takes fright from hearing the story of Lazarus read—"And I am so frightened that they are afterwards obliged to take me out of bed, and show me the quiet churchyard out of the bedroom window, with the dead all lying in their graves at rest, below the solemn moon" (*DC*, ch. 2). Master Humphrey, pondering on "that constant pacing to and fro, that never ending restlessness, that incessant tread of feet wearing the rough stones smooth and glossy," which marks the passage of humanity throughout time, wonders how a sick man with his heightened sensitivity could endure the sound: "think of the hum and noise being always present to his senses, and of the stream of life that will not stop, pouring on, on, on, through all his restless dreams, as if he were condemned to lie, dead but conscious, in a noisy churchyard, and had no hope of rest for centuries to come!" (*OCS*, ch. 1). Here the sick man becomes suggestively confused with the people in the "noisy" graveyard, and it is difficult to determine whether a live man is looking at the dead, or *vice-versa*. This is an effect that seems to have interested Dickens.[1] In *Our Mutual Friend*, a similar thought gives John Harmon pause as he lingers by Limehouse Church graveyard while attempting to solve the riddle of his own supposed murder:

> "It is a sensation not experienced by many mortals," said he, "to be looking into a churchyard on a wild windy night, and to feel that I no more hold a place among the living than these dead do, and even to know that I lie buried somewhere else, as they lie buried here. Nothing uses me to it. A spirit that was once a man could hardly feel stranger or lonelier, going unrecognized among mankind, than I feel." (*OMF*, bk. II, ch. 13)

His identification with the past is an immediately felt experience with uncanny insight into the relatedness of all humanity—even to the interchangeability of their experience.

The restless graveyard, then, is one way of repudiating the pastness of the past. A second picture, developed most fully and allegorically in the Christmas book for 1846, entitled The Battle of Life, might be called the ancient battleground. The story begins with an extensive account of a great battle fought many years ago on the very spot where the events of the present story take place—a bloody battle from which "the painted butterfly took blood into the air upon the edges of its wings"; "the trodden ground became a quagmire" with sullen pools whose "one prevailing hue still lowered and glimmered in the sun"; and the plain was "strewn with upturned faces." For a time, a "tainted wind . . . blew across the scene of that day's work and that night's death and suffering." Traces of the fight lingered—and were fearfully regarded—for a still longer time, in "deep green patches in the growing corn"; in "great worms abounding there"; in "wounded trees" and "scraps of hacked and broken fence and wall, where deadly struggle had been made." But eventually memory fades. Finally the last of the wounded trees have fallen into ashes as Christmas logs and "the deep green patches were no greener now than the memory[2] of those who lay in dust below" (BL, Part the First).

Failure of memory, however, cannot erase the fact that the present act of human life is played out on the same battlefield.

> If the host slain upon the field could have been for a moment reanimated in the forms in which they fell each upon the spot that was the bed of his untimely death, gashed and ghastly soldiers would have stared in, hundreds deep, at household door and window; and would have risen on the hearths of quiet homes; and would have been the garnered store of barns and granaries; and would have started up between the cradled infant and its nurse; and would have floated with the stream, and whirled round on the mill, and crowded the orchard, and burdened the meadow, and piled the rickyard high with dying men. (Part the First)

Now a further refinement on the basic idea is caught in this picture of a past life intermingling with the present: it also penetrates and permeates it in the blowing dust[3] and as a part of the very nourishment of the present passed on through many seasons of garnered stores in barns and granaries. Once again it would be impossible to say where the dead leave off and the living begin. Here is the societal extension of a personal image already familiar, one that also repudiates the pastness of the individual past by implying the procession of figures that every adult carries along as a present reality throughout life.

*The Mystery of Edwin Drood* also contains an example of this fusion of restless graveyard and ancient battleground. Cloisterham (a fictitious name, says the narrator, thereby suggesting a timeless universality) is an old cathedral town—"once possibly known to the Druids by another name, and certainly to the Romans by another, and to the Saxons by another, and to the Normans by another; and a name more or less in the course of many centuries can be of little moment to its dusty chronicles" (*MED,* ch. 3). The children of Cloisterham, we are told, grow "small salad in the dust of abbots and abbesses, and make dirt-pies of nuns and friars" in this ancient town where "every ploughman in its outlying fields renders to once puissant Lord Treasurers, Archbishops, Bishops, and such-like, the attention which the Ogre in the story-book desired to render to his unbidden visitor, and grinds their bones to make his bread." They, in turn, work their way into his thinking: "Fragments of old wall, saint's chapel, chapter-house, convent and monastery, have got incongruously or obstructively built into many of its houses and gardens, much as kindred jumbled notions have become incorporated into many of its citizens' minds. All things in it are of the past." In this striking parallel to the imagined scene on the ancient battlefield, once more past life invades, penetrates, and nourishes—or stifles—the present.

Looming over the city of Cloisterham is the cathedral tower, whose vicinity is avoided after dark by the citizens of the town. Even though they might deny their belief in ghosts, their avoidance betrays "the innate shrinking of dust with the breath of life in it from dust out of which the breath of life has passed," though both are simultaneously "dust." It also suggests the widely diffused reflection: "'If the dead do, under any circumstances, become visible to the living, these are such likely surroundings for the purpose that I, the living, will get out of them as soon as I can'" (ch. 12).

Perhaps the most interesting thing about these fearfully apprehended ghosts is that they never actually materialize from such likely surroundings of battlefield or graveyard: their value in such contexts is purely affective.[4] The ghosts that haunt the works of Dickens arise from a radically different source. In a letter to Mrs.

Gaskell (November 25, 1851), Dickens defines the function of ghost stories as "illustrating particular states of mind and processes of the imagination"[5]—the function they invariably serve for him.

A second set of images, then, exploring the past as it lives in memory, analogizes the states of mind and processes of the imagination that sometimes result in people seeing ghosts. In summary, these mental states all enable their possessors to see the egocentric present in a multiple perspective, projected against past, extended present (that is, across space), and future; for as Scrooge learned, not all ghosts are of the past. The ghost of the future, in fact, may be the most compelling of all.

The person who looks into a mirror and sees something there besides the expected image is in a state of mind to see ghosts. One of the most instructive references to the mirror appears in a letter from Dickens to Lady Eastlake—undated, but possibly referring to an illness of June 1853:

> I have been ill of six days in bed, for the first time in my life. Since Monday last I have been shaving a man every morning—a stranger to me, with big gaunt eyes and a hollow-cheek—whose appearance was rather irksome and oppressive. I am happy to say that he has at last retired from the looking-glass and is replaced by the familiar personage whom I have lathered and scraped these twenty years.[6]

With "big gaunt eyes" and "hollow cheek," this stranger's resemblance to the "dreadful Mask" is sufficiently striking to account for its "irksome and oppressive" effect upon a sick man already susceptible to thoughts of the figure who will finally complete his procession.

Dickens transforms this phenomenon into a magical mirror in "The Haunted House" (Christmas story for 1859), though here its influence runs through time in the opposite direction. The narrator of the story has taken up residence in a house haunted by "Master B." after disclaimers of belief resembling Dickens's own. Six nights have produced only phenomena that could be "scientifically" explained away. Nonetheless, the suspense and the focus of attention upon the resuscitated dead put him into a state of mind for seeing ghosts; that is, susceptible to the influence of the past. On the seventh morning, "I began to perceive that things were going wrong": "The first appearance that presented itself was early in the morning when it was but just daylight and no more. I was standing shaving at my glass, when I suddenly discovered, to my consternation and amazement, that I was shaving—not myself—I am fifty—but a boy. Apparently Master B.!" (HH, ch. 2). Greatly disturbed, the narrator takes a few turns around the room before resuming.

> Opening my eyes, which I had shut while recovering my firmness, I now met in the glass, looking straight at me, the eyes of a young man of four or five and twenty. Terrified by this new ghost, I closed my eyes, and made a strong effort to recover myself. Opening them again, I saw, shaving his cheek in the glass, my father, who has been long dead. Nay, I even saw my grandfather, too, whom I never did see in my life. (ch. 2)

Thus the images from his personal and familial past trail before him across the mirror.

That night, he has a second visitation when, "waking from an uneasy sleep at exactly two o'clock in the morning, what were my feelings to find that I was sharing my bed with the skeleton of Master B.!" The ghost of Master B. now appears before his eyes, amidst his protestations of disbelief, to explain the meaning of both the figures in the mirror and the skeleton. "'Barber!' it apostrophised me when I had finished. . . . 'Condemned,' said the ghost, 'to shave a constant change of customers—now, me—now, a young man—now, thyself as thou art—now, thy father—now, thy grandfather; condemned, too, to lie down with a skeleton every night, and to rise with it every morning—'" In explaining his experience, the narrator in retrospect identifies his visitor as "the ghost of my own childhood, the ghost of my own innocence, the ghost of my own airy belief"—a phantom of the past to be pursued often; but "never with these man's hands of mine to touch, . . . never more to this man's heart of mine to hold it in its purity. And here you see me working out, as cheerfully and thankfully as I may, my doom of shaving in the glass a constant change of customers, and of lying down and rising up with the skeleton allotted to me for my mortal companion" (ch. 2). Although Dickens here substitutes the skeleton for the mirrored mask, they are clearly analogues and the unified procession hovers in the imaginative background. In short, the narrator is now a person continuously mindful of both past and future as he pursues his affairs in the present.

Whether appearing as erratic images in a mirror or in their more traditional form, ghosts are always a warning against living unreflectively in the present—an idea more baldly stated in A Christmas

Carol (Christmas book for 1843) by a humanized Scrooge: "'I will live in the Past, the Present, and the Future. The Spirits of all Three shall strive within me. I will not shut out the lessons that they teach'" (CC, stave IV).

The truth Scrooge learns must also be taught to the chemist Redlaw of The Haunted Man (Christmas book for 1848), who insists that "The past is past" and wishes that he might dispose once and for all of painful remembrance, that "tissue of sorrow and trouble" with its reminders of suffering and loss. When eighty-seven-year-old Philip finds his recollections "merry and happy" and speaks with pleasure of the old motto under the ancient portrait in the great Dinner Hall of the school: "Lord! Keep my memory green" (HM, ch. 1), Redlaw is agitated into the reflective state of mind conducive to seeing ghosts. "My memory" as a faculty he personally possesses begins to slide into the motto meaning of "memory of me" and he is led to reflect on what that memory will be.

When the phantom appears (seen first in the mirror) he and Redlaw scrutinize each other: "The living man, and the animated image of himself dead, might so have looked, the one upon the other." Redlaw thus most significantly "remembers" first the future when he will be dead.

Redlaw insists to the phantom, who is "the animated image of himself dead," that his wish to abolish memory is a benevolent wish for all mankind, who would be far happier without memory of past happiness and misery. Now the phantom not only grants him his personal wish, but also adds the "Gift" that Redlaw's very presence will henceforth destroy memory in all those whom he approaches. He is taken, like Scrooge, on a journey through his familiar world to see the difference made in a humanity without memory and guided only by the circumstances of the present moment: love and compassion, which bind human beings together, have vanished from the race.

With increasing horror, Redlaw sees his philosophy, his touch, contaminate all about him. The monster child (see ch. VI) alone remains impervious to his influence because what he has wished to be, this child already is:

> "the last, completest illustration of a human creature, utterly bereft of such remembrances as you have yielded up. . . . Your influence is powerless here, because from this child's bosom you can banish nothing. His thoughts have been in "terrible companionship" with yours,

> because you have gone down to his unnatural level. He is the growth of man's indifference; you are the growth of man's presumption. The beneficent design of Heaven is, in each case, overthrown, and from the two poles of the immaterial world you come together." (ch. 3)

And what has this child lost?

> "No softening memory of sorrow, wrong, or trouble enters here, because this wretched mortal from his birth has been abandoned to a worse condition than the beasts, and has, within his knowledge, no one contrast, no humanising touch, to make a grain of such a memory spring up in his hardened breast.
>
> All within this desolate creature is barren wilderness. All within the man bereft of what you have resigned, is the same barren wilderness." (ch. 3)

Phantom and child have shown the chemist that what he himself has taught as true in the material world is likewise true in the immaterial one: "No step or atom in the wondrous structure could be lost, without a blank being made in the great universe. I know, now, that it is the same with good and evil, happiness and sorrow, in the memories of men" (ch. 2). Memory, then, "green" to symbolize continued and full life, joins the fancies and wondering visions of childhood in the humanizing dream world of the spirit, growing ever longer and more important as the individual proceeds through life. Without it, life is a "barren wilderness."

Another set of images exploring memory analogizes the fact that recollection, like the child's dream of the future, makes little distinction between what was "only" fancied and dreamed about, and what "really" happened. Both orders of existence play equally decisive roles in shaping the life of an individual, and remembered dreams maintain an integrity of reality at least equivalent to that of remembered events. In his Christmas story for 1851, "What Christmas Is as We Grow Older," Dickens develops this idea in its discursive form. "Time was, with most of us," he writes, "when Christmas Day encircling all our limited world like a magic ring, left nothing out for us to miss or seek"—those Christmases of childhood, which as yet made no distinctions between dream and reality—"That was the time for the beatified enjoyment of the things that were to be, and never were, and yet the things that were so real in our resolute hope that it would be hard to say, now, what realities achieved since, have been stronger!" So strong and influential are the visions, in fact, that it is difficult sometimes to realize that the things dreamed of never actually come to pass:

> [I]s our life here [he speculates], at the best, so constituted that, pausing as we advance at such a noticeable mile-stone in the track as this great birthday, we look back on the things that never were, as naturally and full as gravely as on the things that have been and are gone, or have been and still are? If it be so, and so it seems to be, must we come to the conclusion that life is little better than a dream, and little worth the loves and strivings we crowd into it? (WCI)

The negative answer supplied for the last question once more asserts the real value of the "unaccomplished visions of our youth" as "our teachers to deal gently even with the impalpable nothings of the earth" as we work our way through life.

Memory sometimes plays a further trick with actuality: not only does it grant identical reality to past things actual and imagined, but it also frequently assumes for "things that never were" an ongoing and continuous life extending into the present. Mr. Twemlow in *Our Mutual Friend,* for example, finds melancholy sustenance for a dreary life in maintaining a youthful dream, ironically unaware of its contradictory counterpart in the actual world:

> For, the poor little harmless gentleman once had his fancy, like the rest of us, and she didn't answer (as she often does not), and he thinks the adorable bridesmaid is like the fancy as she was then (which she is not at all), and that if the fancy had not married some one else for money, but had married him for love, he and she would have been happy (which they wouldn't have been), and that she has a tenderness for him still (whereas her toughness is a proverb). (*OMF,* bk. I, ch. 10)

Similarly, the narrator of "The Poor Relation's Story" (Christmas story for 1852) lives a rich double life. While superficially the poor relation, his "real" life, he explains, is spent in the "Castle . . . in the Air," where the dreams of his youth have confounded actuality to be privately fulfilled. "I really do not know, in my Castle," he continues, "what loneliness is." This airy castle, which must be vacated if one is to mature, may, it seems, be reinhabited as a kind of haven from the insupportable disappointments of life. Yet an air of sadness and dessicated futility lingers about the persons of Twemlow and the Poor Relation, who must withdraw from life to find any happiness in it. Arthur Clennam, on the other hand, is picking up the threads of life once more when he perceives the gap between the extended life he has provided for the dream and the unextended life of the actuality: the eighteen-year-old "dream" looks simpering and silly in the middle-aged person of the actual Flora Finching.[7]

The same process of extending the dream, however, may color the thinking even of persons vigorously involved in life, providing them with an endearing or amusing eccentricity. Aunt Betsey Trotwood, never shaken in her affectionate belief in the reality of her niece, Miss Betsey Copperfield, holds up that exemplary person as a model for runaway David. "His sister, Betsey Trotwood, never would have run away," she exclaims. "She would have lived with her godmother, and we should have been devoted to one another" (*DC*, ch. 13). With similar reasoning she continues to protect and give money to her former husband on the grounds that "for the sake of what I once believed him to be, I wouldn't have even this shadow of my idle fancy hardly dealt with" (ch. 47). Thus unreal dreams may have permanently real significance in the lives of their possessors.

Another crucial characteristic of memory is its refusal to define experience as a point or moment in time. Actual persons and events of the past, the present, and the future have a contemporaneous reality regardless of intervening change. Furthermore, like oneself, the people one knows are made up of a succession of figures through time. Particularly when asleep, or in illness, or when dead, people slip readily back through time and "are" what they once were, a complex accumulation of all they have ever been that also prefigures what they will be. Two examples will illustrate this point adequately. In "The Haunted House," the narrator comments on the heightened solemnity of things for him in the early morning hours:

> There is something awful in the being surrounded by familiar faces asleep—in the knowledge that those who are dearest to us and to whom we are dearest, are profoundly unconscious of us, in an impassive state, anticipative of that mysterious condition to which we are all tending—the stopped life, the broken threads of yesterday, the deserted seat, the closed book, the unfinished but abandoned occupation, all are images of Death. (HH, ch. 1)

But even as the sleeping face prefigures the "dreadful Mask," the dead face recapitulates life: "[A] certain air that familiar household objects take upon them when they first emerge from the shadows of the night into the morning, of being newer, and as they used to be long ago, has its counterpart in the subsidence of the worn face of maturity or age, in death, into the old youthful look." Comparably, as the adult David Copperfield progresses through life, he envisions the infant in his procession securely asleep in his mother's arms: "The mother who lay in the grave, was the mother of my infancy; the little creature in her arms, was myself, as I had once been, hushed for ever on her bosom" (*DC*, ch. 19).

In all its aspects, it seems, memory vigorously reaffirms the dream world's transcendency over the actual one. The difference, however, between youthful airy visions and memory is profound. In between, the actual world has been not repudiated, but absorbed. When the momentary event, happy or unhappy, is accepted into memory, its meaning expands and develops and it remains permanently alive, like the figures in the procession. Furthermore, although experience has taught the impossibility of personal dream fulfillment, dreams for the future become revitalized by the enlarged view of life, which once more brings childhood and children into the picture. Dickens explains this in his most sententious fashion in "What Christmas Is as We Grow Older" as he welcomes "old aspirations, glittering creatures of an ardent fancy" to their place under the holly:

> Welcome, all that was ever real to our hearts; and for the earnestness that made you real, thanks to Heaven! Do we build no Christmas castles in the clouds now? Let our thoughts, fluttering like butterflies among these flowers of children, bear witness! Before this boy, there stretches out a Future, brighter than we ever looked on in our old romantic time, but bright with honour and with truth. . . . We see how, when our graves are old, other hopes than ours are young, other hearts than ours are moved; how other ways are smoothed; how other happiness blooms, ripens, and decays—no, not decays, for other homes and other bands of children, not yet in being nor for ages yet to be, arise, and bloom and ripen to the end of all! (WCI)

The equally sententious Mr. Micawber, "full of eloquence," similarly justifies the addition of a new member to his family: "He gave us to understand," writes David, "that in our children we lived again, and that, under the pressure of pecuniary difficulties, any addition to their number was doubly welcome" (*DC*, ch. 28). It is a persistent idea with Micawber, as he later explains to David that in Miss Micawber "her mother renewed her youth, like the Phoenix" (ch. 36). Ada similarly renews hope in her unborn child. That our children renew our lives is a commonplace idea, to be sure, but one that lies constantly behind Dickens's portraits of children. Seen in this light, Jo, the soulless child of "The Haunted Man," and little

Nell all signify as allegorical figures as well as actual children. In children, Dickens preaches, lie our only possible mature hopes and dreams for the future; in each new generation death is joyously negated. In the state or condition of its children is embodied the state or condition of humankind itself.

In the inner world of memory and hope, then, lives all of human experience. The individual who carries such a world within has a perspective that reduces personal mortality to a natural, undisturbing fact. This individual lives in a present dwarfed by the past and the future; yet, paradoxically, that long view charges each present moment with significance. Such a person carries within, in fact, something analogous to the warm, bright fire on the hearth.

It may be that only people who have tried to cope with English damp and cold without benefit of central heating could appreciate fully the centrality of the fireplace in the Dickens imagery. Manner turns dependably into mannerism as every Dickens traveller fleeing from the damp and cold is drawn by lighted window and peers down onto a scene of human congeniality around the cheerful fire on the hearth; and as every householder closes doors and shutters windows to close in light and warmth and push back the freezing dark extending through graveyard and across marsh—no congenial environment for living people.

Betty Higden, a wanderer outside of houses, thinks it a little hard in them when families gathering together for the night close the shutters and blacken the flame. "'Ah me!' she said to herself. 'The dead and I seem to have it pretty much to ourselves in the dark and in this weather'" (*OMF,* bk. III, ch. 8). David similarly recalls his first childish association with his father's white gravestone in the churchyard and "the indefinable compassion I used to feel for it lying out alone there in the dark night, when our little parlour was warm and bright with fire and candle, and the doors of our house were—almost cruelly, it seemed to me sometimes—bolted and locked against it" (*DC,* ch. 1).

Yet, granted the realistic force of the fireplace image, its real power lies in its emblematic and symbolic meanings. Indeed, in the passages just quoted, meaning has already burst its literal bounds and expanded into societal connotations: At the center of the house of life is the fireplace around which human beings gather together and from whose vitalizing warmth none should be excluded.

An even more pervasive analogy, however, is that between the burning fireplace and the living human soul passing through time.

This analogy is hyperbolically and comically depicted in the literal-minded obsession of Mrs. Fibbitson in *David Copperfield.* The boy David encounters her sitting by the fire with another old woman: "'Ah, she's poorly,' said the first old woman. 'It's one of her bad days. If the fire was to go out, through any accident, I verily believe she'd go out too, and never come to life again'" (*DC,* ch. 5). Though it is a warm day, marvels David, she thinks of nothing but the fire—is "jealous even of the saucepan on it"—and sits "screening the fire as if she were sedulously keeping *it* warm, instead of it keeping her warm, and watching it in a most distrustful manner." The completion of David's breakfast, "by relieving the fire, gave her such extreme joy that she laughed aloud." Mrs. Fibbitson, to be sure, is a caricature. But more thoughtful characters in Dickens's stories are humanized and complete people, or are on their way to being so, when they find personal meaning in the fire. Those who, like Sir Leicester, sit unaware by the burning fire full of signs and omens are dehumanized or subhuman.

The total fire-fireplace configuration is perhaps the most complex in the entire Dickens tapestry. In the fireplace itself, burning wood or coal not only emblematizes one's own life falling away into ashes; it also recalls one's connection with a remote past when the wood stood as living trees not yet felled and coal stood as living trees not yet fallen in the swamp—"Dedlock timber and antediluvian forest." The actual instant at which a large-souled person stares into the fire provides only a point upon which to suspend momentarily the *durée* that makes up "real" life. In the fire, the present moment is projected against the past and future. Here sensitive people find memory and hope, and see their lives in total perspective.

One of the most extended and complete examples of the fireplace associations runs through *Hard Times,* where inability to catch the analogies becomes a gauge of the souls of Mr. Gradgrind and Tom. In the fireplace also is traced the evidence of Louisa's irrepressible soul. The "Ogre" Gradgrind, predictably enough, is singularly insensitive as he tries unsuccessfully to fathom (even with "his cavernous eyes on the fire") what has fostered Louisa's "idle imagination" (see ch. VI). He postulates a corrupting instructor, or an "idle storybook," but the intrusion into his well-ordered household of a "wondering" child is beyond his understanding. The truth of the matter is that he is staring blindly at the culprit, for Louisa finds in the sympathetic fire the only sustenance for her starved soul. Mrs. Gradgrind, similarly puzzled by her daughter, blames Tom for encouraging her derelictions into the world of fancy. But Louisa quickly explains it otherwise: "'I was encouraged by nothing, Mother, but by looking at the red sparks dropping out of the fire, and whitening and dying. It made me think, after all, how short my life would be, and how little I could hope to do in it'" (*HT,* bk. I, ch. 8). Thus the log consumed by fire becomes to Louisa analogous to her own life. As the felled tree drops in flakes into the nothingness of dead ashes, she sees her life burning meaninglessly toward death.[8]

Although Thomas's soul is a weak thing, he takes some strength from Louisa. As they sit by the fire, he rests "his sulky face on his arms," while she watches the bright sparks as they drop upon the hearth. Tom expresses his desperate hatred of everything in his life except his sister. He speaks with special detestation of Mr. Bounderby, with whom it has been arranged he is going to live. As they talk, the fire defines their shadows on the wall and ceiling "as if the brother and sister were overhung by a dark cavern.[9] Or, a fanciful imagination—if such treason could have been there—might have made it out to be the shadow of their subject, and of its lowering association with their future" (bk. I, ch. 8). But in the very shadow of the "Giant" Bounderby and his dark cavern, Loo (Louisa) sits engaged in the forbidden practice of wondering:

> "Have you gone to sleep, Loo?"
>
> "No, Tom. I am looking at the fire."
>
> "You seem to find more to look at in it than ever I could find," said Tom. "Another of the advantages, I suppose, of being a girl." (bk. I, ch. 8)

A little later:

> Tom went and leaned on the back of her chair, to contemplate the fire which so engrossed her, from her point of view, and see what he could make of it.
>
> "Except that it is a fire," said Tom, "it looks to me as stupid and blank as everything else looks. What do you see in it? Not a circus?"[10]
>
> "I don't see anything in it, Tom, particularly. But since I have been looking at it, I have been wondering about you and me, grown up."
>
> "Wondering again!" said Tom.
>
> "I have such unmanageable thoughts," returned his sister, "that they *will* wonder." (bk. I, ch. 8)

For the young Louisa, "wondering" about the future brings little hope. But in the calm aftermath of *Hard Times,* after much suffering and learning, an adult Louisa seems to find more happy predictions in the fire. She once more sits "watching the fire as in days of yore, though with a gentler and humbler face. How much of the future might arise before *her* vision?" (bk. III, ch. 9). It will be a future of serenity, not of fairy-tale happiness, but with both a father and a brother returned to humanity.

Most of all, she might see herself among children. The first sight meeting her eyes after the unconsciousness into which she falls on the night she returns to her father is an emblem of reviving hope: her young sister Jane. ("'What a beaming face you have, Jane!' said Louisa, as her young sister—timidly still—bent down to kiss her. 'Have I? I am very glad you think so. I am sure it must be Sissy's doing'" [bk. III, ch. 1].) This one resource comes to be completely restored for Louisa: the perpetual hope to be found in children in the idyllic garden—although they are not to be hers. Had they been, she knows she would have been "very careful that they should have a childhood of the mind no less than a childhood of the body":

> But, happy Sissy's happy children loving her; all children loving her; she, grown learned in childish lore; thinking no innocent and pretty fancy ever to be despised; trying hard to know her humbler fellow-creatures, and to beautify their lives of machinery and reality with those imaginative graces and delights without which the heart of infancy will wither up, the sturdiest physical manhood will be morally stark death, and the plainest national prosperity figures can show will be the writing on the Wall—she holding this course as part of no fantastic vow, or bond, or brotherhood, or sisterhood, or pledge, or covenant, or fancy dress, or fancy fair, but simply as a duty to be done. (bk. III, ch. 9)

As personal dreams of happiness have been relinquished to be replaced by the hope to be found in renewed generations, Louisa can now find in the fire a future life of serene contentment invested with enlarged meaning.[11]

Lizzie Hexam, too, is given to seeing pictures in the fire. Like Louisa, she gently encourages the more sluggish soul of her brother in an interchange of ideas as they sit before the fire. Lizzie is thoughtful:

> ". . . as I sit a looking at the fire, I seem to see in the burning coal—like where that glow is now—"
>
> "That's gas, that is," said the boy, "coming out of a bit of forest that's been under the mud that was under the water in the days of

> Noah's Ark. Look here! When I take the poker—so—and give it a dig—"
>
> "Don't disturb it, Charley, or it'll be all in a blaze. It's that dull glow near it, coming and going that I mean. When I look at it of an evening, it comes like pictures to me, Charley."
>
> "Show us a picture," said the boy. "Tell us where to look."
>
> "Ah! It wants my eyes, Charley."
>
> "Cut away then, and tell us what your eyes make of it." (*OMF*, bk. I, ch. 3)

Charley's practical interpretation of the glow is more than an evidence of his factual turn of mind: his association of it with "the mud that was under the water in the days of Noah's Ark" unmistakably brings in the primitive savage world of subhuman amphibians. In response to Charley's request, Lizzie "cuts away" to paint for him a picture of childhood experiences shared in their memories; and in response to another request to "cut away again . . . and give us a fortune-telling one; a future one," she depicts her dreams for their future. For Lizzie, both memory and hope live in "the hollow down by the flare" (bk. I, ch. 3).

Like Tom, Charley will never see with his sister's eyes. In a later day, as an ambitious youth who lives opportunistically in the present, Charley complains petulantly against his sister's reminders of the past, declaring that "'What we have got to do is, to turn our faces full in our new direction, and keep straight on'":[12] "'You are such a dreamer,' said the boy. . . . 'It was all very well when we sat before the fire—when we looked into the hollow down by the flare—but we are looking into the real world, now'" (bk. II, ch. 1). To which Lizzie replies: "'Ah, we were looking into the real world then, Charley.'"

For David Copperfield, also, the fire provides a meeting ground for the past and future as he tries to reconstruct his life after the death of Dora:

> I gradually fell . . . to tracing prospects in the live-coals, and to thinking, as they broke and changed, of the principal vicissitudes and separations that had marked my life. I had not seen a coal fire, since I had left England three years ago: though many a wood fire had I watched, as it crumbled into hoary ashes,[13] and mingled with the feathery heap upon the hearth, which not inaptly figured to me, in my despondency, my own dead hopes.
>
> I could think of the past now, gravely, but not bitterly; and could contemplate the future in a brave spirit. (*DC*, ch. 59)

In all of these interpretations there is the common core of meaning that the world of dreams and the world of actuality coalesce in the fireplace, where they both acquire their significant "reality" through memory and hope.

Other configurations in which fire appears touch and interrelate with the fireplace patterns in rich new ways responding to Dickens's associative imagination. The burning away of human life within the confined, steady control of the fireplace contrasts sharply with the death emblematized in the wild and destructive burning of the warehouse whose flames cast a lurid light across the death struggle of Daniel Quilp; or with the violent and sudden death analogized in the blood-red marsh sunrise or sunset, which seems "filled with the ruins of a forest it had set on fire" (bk. I, ch. 6).

The contrast hovers in young Louisa's mind as she looks across the chimneys of Coketown with their serpents of smoke. Louisa, "so much given to watching the bright ashes at twilight as they fell into the grate and became extinct," tries to discover "first in her own fire within the house and then in the fiery haze without what kind of woof Old Time, that greatest and longest-established spinner of all, would weave from the threads he had already spun into a woman" (*HT*, bk. I, ch. 14). For suddenly Louisa is a woman, and Mr. Bounderby has proposed marriage. Now, as we have seen, Louisa finds in the smoking chimneys of Coketown a prophetic similarity to herself. Her own repressed fires, Louisa senses, instead of yielding life-giving light and warmth, might explode into a frightening and ravaging force to consume instantly the log in which they burn: "I have often thought that life is very short." But her father, looking unseeingly into the fireplace, can't be expected to see the remark's application.

The burning fireplace and the felled tree are of course inseparable; hence, all configurations in which the tree is featured are drawn into this one as well. The mysterious merging of these patterns in the imagination of both writer and reader may well account for some of the crackle of language noted by John Gross (see Introduction) as part of the electrifying effects Dickens can at times produce in his readers. The relevant characteristics of the tree are its greenness, its felling, its burning, and its falling into ashes. Greenness is life; it is also memory. The conventional meaning of the Christmas tree falls readily into the Dickens imagery: its greenness is a reminder of the continued life of Christ and the continued life in his teachings. In "A Christmas Tree," Dickens reports "a whisper going through the leaves" of the tree as it sinks into the ground: "This, in commemoration of the law of love and kindness, mercy and compassion. This, in remembrance of Me!" One remembers that in The Battle of Life, although the green patches on the ancient battlefield kept memory alive for years, ultimately the "wounded trees had long ago made Christmas logs, and blazed and roared away. The deep green patches were no greener now than the memory of those who lay in dust below." Echo recalls Redlaw and the old motto under the portrait in the great Dinner Hall of his school: "Lord! Keep my memory green." Once more comes the subtle fusing of trees and human beings so frequently observed during the course of this study.

Now with a slight shift in point of view, a new pattern emerges. When is the life of the tree really over? The felled Christmas tree is still green. The Yule log burns with vital light and warmth. So does the coal from the antediluvian forest. Is there not comfort in the extended analogy between human life and tree? The individual who in one sense can see life burning away to ashes like the log in the fireplace, in another sense may perceive that the light and warmth that make the ancient life still glow with vitality may have some personal relevance. One's own green memory, it suggests, may be prolonged if one so lives as to furnish analogous light and warmth for future generations.

For the picture in the fireplace created by the burning log or coal symbolizes the light- and warmth-giving significance of the burning human life. Memory is doubly crucial to the perception of this significance. Within an individual's own perception, memory of the past, both personal and cultural, humanizes that person so that life possesses these life-giving qualities; in the memory of those who come after rest hopes for personal immortality. The restless ghosts clamoring for recognition are all reiterating the same plea for continued life: "Lord, keep my memory green."

What, then, is finally the relationship between dream and actuality? Although the actual world is unquestionably the stuff of life, the dream world, by awakening, nourishing, and sustaining the human soul, gives this actuality its meaning. Through childhood fancy, wonder, and airy visions an ideal of human happiness is conceived; through adult memory and hope, the egocentric dream of personal fulfillment and immortality is replaced by an altruistic sense of vital participation in a perennially resurgent human life. Such a reconciliation of the two worlds comes in natural stages for the fortunate. Some achieve it only after great travail. Some, permanently unable or unwilling to make the transition into full human beings, remain subhuman or dehumanized. For such allegorical characters as Scrooge or Redlaw, the truth, appearing dramatically as supernatural revelation, thaws out the frozen soul to bring about an exhilarating rebirth into the life of society.

Since these views obviously endorse the teachings of Christ, it is not surprising that they find their most overt expression in the Christmas books and stories. But it is worth noting that the images of the Christmas season that attract Dickens are those in harmony with his imaginative mode of experience rather than those heavy with religious symbolism: the Christmas tree rather than the creche; the frozen season giving way to yielding warmth, which brings springtime to this world more than it gives promise of a future existence. It attests to the brotherhood of man, which is a social and humanistic idea, and largely ignores the theological question of the fatherhood of God. The life it celebrates is the essentially comic rhythmic cycle of ongoing humanity.

# IX

## *Summary and Conclusions*

ALLEGORY CAN NEVER be judged by its novelty. To criticize Dickens for lack of originality in his perceptions and analogies is to divert attention from the very source of his power, of the power of any allegorist. What lives in his consciousness as his mode of experience is probably not too different from what lives subliminally in the consciousnesses of readers subject to the same cultural conditioning. It is this very universality of human experience in a given time and place that completes the process of communication of life entirely lived and felt. There would be no power in the image-making consciousness of the writer without responsiveness in kind from the reader. With it comes the imaginative power that characterizes the poet.

But what conclusions can be drawn concerning Dickens's allegorical writing as a totality? This study has sought to discover the "comprehensive and self-consistent mode of experience" that lies behind the created world of Dickens: his perceptual universe. Perceived by the reader directly through inference, descriptions of all kinds of experience have communicated appropriate emotional responses to him in the "kind of speculative thought which," as Murry says, "differs from the speculative thought of the philosopher by its working from particular to particular." Such thoughts, felt experience rather than didactic lessons, become a complex mosaic. Can the pieces be put together to form a "Dickens *Weltanschauung*"?

With much admitted sacrifice of complexity, the story of the tapestried imagination can readily be organized into logical discourse and can be retold as the allegory of a nineteenth-century

Everyman. This Everyman has a significantly contemporary look, quite unlike that of his otherworldly fifteenth-century counterpart. For Dickens's Everyman provides emotional responses to the same elements in contemporary life and thought for which Tennyson agonizingly sought answers. Given their different assumptions and attitudes, however, the problems and questions look quite different. The pragmatic Dickens, in and of this world, accepted without apparent anguish the discoveries of contemporary science, which brought man out of primitive beginnings and which threw doubts on his personal immortality. He was content to leave mystery as mystery, but he found in the new ideas imaginative materials with which to illuminate life here and now—to show that the real terror is death-in-life: not to be descended from primitive monsters, but to be and act like them. Even as he points out the death-related concepts, he likewise shows the way to escape from them and therefore also from death. If Tennyson comes laboriously to faith through honest doubt, Dickens spontaneously assumes an infectious faith in life itself. From life fully lived springs freedom, contentment, and hope. The future can then take care of itself. These views were perhaps more happily communicated to most Victorians, who shivered in the contemporary climate of opinion, than were the mental lucubrations of the more cerebral artists of the day. Indeed, they may speak even more readily to the twentieth century, which regards Tennyson as a little quaint.

In Dickens's view, Everyman comes out of and goes back into mystery. He emerges from the mists, travels steadily along the road or river in a series of changing figures he carries along with him, and in due time passes back into the mists. Awareness of this pattern makes him conscious of an intimate kinship with all the other shadowy human figures set along the same path from the beginning of time to its end. This is a pattern over which he has no control, but which he is doomed to trace out.

While he is on the road, however, he does have the power to make life joyous and vital, to invest it with meaning. To do so, he must find the wisdom to permit the natural processes of life, both for himself and for others whom he touches, the freedom to develop, mature, come to fruition, and decay. Attempts to force or to deny any part of the process lead to blight and death-in-life. In this natural order of development, Everyman must learn to reconcile the free and ideal world of dream with the circumscribed and imperfect world of fact, neither of which may be denied in the fully alive human being. Along the way, Everyman will encounter a host of eccentric and grotesque half-adults whose example he must shun: dehumanized creatures who have egocentrically attempted to resolve the dualism without effort or pain by repudiating one world or the other. On the one hand are those who have rejected the world of fact to live undisturbed in a private inner world of dreams—unnatural children and self-centered parasites like Skimpole or Dedlock; frozen caricatures of people like Belinda Pocket. On the other hand are those who insist upon the exclusiveness of the world of fact and deny the world of dream—cruel tyrants and ogres like Dombey and Gradgrind; ludicrously vicious yet powerless dolls like Smallweed and his family; primitive monsters without feelings or conscience like Rogue Riderhood. Along the way he will also encounter a multitude of partial human beings—subhuman savages, pathetic innocents, dolls and puppets who have been unable to claim their human heritage because of deprivation, exploitation, or their own limitations of strength and will. These are adults *manqué* like Magwitch, Gaffer, Charley, Nancy, Jo, and Dora.

In the natural process of human development, however, Everyman first learns to wonder and to dream, for, as he will one day perceive, the capacity to do so provides the "fireplace" of his soul. He first formulates the ideal good as a selfish dream; its achievement is in personal terms of fulfilled happiness. First contact with the "real" world comes by way of presentiment through the threatening "Mask" and the images of guilt. Everyman comes to an intuitive understanding that what humanity calls evil is another term for the circumscription and imperfection of human life: physical limitations, pain, and death on the one hand; human limitation and susceptibility to error on the other. With the knowledge of his perfect dreams upon him, he becomes increasingly aware of his own complicity in imperfection and thus becomes ridden with feelings of guilt, both as an individual and as a member of society. Everyman must learn to live with this knowledge of evil; of boundaries, of unfulfilled and compromised ideals. When he has fully assimilated these limiting ideas, he is ready to take on the full adult life of involvement and responsibility.

Now the ideal transmutes from the selfish and egocentric dream to radiate outward toward the rest of humanity. The good life takes on its real meaning as Everyman attempts to make the ideal a reality for others. He finds his hopes and dreams perpetuated in the coming generations, and for them will continue to raise castles in the air to give life a joy and warmth possible only when he has relinquished his private dreams of personal fulfillment. As a naturally maturing individual, he constantly readjusts his concept of time, the most basic of all his concepts. Without time, life is inconceivable. With time, as he will see, come creation, change, diversity, action, and movement—but to have these, he must also accept danger, decay, and dissolution. To have life, he must acquiesce in death. The present moment—a pinpoint in time—becomes less and less crucial to him as the life in his memory stretches out longer behind him, and as the life of hope and dream reaches out more comprehensively into the future.

As a mature adult, Everyman may appear to have come about full circle when he is ready to say, with Lizzie, that the "real" world is the one that exists in the mind. Actually, he has moved miraculously forward for, as experience has brought the outside world of fact within his consciousness to be synthesized into memory and hope, he has not repudiated the outside world but has absorbed it. Personal death for him has lost its threatening quality, and he sees his life being perpetually revitalized in humanity's ongoing life. Whereas the egocentric being shrinks into a frozen or mechanical imitation of human life, the being of Everyman has expanded to assimilate the whole of humanity.

This, in these terms, is the total allegory—the ordered interpretation of experience—contained in the configurations. Whether or not Dickens "thought" about it when writing a story, it was there as the framework and flesh of his mode of experience, it helped to determine what he would see about him, and it colored every step of the composition. The appropriate analogies and associations rose selectively to the surface of his mind to appear as setting, characters, plot, theme, and language—to provide what might be called the substance of his style: that part of it that "is the man."

Dickens gives frequent notice of his allegorical intent. From the simple short pieces, such as "A Child's Story" or "Nobody's Story" to the big complex novels, such as *Bleak House* and *Little Dorrit,* he points the "finger of Allegory." As he creates the characters, situations, and actions that fill his novels with bustling life and reality, he understands full well that he is "reweaving" parts or all of the total allegory of the pilgrimage of life. David Copperfield glancingly alludes to this fact (see ch. VII) when he says he was "balanced curiously" between "two irreconcilable conclusions": "the one, that what I felt was general and unavoidable; the other, that it was particular to me, and might have been different." What this statement seems to record is Dickens's reminder that he could have woven David's tale in such fashion that it would have turned out otherwise.

Nowhere else in his novels did Dickens so openly declare his allegorical purposes as in *Little Dorrit.* After the travellers in quarantine in Marseilles have been released to resume their individual journeys, the narrator notes that by nightfall

> the caravan of the morning, all dispersed, went their appointed ways. And thus ever, by day and night, under the sun and under the stars, climbing the dusty hills and toiling along the weary plains, journeying by land and journeying by sea, coming and going so strangely, to meet and to act and react on one another, move all we restless travellers through the pilgrimage of life. (*LD,* bk. I, ch. 2)

Two unlikely characters are Dickens's further voices, one at the beginning and one at the end of the novel. Miss Wade is first. As the travellers part, she makes a "composed" statement: "'In our course through life we shall meet the people who are coming to meet *us,* from many strange places and by many strange roads . . . and what is set to us to do to them, and what is set to them to do to us, will all be done.'" (bk. I, ch. 2).

The summarizing statement at the end falls unexpectedly from the lips of Flora Finching. Like Lucky in *Waiting for Godot,* Flora is a repository of insight once one unravels her tangled language. She is speaking to Little Dorrit.

> "I earnestly beg you as the dearest thing that ever was if you'll still excuse the familiarity from one who moves in very different circles to let Arthur understand that I don't know after all whether it wasn't all nonsense between us though pleasant at the time and trying too and certainly Mr. F did work a change and the spell being broken nothing could be expected to take place without weaving it afresh which various circumstances have combined to prevent of which perhaps not the least powerful was that it was not to be." (bk. II, ch. 34)

Flora, it seems, like her creator understands that how the tale is woven determines its outcome. She and Arthur, similarly suspended in childhood at the beginning of the novel, have suffered opposite fates. For him, given a second chance to live through the adolescent experience by "weaving it afresh," the story this time turns out differently. For her, "it was not to be." Similarly, Tattycoram, for whom the story of Miss Wade has been rewoven, finds within herself what is needed to change its ending.

In his last years, as the events in Dickens's life must have deepened his personal feelings of guilt and non-fulfillment and failure, there are certainly grounds for describing a darkened outlook in his final novels. Nonetheless, there is likewise evidence in *The Mystery of Edwin Drood* that his faith in the *Weltanschauung* he had developed remained unshaken. He still could muster the perspective to see beyond his own diminished actual world to reaffirm the real significance of human dreams and values.

Edwin—not Jasper—becomes the vehicle for putting the dismal Cloisterham world into perspective. In this Cloisterham, the narrator has earlier observed: "Even its single pawnbroker takes in no pledges, nor has he for a long time, but offers vainly an unredeemed stock for sale, of which the costlier articles are dim and pale old watches apparently in a cold perspiration, tarnished sugar-tongs with ineffectual legs, and odd volumes of dismal books" (*MED*, ch. 3). The "pale old watches," the "ineffectual legs," and the "volumes of dismal books" are emblems of a nineteenth-century human community that for the time being has lost its way.

On a later occasion, after Rosa and Edwin have decided to go their separate ways, Edwin decides to return to Mr. Grewgious the "sorrowful jewels" he had planned to give Rosa as his fiancée. He explains his decision to Grewgious:

> They were but a sign of broken joys and baseless projects; in their very beauty they were . . . almost a cruel satire on the loves, hopes, plans, of humanity, which are able to forecast nothing, and are so much brittle dust. Let them be. He would restore them to her guardian when he came down; he in his turn would restore them to the cabinet from which he had unwillingly taken them; and there, like old letters or old vows, or other records of old aspirations come to nothing, they would be disregarded, until, being valuable, they were sold into circulation again, to repeat their former round. (ch. 13)

The note struck here is a sad one because at the moment the human dream seems bankrupt, without value on the market. Despite the biographical evidence to suggest that Dickens's view at the end was a "dark" one, this idea might have appeared anywhere in Dickens. Its implications go beyond either the optimistic or the pessimistic: they may be viewed as predominantly either sad or happy depending on the current state of the dream; on which part of the total allegory one is exploring at the moment and how it is being woven. Yet whichever is predominant, the opposite possibility lingers in the background to communicate the bittersweet interpretation of life. In the world about him, Dickens found an inexhaustible supply of variations on his allegory of life. The bustling specificity of his novels may sometimes obscure the universal representation; yet the universal, once seen, is thereafter clearly visible through the circumstantial.

Recognizing the unified mode of experience controlling and stabilizing the richly varied materials of life that burst from his novels leads finally to a new respect for the mind of Charles Dickens. His interpretation of life remains strikingly valid, unsentimental, and relevant a century and more after its inception. He shared with Shakespeare and Arnold's Greeks one fundamental quality of spirit: the capacity to see life steadily and see it whole. Life is tragedy, but it is also comedy. If it is sad that human dreams and aspirations come to nothing, it is a joyous miracle that they can and will be sold into circulation again to repeat their former rounds. Again as in Shakespeare, the world of Dickens's novels, though pervaded by mysterious forces over which humanity has little or no control, is the world of time, bustling with the things and activity of this life, and finding the meaning of life in the quality an individual brings to its living. The fact that dreams can be revitalized for every oncoming human being ensures that human life can continue to be existentially invested with the qualities necessary to give it significance.

# *Notes*

## CHAPTER I

1. J. Middleton Murry, *The Problem of Style* (London: Oxford Univ. Press, 1922), pp. 23–25.

2. "Prolegomena to the Analysis of Prose Style," in *Style in Prose Fiction,* Harold C. Martin, ed. (English Institute Essays, 1958), p. 6. In this essay, Ohmann analyzes the process of selection and ordering as an intuitive, primitive function of the human consciousness endeavoring to impose meaning on raw experience. "The perceiver," he explains,

> shapes the world by choosing from it whatever perceptual forms are most useful to him—though most often the choice is unconscious and inevitable . . . the selections are initially free, in an important sense. . . . In these multifarious Ur-choices, these pre-verbal and verbal pigeon-holings, style has its beginnings. If the critic is able to isolate and examine the most primitive choices which lie behind a work of prose, they can reveal to him the very roots of a writer's epistemology, the way in which he breaks up for manipulation the refractory surge of sensations which challenges all writers and perceivers. In this Heraclitean flux, and not in the elusive forms of thought, is the common source of all perceptions, all sentences, all prose. (p. 9)

3. Note how aptly this likewise describes Kant's "Intuitions."

4. *Philosophy in a New Key* (Cambridge, MA: Harvard Univ. Press, 1942), p. 93.

5. *Feeling and Form, A Theory of Art* (New York: Scribners, 1953), p. 291.

6. *The Problem of Style,* p. 85.

7. Here I am indebted to John Romano for his discussion of closure/ openness in *Dickens and Reality* (New York: Columbia University Press, 1978; for a more extended review, see "Bibliographical Essay"). Romano begins this particular discussion with the premise that all novels represent a "closed" world or system of some kind, if only in respect to form: to shape into form is to exclude the surrounding world. Yet the surrounding world is "reality." Dickens is an artist who, realizing the artificiality of the forms he has created, finds means of "exploding" them by the intrusion of some uncontrollable reality. If novels are in a sense "games" or "systems," such intrusions momentarily scatter or knock the pieces off the board. Then, as they themselves become a part of the form, some new "devastation" must occur: "the repeated devastations themselves become a metaphor . . . for the vulnerability of any creation of human consciousness . . . to the disordering impact of actuality" (p. 20).

8. When the symbol *is* an analogy, the discrimination described makes no real difference. But when something like a white horse, for instance, is established as a symbol standing for tradition, then the rules of the game have been confusingly violated when it suddenly stands for something else—or for nothing at all beyond itself. This type of arbitrary symbol is, I think, quite absent from Dickens.

9. In "*Pickwick:* Dickens and the Art of Fiction," in *Dickens and the Twentieth Century.* (London: Routledge and Kegan Paul, 1962), Killham provides an instructive analysis that clarifies the functioning of Dickens's images:

> We find clear anticipation in *Pickwick* of that so-called symbolism represented in later work by the railway (said by some to hint at the ruthlessness of Dombey, by others at the change from commerce to industry which was to oust Dombey); by the fog, the caged birds, the dust-heap, and perhaps the river in *Our Mutual Friend.* Dickens uses one of Tennyson's favourite words to refer to the railway train in *Dombey*—he calls it 'a *type* of the triumphant monster, Death.' Mr. Wilson, who saw a more complicated symbolism in Dickens's characters, refers to such things as this as 'metaphors that hang as emblems over the door.' 'Emblems' is an excellent word to use, for they are not really symbols acting as signs for the total insights of the novels in which they occur. A symbol does not *resemble* what it signifies, as does—in some significant respect—an image or emblem. So it is a pity to use the term symbol, perfectly suited to indicating the function of, say, the idea of 'the wings of the dove' in James's novel, in reference to something which is so different in kind. "Emblem" justly indicates their traditional nature, and has, too, the additional merit of being Dickens's own word to describe, in *Pickwick,* a withered plant vainly watered by the wife of a prisoner in the Fleet—'too true an emblem, perhaps, of the office she had come there to discharge.' When Mr. Pickwick was greeted on his first arrival in the prison by the sight of a Dutch clock and a bird-cage, Sam Weller was quick to point out the meaning of these objects. 'Veels within Veels, a prison in a prison. . . .'
>
> Dickens does not of course allow his emblems to arrest his narrative as does Bunyan. The dust-heap in *Our Mutual Friend* plays its part in the narrative very well; but it is clear that it is to bear from time to time a pejorative construction as an analogue for filthy lucre. That it is an emblem rather than a symbol is shown by the fact that its meaning (over and above that required in the fiction) is to be taken at some times and not at others. Dickens does not examine the merits of being allowed to inherit large unearned incomes, only the legality of so doing. Consequently the Harmon money comes in the end to the virtuous Rokesmith and Bella, its disagreeable origin, as emblematically represented, no longer felt to be disturbing. Obviously we cannot say, as we might say of the bullfight in *The Sun Also Rises,* for example, that it is a symbolic control enabling the author to reinforce the *plot,* for at times the analogue could, if remembered too long, actually oppose it. (pp. 38–39)

10. Although it has been customary to treat *imagination* and *fancy* as interchangeable when considering Dickens, I believe it is helpful to preserve Coleridge's distinctions between these two imaginative faculties. In discussing imagination, Coleridge describes "that synthetic and magical

power, to which I would exclusively appropriate the name of Imagination." This power "reveals itself in the balance or reconcilement of opposite or discordant qualities: the sameness, with difference; of the general with the concrete; the idea with the image; the individual with the representative; the sense of novelty and freshness with old and familiar objects; a more than usual state of emotion with more than usual order. . . ." While imagination is "the Soul [of poetic genius] that is everywhere, and in each," fancy is "its Drapery." Fancy he describes as "no other than a mode of memory emancipated from the order of time and space; while it is blended with, and modified by that empirical phenomenon of the will, which we express by the word Choice. But equally with the ordinary memory the Fancy must receive all its materials ready made from the law of association" (*Biographia Literaria,* chs. 13 and 14).

These distinctions seem admirably suited for considering the imaginative faculties of Charles Dickens. *Imagination* (a synthesizing power capable of fusing into a unity the "opposite or discordant," revealing itself through its ability to balance or reconcile sameness/difference, general/concrete, idea/image, individual/representative, new/old, emotion/order) is that faculty of the mind creating significance or meaning through its ability to fuse reports from its two sources of knowledge: the chaotic phenomena from the sense world outside, and the ordering concepts of the idea world inside. This imagination "invents" nothing: its images are limited to the multifarious but still finite "real" experiences of its owner. Its products have a coherent stability capable of unifying experience into a controlled interpretation of life: what in this study is referred to as Dickens's "mode of experience." *Fancy,* on the other hand, "no other than a mode of memory" that must "receive all its materials ready made from the law of association" yet ranges freely, unrestricted by bondage to Time and Space, which condition all experience in the "real" sense world. Fancy *invents* its images; its product, according to Herbert Read, is "fantasy," which is distinguished by objectivity and apparent arbitrariness, is notably expressed in the fairy tale, is primitive or at least innocent, dispenses with all logic and habit, and relies on the force of wonder alone. "Fancy and imagination," says Read, "are to be regarded as equal and opposite faculties, directly related to the general opposition of discursive and non-discursive thought" (*English Prose Style* [Boston: Beacon Press, 1963], ch. 9). The wonderful inventiveness of Dickens's fancy can easily conceal its complete dependence upon the controlling imagination that gives fantasy its tie with reality. The "apparent arbitrariness" of his fancy's products turns out upon analysis to be after all a "mode of memory," disguised as dream images mask their origins.

## CHAPTER II

1. For instance, "The Child's Story" (Christmas story for 1852), which is frankly an allegory, is structured in this analogy:

> Once upon a time a good many years ago, there was a traveller, and he set out upon a journey. It was a magic journey, and was to seem very long when he began it, and very short when he got half way through. . . . The whole journey was through a wood, only it had been open and green at first, like a wood in spring; and now began to be thick and dark, like a wood in summer. . . . And now the wood was yellow; and now brown; and the leaves, even of the forest trees, began to fall [etc.]. (CS)

2. To understand the role of these images in a totally conceived *Weltanschauung,* it might be instructive to note a common interpretation of the sea that Dickens avoids. The linear journey of life is never viewed as a sea voyage. People go off on sea journeys, to be sure, but most of these are literal. (Bella Rokesmith gives the idea a different figurative value when she explains to her husband that "'there is a ship upon the ocean'" bringing them a baby [*OMF,* bk. IV, ch. 5].)

It is further important to maintain a distinction between the literal and figurative uses of the river imagery, since people roam freely up and down the literal rivers flowing through Dickens's novels and stories. But in the figurative sense, people never go back up the river: the "everlastingly-green garden" not only seems but *is* "left for everlasting, unregainable, and far away." The point here is that Dickens's use of commonplace images and analogies is selective and purposeful, marking not the thoughtlessness of common use, but the usage of concretely formulated thought.

3. See also chapter VII, which follows this allegory into the story of Arthur Clennam in *Little Dorrit.*

4. The context here, as always, makes clear whether the literal or figurative imagery is applicable. For example, Mr. Guppy (see following discussion), while *literally* on the lower river, is *figuratively* on the upper river. Rogue Riderhood, on the other hand (see ch. III), while literally on the upper river is figuratively described in lower-river terms.

5. This "stream of life that will not stop" becomes in *A Tale of Two Cities* the footsteps of the downtrodden populace, which echo through its pages. Foreshadowed first on the quaint corner in London where Dr. Manette lived—"a wonderful place for echoes"—they trace the restless rebellion of the common people through its explosion in the bloody events of the Terror. Here in London, even the withdrawn corner of Dr. Manette "had begun to echo . . . resoundingly to the tread of coming feet. . . . Not only would the echoes die away, as though the steps had gone; but, echoes of other steps that never came would be heard in their stead" (*T2C,* bk. II, ch. 6). In France, the roadways are filled with a "myriad of small creatures," pedestrians all, who watch and wait and finally act. The last chapter of the novel relates the events of the day when "The Footsteps Die out for Ever." Twenty-three aristocratic heads are to roll on this day. In front of La Guillotine, a number of women "seated in chairs, as in a garden of public diversion," knit busily. (Cf. the spectators at Sikes's and Fagin's deaths.) As the heads fall, the women count. "The murmuring of many voices, the

upturning of many faces, the pressing of many footsteps in the outskirts of the crowd, so that it swells forward in a mass, like one great heave of water, all flashes away" (bk. III, ch. 15). It is now all over.

(With the single exception in chapter IV, I have included all references to *A Tale of Two Cities* in the notes rather than at the appropriate places in the text to emphasize the pervasive and encompassing presence of Dickens's mode of experience in this late "historical" novel.)

6. Some twelve years after writing this observation, I came across this corroborative piece of testimony from Dickens himself in a letter to G. H. Lewes, assigned the probable date of 9 June, 1838:

> With reference to that question of yours [unidentified] concerning Oliver Twist I scarcely know what answer I can give you. I suppose like most authors I look over what I write with exceeding pleasure and think (to use the words of the elder Mr. Weller) "in my innocence that it's all wery capital". I thought that passage a good one *when* I wrote it, certainly, and I felt it strongly (as I do almost every word I put on paper) *while* I wrote it, but how it came I can't tell. It came like all my other ideas, such as they are, ready made to the point of the pen—and down it went. Draw your own conclusion and hug the theory closely. (Madeline House and Graham Storey, *The Letters of Charles Dickens* [Cambridge, MA: Oxford Univ. Press, 1965], I, 403).

Why it came "ready made to the point of the pen" can be referred to his mode of experience.

7. The "Surrey side" of the river carries special significance apparently even in this early work. Later, its relationship to a recurring Dickens use of it is *presumably* accounted for in a journalistic piece called "Down with the Tide" (February 5, 1853), in which Dickens discusses the use of bridges by suicidal persons. The story's narrator, a young reporter, receives a full macabre report from the keeper of Waterloo Bridge—a bridge favored by the desperate. After several vivid anecdotes, the reporter asks the keeper "if there were a favorite side of his bridge for this dreadful purpose? He reflected, and thought yes, there was. He should say the Surrey side." Crossing to the Surrey side, then, carries added suggestion of violent death, usually self-inflicted.

8. "Coaches," in contrast, seem to represent incursions into the actual world. For instance, the members of the Pickwick Club travel by coach through their contemporary world.

Coaches figure even more prominently in *A Tale of Two Cities* as they carry travellers along the highways between London and Paris as well as to other destinations in the troubled period before the French Revolution. Along those same highways and byways travel the "carriages" of "their Greatnesses," the aristocracy. These carriages, in contrast, encapsulate their occupants against the reality of the pedestrians (cf. note 5) lining their path—the "myriads of small creatures" whose eyes follow the passage of the carriages whirling recklessly past them. Today, for example, the Marquis is conveyed swiftly along the road between Paris and his country château. He remains stonily indifferent to the child killed beneath the wheels of his carriage as it swoops around a street corner by a fountain around which peasants are gathered. Carelessly, he tosses a coin to the grieving father and reacts with cold anger when somebody sends it flying back into his carriage. Regarding the cowed group, he says smoothly: "I would ride over any of you very willingly and exterminate you from the earth" (*T2C*, bk. II, ch. 7).

The Marquis cannot foresee that the roads shared by travellers, pedestrians, and aristocracy—all intent on their own purposes—are the routes leading to the French Revolution. In this light, the name of the revolutionary figure known only as "a mender of roads" takes on heightened significance.

9. The implications of this indifference to time are developed in chapter IV.

10. David Copperfield has a related experience in recalling his youthful love for Dora (see ch. V). The initial impulse of the adult toward "contemptuous recollection" of the "lackadaisical young spooney" is succeeded by a deeper empathic look at himself.

11. Certain terms signifying this monotony are repeatedly encountered in descriptions of marshes: *weary, dreary, bleak, dismal,* and *melancholy* will be seen to interplay in many ways, both obvious and subtle.

12. A striking example of the non-discursive method in operation. By mentioning the *absence* of mounds, he brings them into the imaginative picture.

13. On another occasion, an interesting interchange between David and Steerforth reminds the reader of the deadly marsh monotony. Aunt Betsy has sent David to Yarmouth to think over what he wants to do with his life.

> "Why, she reminds me, Steerforth" said I, "that I came out on this expedition to look about me, and to think a little."
>
> "Which, of course, you have done?"
>
> "Indeed I can't say I have, particularly. To tell you the truth, I am afraid I had forgotten it."
>
> "Well! look about you now, and make up for the negligence," said Steerforth. "Look to the right, and you'll see a flat country, with a good deal of marsh in it; look to the left, and you'll see the same. Look to the front, and you'll find no difference; look to the rear, and there it is still."
>
> I laughed, and replied that I saw no suitable profession in the whole prospect, which was perhaps to be attributed to its flatness. (*DC*, ch. 23)

14. Note how Lizzie's shiver has been dissociated from her to become the depersonalized shudder attached to the general picture.

15. Similar fusions occur in two places in *A Tale of Two Cities*. Both relate to the story of the Marquis. On the evening of the day his carriage runs over the child (see note 8), it passes at sunset through the village near his château. Striking "brilliantly" into the travelling carriage, the setting sun

has "steeped [its occupant] in crimson." Glancing at his hands, the Marquis is unconcerned by their hue: "It will die out," he says, "directly." As the carriage slides down over the hill, sun and Marquis "go . . . down together" (*T2C*, bk. II, ch. 8).

The other fusion is more complex and subtle. In the village near the château, "pedestrian" figures at all times cluster around the fountain for necessary refreshment. As both punishment for the death of the Marquis and as a warning to the rebellious populace, his murderer has been hanged on a gallows raised for the occasion "forty feet high" beside the fountain—"and is left hanging, poisoning the water" (bk. II, ch. 15). Then, one black night, "the château began to make itself strangely visible by some light of its own. . . ." A flickering streak soars higher and higher. Stone faces, awakened, stare out of fire. "The mender of roads, and two hundred and fifty particular friends, stood with folded arms at the fountain, looking at the pillar of fire in the sky. 'It must be forty feet high,' said they, grimly; and never moved" (bk. II, ch. 23). One fancies that the red pillar of fire has stained the waters of the fountain into a torrent of blood.

16. These analogies relating the destruction of human beings to that of trees are the first of many references to the relationship to be found throughout this study. The whole complex analogy will be most fully developed in chapter VIII.

17. The death-related meanings of the "arched" bridge attach to other arched things. References to "arching trees," the arch of a cathedral, or the "arched thoroughfare" of the next quotation set vibrating the affective meanings of the lower-river configurations.

18. A comparable staining works as a leitmotif throughout *A Tale of Two Cities.* It is 1775. In the street before the wine shop of Monsieur Defarge in the Paris suburb of St. Antoine, a large cask of wine has been dropped and broken, spilling its red contents everywhere. Suddenly, scavengers appear, to kneel down, make scoops of their hands, dip in the puddles with little mugs or head kerchiefs, "while the wine game lasted." Then they are quickly gone, and fingers rake the area back into a gridiron pattern. But the stains are everywhere. The wine has stained the ground of the narrow street, has stained many faces and naked feet, and has stained the hands of the man who saws the wood. Now someone has "scrawled upon a wall with his finger dipped in muddy wine-lees—BLOOD. The time was to come, when that wine too would be spilled on the street-stones, and the stain of it would be red upon many there" (*T2C,* bk. I, ch. 5).

19. Although *showing* is by no means inherently superior to *telling,* when Dickens entrusts his meaning to the non-discursive imagery, to add a discursive explanation lessens its artistic effectiveness.

20. Why not a "light"? The substitution of the fire image deserves mention, for fire creates both light and heat. As the lighthouse promises safety, the fireplace promises a warm sanctuary against the threatening elements. Both promises are cruelly deceptive here.

21. And yet not so displaced either, since "coke" is the direct product of a long-ago marsh.

22. Cf. the view of Mr. Podsnap, who has a very froglike aspect: "the world got up at eight, shaved close at a quarter-past, breakfasted at nine, went to the City at ten, came home at half-past five, and dined at seven. Mr. Podsnap's notions of the Arts in their integrity might have been stated thus" (*OMF,* bk. I, ch. 11).

23. Could Eliot have had this passage in mind when he has Prufrock say: "I should have been a pair of ragged claws / Scuttling across the floors of silent seas"?

24. Dickens substitutes his own marsh word for Pope's less pointed "slow": "A needless Alexandrine ends the song / That, like a wounded snake, drags its slow length along" ("An Essay on Criticism," ll. 356–57).

25. Note the echoing variants on the "bleak place" that Pip uses to describe the marsh (*GE,* ch. 1).

26. Since Lincolnshire covers a territory at one time actually marshland, we are not permitted to forget that the Dedlock place is situated there, though no point is made of the same fact in reference to its neighbors.

27. The only reference to this subject I have been able to find appears as the postscript of a letter to Angela Burdett-Coutts, dated October 30, 1852 (#159 in Edgar Johnson, *The Heart of Charles Dickens,* New York: Duell, Sloan and Pearce, 1952): "I think of doing something about the Thames Police, and had some of the Toll takers at Waterloo Bridge at the office yesterday to put some questions to them about their experience of Suicide. Their answers were rather curious. Almost all the attempts are by women—a man quite a rarity." Although Johnson adds as a footnote: "Dickens does not seem to have written anything on this subject" it was, as a matter of fact, published on February 5, 1853, as "Down with the Tide." *If,* as I now suspect, the interview referred to was the main source of information for the article, the fortuitous adaptation of details to his mode of experience is readily accounted for: they were entirely products of his imagination rather than partly reports of observation.

## CHAPTER III

1. Magwitch, returning years later to make himself known to Pip, and mistaking as a failure of memory Pip's reluctance to recognize him, tries to jog the young man's recollection with a dumb play that would have required an uncanny knowledge of Pip's perceptions on this occasion of their first meeting. Pip writes:

> If the wind and the rain had driven away the intervening years, had scattered all the intervening objects, had swept up to the churchyard where we first stood face to face on such different levels, I could not have known my convict more distinctly than I knew him now, as he sat in the chair before the fire. No need to take a file from his pocket and show it to me; no need to take the

> handkerchief from his neck and twist it round his head; no need to hug himself with both his arms, and take a shivering turn across the room, looking back at me for recognition. I knew him before he gave me one of those aids. (*GE*, ch. 39)

Except for the file (experientially shared by them), Magwitch's choice of details reflects that this emblematic image cluster was indelibly printed in Dickens's imagination to help define the convict.

2. Such a person is the Marquis, who fittingly lives in a stony château.

> It was a heavy mass of building, that château of Monsieur the Marquis, with a large stone court-yard before it, and two stone sweeps of staircase meeting in a stone terrace before the principal door. A stony business altogether, with heavy stone balustrades, and stone urns, and stone flowers, and stone faces of men, and stone heads of lions, in all directions. As if the Gorgon's head had surveyed it, when it was finished, two centuries ago. (*T2C*, bk. I, ch. 9)

On the morning after the Marquis is murdered, unusual activity in the village seems to promise some unusual discovery. "What did all this portend?": "It portended that there was one stone face too many, up at the château. The Gorgon had surveyed the building again in the night, and had added the one stone face wanting; the stone face for which it had waited through about two hundred years" (bk. I, ch. 9).

Stony people are often recognized by their stony names: Murdstone, Headstone, Carstone, Jasper, Claypole.

3. Oliver needs a similar graphic instruction in order to follow an otherwise cryptic conversation with Charley Bates.

> "It's naughty, ain't it, Oliver?" inquired Charley Bates. "He'll come to be scragged, won't he?"
>
> "I don't know what that means," replied Oliver.
>
> "Something in this way, old feller," said Charley. As he said it, Master Bates caught up an end of his neckerchief and, holding it erect in the air, dropped his head on his shoulder and jerked a curious sound through his teeth, thereby indicating, by a lively pantomimic representation, that scragging and hanging were one and the same thing. (*OT*, ch. 18)

4. A shift to be encountered much more subtly in the later portrayal of John Jasper.

5. Mr. Flintwinch, of *Little Dorrit*, is similarly described. This crablike old man has a "neck so twisted, that the knotted ends of his white cravat usually dangled under one ear" to give his features "a swollen and suffused look. . . . Altogether he had a weird appearance of having hanged himself at one time or other, and of having gone about ever since, halter and all, exactly as some timely hand had cut him down" (*LD*, bk. I, ch. 3).

6. The comparison with Flintwinch continues. Arthur Clennam has arrived at his mother's house "to find the door open, and Mr. Flintwinch smoking a pipe on the steps. . . . The smoke came crookedly out of Mr. Flintwinch's mouth, as if it circulated through the whole of his wry figure and came back by his wry throat, before coming forth to mingle with the

smoke from the crooked chimneys and the mists from the crooked river" (*LD,* bk. II, ch. 23).

As Arthur regards him, "Mr. Flintwinch, regarding the opposite house over the gateway with his neck twisted and one eye shut up, stood smoking with a vicious expression upon him; more as if he were trying to bite off the stem of his pipe, than as if he were enjoying it."

7. Dickens's obvious awareness of the primal elements here draws attention to the conspicuous role they play in the primitive river and marsh allusions. The way in which these elements appear in combination is particularly noteworthy (i.e., fire visually mingling with water to suggest blood; air and water mixing for fog, rain, snow, hail; water and earth combining into mud; earth and air mingling in flying particles of dust).

8. Echo insists that there must be some relationship between this flight, Miss Flite, the flightiness of Richard, and Lady Dedlock's final flight.

9. It is interesting to note here once again how the associational nondiscursive method works. Although it speaks of "departed" monsters, what the passage actually does is *bring them in,* comparing them to passions most inappropriate for the context, since the departed monsters were predominantly cold-blooded. Their real effect is to suggest the marsh.

10. It should be noted that the people described as related to the marsh by monotony have already been environmentally associated with it (see ch. II). The Lincolnshire place, Daniel Quilp's counting-house, the Chancery Court, Coketown, and Cloisterham furnish the environmental backgrounds for each of these people respectively.

11. Dickens employs an effective device of punctuation here to enhance the feeling of undependable dream logic. A stricter logic would surely reverse the exclamation points and the question marks in these first four statements.

12. The full meaning of this allusion will not be clear until chapter V.

13. Late in the story, this association is made explicit. The haggard woman of the opium den, spying on John Jasper, is making inquiries about him. "'Has he a calling, good gentleman?' 'Calling? Yes. Sings in the choir.' 'In the spire?' 'Choir'" (*MED,* ch. 23).

14. This house interestingly fuses past, present, future to reinforce Durdles's timelessness: an antiquated house built of stones from a remote past, to be finished, if ever, at some vague future time.

15. Compare the sensitivity of Fagin's throat (et al.).

16. Earle Davis points out in *The Flint and the Flame* ([Columbia: Univ. of Missouri Press, 1963], pp. 191–96) that this practice of building a case to be destroyed with a surprise ending is one of the very few actual influences of Wilkie Collins on Dickens. Davis therefore also considers the strong possibility that Jasper would be proved innocent.

17. I suspect the passage means that Jasper suddenly realizes the triviality of "it," his desire for his nephew's death: a realization that will destroy the effectiveness of the opium dream.

18. Dickens's marsh creatures belong with other Victorian aborigines (the antitheses of the romantic noble savage). Compare especially Browning's Caliban.

## CHAPTER IV

1. Despite its corruption, the city is the center of human society, the place for the traveller to throw his lot in with "the common stock of people."

2. This idea is discussed in chapter VI.

3. In direct contrast, in *A Tale of Two Cities* a clue to Charles Darnay's true character is given on his first appearance in the prisoner's dock through his gentle relationship to plant growth. "He was quiet and attentive; watched the opening proceedings with a grave interest; and stood with his hands resting on the slab of wood before him, so composedly, that they had not displaced a leaf of the herbs with which it was strewn" (*T2C,* bk. II, ch. 2).

As he stands there, "some passing thought of the infamy and disgrace" for which this court has been reserved crosses his mind, "his face flushe[s], and his right hand pushe[s] the herbs away." Later in the proceedings, when Miss Manette is charged to look upon the prisoner:

> To be confronted with such pity, and such earnest youth and beauty, was far more trying to the accused than to be confronted with all the crowd. Standing, as it were, apart with her on the edge of his grave, not all the staring curiosity that looked on, could, for the moment, nerve him to remain quite still. His hurried right hand parcelled out the herbs before him into imaginary beds of flowers in a garden: and his efforts to control and steady his breathing shook the lips from which the colour rushed to his heart. (bk. II, ch. 3)

4. Compare the description of Mr. Lorry in *A Tale of Two Cities:* "Very orderly and methodical he looked, with a hand on each knee, and a loud watch ticking a sonorous sermon under his flapped waistcoat as though it pitted its gravity and longevity against the levity and evanescence of the brisk fire" (bk. I, ch. 4). He, too, is wearing Time as a man of precise and orderly control. But whereas Dombey's watch is "pitted against" that of Dr. Parker Peps in the ensuing discussion, Lorry's watch is in some kind of contest with the "brisk fire" that replaces "the feeble rays of the distant fire." The full meaning of the fire imagery will be examined in chapter VIII.

## CHAPTER V

1. Although Dickens almost invariably uses the masculine gender in his allegorical accounts, his interpretations are not as sexist as the practice might imply, but rather emphasize their probable self-reference. As will be demonstrated, girls as well as boys, women as well as men, suffer similar

effects from their experience in the childhood garden. For simplicity, Dickens's style is followed in this analysis in chs. V–VII, and in the summary in ch. IX.

2. Cf. the titles Dickens gives to the three "books" of *Hard Times*—"Sowing," "Reaping," and "Garnering"—in which he carries through the garden imagery.

3. Cf. Mrs. Clennam.

4. The Doll's house is Dickens's emblem for the remembered lost home described by Arthur Miller in his essay, "The Family in Modern Drama," (reprinted in *Modern Drama: Essays in Criticism,* Travis Bogard and Wm. Oliver, eds. [London, Oxford Univ. Press, 1965]). Compare Miller's description of the universal experience:

> It has been said often that the central theme of the modern repertoire is the alienation of man, but the idea usually halts at the social alienation—he cannot find a satisfying role in society. What I am suggesting . . . is that while this is true of our plays, the more or less hidden impulse antedating social alienation, the unsaid premise of the very idea of "satisfaction," is the memory of both playwright and audience of an enfolding family and of childhood. It is as though both playwright and audience believed that they had once had an identity, a *being,* somewhere in the past which in the present has lost its completeness, its definitiveness, so that the central force making for pathos in these large and thrusting plays is the paradox which Time bequeaths to us all: we cannot go home again, and the world we live in is an alien place. (pp. 223–24)

5. For the significance of the crocodile book, see discussion in chapter III.

6. This scenario works variously into the novels. See particularly the discussion of *Dombey and Son* in chapter VI.

7. It is now possible to make greater sense of some of the images in the opium dream of John Jasper (see ch. III).

8. Cf. the account of Clara Copperfield's death and its consequences for David in *David Copperfield,* chapter 9.

9. Dickens's preoccupation with betrayal of benefactors may account for his attachment to this old play. For another use of it, see *Great Expectations,* ch. 15: Pip's felt guilt here foreshadows his guilt over both Joe and Magwitch.

## CHAPTER VI

1. Cf. Paul Dombey, whose capacity of soul is indicated by his ability to see such quadrupeds even when they aren't literally pictured: "He was intimate with all the paperhanging in the house; saw things that no one else saw in the patterns; found out miniature tigers and lions running up the bed-room walls, and squinting faces leering in the squares and diamonds of the floor-cloth" (DS, ch. 12).

2. These stories of children surrounded by tyrannical giants must strike a sympathetic chord of truth for any child or for any imaginative adult who recalls literally living in such a world.

3. Note how, in his developed use of "forcing," "cultivating," and "spoiling," Dickens has restored to life the commonly used dead metaphors. "Spoiling" will receive treatment in chapter VII.

4. A singular example of giving reality to figures "existing" elsewhere on the time continuum. Where David remembers past figures, here a future figure exists.

5. It is difficult not to associate this emblem of Dickens with the Freudian concept of "fixation." Both are related to the fairy-tale condition of "enchantment": all natural processes are suspended until removal of the condition.

6. This road imagery figures prominently in *A Tale of Two Cities,* where it becomes a dominant motif.

7. For a complete discussion of the fire-fireplace configuration, see chapter VIII.

8. This horse symbolism also shines an amusing light on Mr. Pecksniff's deficiencies in *Martin Chuzzlewit.* In an early chapter, the reader is informed that Pecksniff

> kept a horse, in whom [his] enemies . . . pretended to detect a fanciful resemblance to his master . . . in his moral character, wherein, said they, he was full of promise, but of no performance. He was always, in a manner, going to go, and never going. When at his slowest rate of travelling, he would sometimes lift up his legs so high, and display such mighty action, that it was difficult to believe he was doing less than fourteen miles an hour; and he was for ever so perfectly satisfied with his own speed, and so little disconcerted by opportunities of comparing himself with the fastest trotters, that the illusion was the more difficult of resistance. He was a kind of animal who infused into the breasts of strangers a lively sense of hope, and possessed all those who knew him better with a grim despair. (*MC,* ch. 5)

Pecksniff, though innocent of any possible application to himself, seems to understand the horse symbolism. Inspired by a journey employing horse and carriage and by "a copious refreshment" from the brandy bottle, he philosophizes: "'What are we?' said Mr. Pecksniff, 'but coaches? Some of us are slow coaches . . . some of us are fast coaches. Our passions are the horses; and rampant animals too'" (*MC,* ch. 8). If one remembers the earlier analogy, the passions of Mr. Pecksniff are far from "rampant." (Cf. the similar treatment of Mrs. Skewton's passions.)

9. Cf. Plato's *Phaedrus,* 246A, translation by R. Hackforth, (New York: Library of Visual Arts, 1952).

> As to the soul's immortality then we have said enough, but as to its nature there is this that must be said: what manner of thing it is would be a long tale to tell, and most assuredly a god alone could tell it; but what it resembles, that a man

> might tell in briefer compass: let this therefore be our discourse. Let it be likened to the union of powers in a team of winged steeds and their winged charioteer. Now all the gods' steeds and all their charioteers are good and of good stock [or, variably with another translator, "wholly good"]; but with other beings it is not wholly so. With us men, in the first place, it is a pair of steeds that the charioteer controls; moreover one of them is noble and good, and of good stock, while the other has opposite character, and his stock is opposite. Hence the task of our charioteer is difficult and troublesome. (p. 69)

Hackforth's commentary on this myth as "the vision of a poet" is particularly pointed in relationship to Dickens also: "For the most part the myth is the vision of a poet whose images are not disguised doctrine but spring from a non-rational intuition: the reader must therefore allow his rational and critical faculty to be suspended as he reads, seeking to feel with the poet rather than 'understand' him and turn his poetry into prose" (p. 72).

10. Mr. Gradgrind on this occasion cannot believe Bitzer's conduct.

> "Bitzer," said Mr. Gradgrind, broken down, and miserably submissive to him, "have you a heart?"
>
> "The circulation, Sir," returned Bitzer, smiling at the oddity of the question, "couldn't be carried on without one. No man, Sir, acquainted with the facts established by Harvey relating to the circulation of the blood, can doubt that I have a heart."
>
> "Is it accessible," cried Mr. Gradgrind, "to any compassionate influence?"
>
> "It is accessible to Reason, Sir," returned the excellent young man, "And to nothing else." (*HT,* bk. III, ch. 8)

Reason has made it clear to Bitzer that he will be rewarded for returning Tom to Mr. Bounderby.

> "If this is solely a question of self-interest with you—" Mr. Gradgrind began.
>
> "I beg your pardon for interrupting you, Sir," returned Bitzer; "but I am sure you know that the whole social system is a question of self-interest. What you must always appeal to, is a person's self-interest. It's your only hold. We are so constituted. I was brought up in that catechism when I was very young, Sir, as you are aware." (bk. III, ch. 8)

Finally in desperation Gradgrind makes a last bid for Bitzer's sympathy:

> "Bitzer, I have but one chance left to soften you. You were many years at my school. If, in remembrance of the pains bestowed upon you there, you can persuade yourself in any degree to disregard your present interest and release my son, I entreat and pray you to give him the benefit of that remembrance."
>
> "I really wonder, Sir," rejoined the old pupil in an argumentative manner, "to find you taking a position so untenable. My schooling was paid for; it was a bargain; and when I came away, the bargain ended."
>
> It was a fundamental principle of the Gradgrind philosophy that everything was to be paid for. Nobody was ever on any account to give anybody anything, or render anybody help without purchase. Gratitude was to be abol-

ished, and the virtues springing from it were not to be. Every inch of the existence of mankind, from birth to death, was to be a bargain across a counter. And if we didn't get to Heaven that way, it was not a politico-economical place, and we had no business there.

"I don't deny," added Bitzer, "that my schooling was cheap. But that comes right, Sir. I was made in the cheapest market, and have to dispose of myself in the dearest." (bk. III, ch. 8)

## CHAPTER VII

1. Cf. the "big head" of the Hindoo baby in a bottle in Venus's specialty shop.

2. This cavalier view of space accompanies the cavalier view of time, as we have seen.

3. This is an interesting sentence. Since Skimpole is clearly endowed with both a strong will and an immense power of business detail (though not in the usual sense), the concealed meaning must be that he possesses them for other purposes than "to throw himself into objects"—quite the contrary. They enable him to will away the whole world of objects where the thought is empty without the fulfilling deed, and yet to enjoy at his ease the comforts and pleasures of the world.

4. Another Wordsworthian echo?

5. This quality of "attaching importance to things" is, as we have seen before, a sign of attachment to life. At the other extreme is not only the carelessness of Harold Skimpole or Mr. Chadband, but also the boredom and indifference of Lady Dedlock or James Harthouse.

6. Such undiscriminating agreeableness asks for Alceste's misanthropic comment: "The friend of mankind is no friend of mine."

7. A particularly ironic instance of the child used to evaluate the adult occurs in *Bleak House*, where Dickens uses his own words to pillory the unctuous Chadband. In the passage below, Chadband has grotesquely warped the innocence characteristic of childhood into the distinguishing characteristic of Jo, produced by him as a defense on all occasions: "I don't know nothink." On this occasion Chadband seizes upon Jo's protestation to deliver a typically high-sounding oration that heartlessly parodies the idea of the perpetual hope inspired by the innocent child in the idyllic garden:

> "My young friend," says Chadband, "you are to us a pearl, you are to us a diamond, you are to us a gem, you are to us a jewel. And why, my young friend?"
>
> "*I* don't know," replies Jo. "I don't know nothink."
>
> "My young friend," says Chadband, "it is because you know nothing that you are to us a gem and a jewel. For what are you, my young friend? Are you a beast of the field? No. A bird of the air? No. A fish of the sea or river? No. You are a human boy, my young friend. A human boy. O glorious to be a human boy! And why glorious, my young friend? Because you are capable of profiting

> by this discourse which I now deliver for your good, because you are not a stick, or a staff, or a stock, or a stone, or a post, or a pillar.
>
> O running stream of sparkling joy
> To be a soaring human boy!
>
> And do you cool yourself in that stream now, my young friend? No. Why do you not cool yourself in that stream now? Because you are in a state of darkness, because . . . (*BH,* ch. 19)

Chadband seems as oblivious to his societal responsibility for Jo's ignorant condition as is Jo himself.

8. It might be interesting to pursue this analogy in the tradition of the artist as an outlaw in society.

9. The combination of the child heart and the fierce exterior surely makes this a tag name.

10. This little parenthesis is important in helping to maintain the distinction Dickens wants made without undoing the character he has set up for Boythorn. It is necessary that this protector of children should unhesitatingly show that his defense is not merely verbal (which would have revealed him as no different from Skimpole, who considers the beneficent thought as good as the deed); but it is also necessary for character consistency that his extreme violence be shown, once more, as *mostly* verbal.

11. In *David Copperfield,* the Micawbers bear a family resemblance to Mrs. Pocket. Whatever the case to be made for Micawber as a fictionalized version of Dickens's father, it seems indubitable that he is David's father in aerial architecture. In fact, both Mr. and Mrs. Micawber live in an aura of great expectations. Mrs. Micawber can never quite get over the surprise that marriage to Mr. Micawber is not the realization of what she was led to expect for her future "when I lived at home with papa and mama." She bravely sets up the hopeful "Mrs. Micawber's Boarding Establishment for Young Ladies," to wait for young ladies who never come, and shares her husband's perennial expectation that something is just about to turn up. Surrounded by children who are "tumbling up," constantly in debt (despite his Polonian advice to David), Micawber is nonetheless, like Boythorn, redeemed by his child heart.

12. Iris Murdoch, in *A Severed Head,* fully exploits these humorous possibilities in the character of Martin Lynch-Gibbon.

13. Michael Kearns (see "Bibliographical Essay") describes the process by which a character must develop control of his own life by first wiping the slate clean through withdrawal into his "own tremendous region."

14. Cf. the utter simplicity of the view of the child David toward the letters of the alphabet. The "characters" have turned from friendly to sinister with the advance of the child from innocence to experience.

15. Although Dickens frequently permits at least a "limited-miracle" ending (as in *Hard Times*), in *Bleak House* there is none. Nemesis continues

its leveling process until all the castles have been utterly destroyed: not one builder of air castles survives into the aftermath.

16. This good and well-meaning man has encouraged his "Pet" to remain a dependent child. One suspects that other doll-like girls have resulted from a similar situation. Both Dora Spenlow and Flora Finching, for example, are only children of doting fathers. Bella Wilfer of *Our Mutual Friend* perhaps should have turned out the same way. As is true with other blighting, however, people with sufficient inner resources of strength and will can avoid its consequences.

17. An interesting tag name, combining the "flower" and the bird, which will later return in the "Finches of the Grove" related to Pip's suspension in air castles.

18. One recalls the Christmas allegory, "Nobody's Story," in which both a general anonymity and a specific individual are implied. When one also notes that "Nobody's Story" appeared less than two years before Dickens began work on *Little Dorrit,* and recalls that Dickens had originally planned a quite different name for his novel, the allegorical intent is even more emphasized.

In a letter to the Honorable Mrs. Richard Watson, Dickens wrote in 1855:

> Catherine tells me that you want to know the name of my new book. I cannot bear that you should know it from anyone but me. It will not be made public until the end of October: the title is:
>
> NOBODY'S FAULT
>
> Keep it as the apple of your eye—an expressive form of speech, though I have not the least idea of what it means." (*The Letters of Charles Dickens,* Mamie Dickins and Georgina Hogarth, eds. [New York: Charles Scribner's Sons, 1879], I, 471)

This proposed title vibrates with ambiguous meaning. Is it meant, either in fact or ironically, to absolve everyone from guilt for the conditions and situations in the novel? Does it suggest that what is "Nobody's Fault" can not pin guilt on anybody specifically because it is really "Everybody's Fault"? Or does it suggest a weakness, like a fault in a rock, which can damage a character? This last interpretation adds meaning to the "Nobody" chapters, which do indeed explore Arthur's weakness, and also could attach to Mr. Merdle's "complaint" as well as to the faults of other characters.

19. In *Our Mutual Friend,* this role is played by what would appear to be an unlikely character, Jenny Wren. Although Lizzie Hexam might seem more likely, when Eugene Wrayburn lies at death's door after his murderous attack, he understands that Jenny is the one person who understands him and will be able to guide him. He therefore asks that she come to his bedside. What Jenny understands is that, in his inability to make a commitment to Lizzie, he betrays an indolence and self-centeredness that relate him to James Harthouse and the doll-like figures like Harold

Skimpole who try to substitute play objects for life. She has refused to make him a doll, which he insisted was for his godchild, when a real woman is waiting for him. Now, with Jenny beside him, Eugene finds both strength and will to make the commitment needed to restore him to life.

20. As in the fairy tales where there is only one room into which one may not look, or only one thing which one may not do, or (even) one tree of which one may not eat. In each case, failure to meet the condition means losing a paradise predicated on innocence. In each case, the injunction is against knowledge.

## CHAPTER VIII

1. The speculation that perhaps the dead are surveying the living, or that the unconscious have thought processes barred from onlookers finds repeated expression. Cf., for instance, the rapt attention of spectators trying to assess where Rogue Riderhood *is* as he lies unconscious and near death (see ch. IV); or the effort by John Jasper to penetrate the thoughts of his fellows in the opium den (see ch. III).

2. One meaning of this word—dead men don't have memories—slides ambiguously into a second meaning: by now nobody remembers them.

3. Cf. the blowing dust from Egypt and the Far East of "Down With the Tide" (see ch. II).

4. In view of Dickens's repeated invocation of ghosts in haunted house and haunted man, it seems only reasonable that some people might mistake his attachment to them for belief in their existence. Mrs. Trollope, for instance, drew upon herself the following stiff and ungracious note in response to her invitation to him to attend an occult visitation:

> I was out of town on Sunday, or I should have answered your note immediately on its arrival. I cannot have the pleasure of seeing the famous "medium" to-night, for I have some theatricals at home. But I fear I shall not in any case be a good subject for the purpose, as I altogether want faith in the thing.
>
> I have not the least belief in the awful unseen world being available for evening parties at so much per night; and, although I should be ready to receive enlightenment from any source, I must say I have very little hope of it from the spirits who express themselves through mediums, as I have never yet observed them to talk anything but nonsense, of which (as Carlyle would say) there is probably enough in these days of ours, and in all days, among mere mortality. (Dickins and Hogarth, *Letters of Dickens,* I, 466)

5. *The Letters of Charles Dickens,* ed. Walter Dexter, II (London [Bloomsbury]: 1938), p. 360.

6. *Letters of Charles Dickens,* p. 527.

7. A still different variation on this theme is provided by Master Humphrey, who maintains a private dream world of air castles, but who simultaneously involves himself meaningfully in the actual world about him.

In the concluding section of *Master Humphrey's Clock* (weekly periodical, 1840–41), Master Humphrey describes the warm fireside at which he sits lovingly surrounded by imagined wife, children, and grandchildren until the clock strikes, and he returns to the actual world where "my chair is in its old spot, and I am alone. What if I be? What if this fireside be tenantless, save for the presence of one weak old man? . . . Let me thank Heaven that I can people my fireside with shadows such as these; with shadows of bright objects that exist in crowds about me; and let me say, "I am alone no more."

8. Paul Dombey, similarly, sees in the fireplace a "ghostly puppet-show" reflecting his own life (see chapter VI).

9. The parallels between this scene (foreshadowed by Gradgrind's unseeing "cavernous eyes") and Plato's Myth of the Soul seem too striking to be accidental. In the following translation note also the *puppets* and *puppet show,* which would make the myth especially appealing to Dickens.

> Next, said I, here is a parable to illustrate the degrees in which our nature may be enlightened or unenlightened. Imagine the condition of men living in a sort of cavernous chamber underground, with an entrance open to the light and a long passage all down the cave. Here they have been from childhood, chained by the leg and also by the neck, so that they cannot move and can see only what is in front of them, because the chains will not let them turn their heads. At some distance higher up is the light of a fire burning behind them; and between the prisoners and the fire is a track with a parapet built along it, like the screen at a puppet-show, which hides the performers while they show their puppets over the top. . . .
>
> Like ourselves . . . prisoners so confined would have seen nothing of themselves or of one another, except the shadows thrown by the fire-light on the wall of the Cave facing them, would they? . . .
>
> Now . . . suppose one of them set free and forced suddenly to stand up, turn his head, and walk with eyes lifted to the light; all these movements would be painful, and he would be too dazzled to make out the objects whose shadows he had been used to see. What do you think he would say, if someone told him that what he had formerly seen was meaningless illusion, but now, being somewhat nearer to reality and turned towards more real objects, he was getting a truer view? . . . Would he not be perplexed and believe the objects now shown him to be not so real as what he formerly saw? . . . And if he were forced to look at the fire-light itself, would not his eyes ache, so that he would try to escape and turn back to the things which he could see distinctly, convinced that they really were clearer than these other objects now being shown to him? (*The Republic of Plato,* Francis M. Cornford, trans. [London: Oxford Univ. Press, 1981], pp. 227–29)

Louisa and Tom would seem to represent the enlightened and the unenlightened views. The remainder of the Platonic myth is equally striking in its parallels with Dickens's belief, particularly in later references to virtue and knowledge.

10. Sleary's circus and the fireplace would naturally merge together in their implications for the living soul.

11. Sydney Carton in *A Tale of Two Cities* manifests striking parallels with Louisa Gradgrind, although at first he seems more to resemble James Harthouse.

During the English trial of Charles Darnay early in the novel, he is described as a "slovenly if not debauched" young man, "especially reckless in his demeanour" and with a "disreputable look." Nonetheless, he bears an amazing likeness to the prisoner, which Darnay's counsel, Mr. Stryver, uses effectively to confound a witness who has identified the prisoner. After the acquittal verdict, Darnay tries to thank Carton for his role in the successful outcome. "'I neither want any thanks, nor merit any,' was the careless rejoinder. 'It was nothing to do, in the first place; and I don't know why I did it, in the second'" (*T2C,* bk. II, ch. 4). He further declares, "'I care for no man on earth, and no man on earth cares for me.'"

This "idlest and most unpromising of men" works for Stryver. It soon appears that some of Stryver's best ideas are really his. "'You were very sound, Sydney, in the matter of those crown witnesses to-day,' Mr. Stryver observes. 'Every question told.'" Carton gives a "deprecatory grunt" by way of response. These two men have known each other since their school days. Stryver, "review[ing] him in the present and the past" says he is "'the old seesaw Sydney. Up one minute and down the next, now in spirits and now in despondency,'" his problem that "'your way is, and always was, a lame way. You summon no energy and purpose'" (bk, II, ch. 5). The narrator expands this assessment:

> Waste forces within him, and a desert all around, this man stood still on his way across a silent terrace, and saw for a moment, lying in the wilderness before him, a mirage of honourable ambition, self-denial, and perseverance. In the fair city of this vision, there were airy galleries from which the loves and graces looked upon him, gardens in which the fruits of life hung ripening, waters of Hope that sparkled in his sight. A moment, and it was gone. Climbing to a high chamber in a well of houses, he threw himself down in his clothes on a neglected bed, and its pillow was wet with wasted tears. (bk. II, ch. 5)

These complexities in Carton's nature foretell that he will eventually be "Recalled to Life" (bk. I) in the most significant sense, though, like Louisa, he will be unable to claim personal happiness.

Meanwhile, he is "moody and morose . . . the cloud of caring for nothing, which overshadowed him with such a fatal darkness, was very rarely pierced by the light within him" (bk. II, ch. 13). He has been singularly stirred by Lucie Manette, despite the "cloud" about him. Her sympathy leads him to an attempt at self-clarification. "'I am like one who died young,'" he explains. "'And yet I have had the weakness, and have still the weakness, to wish you to know with what a sudden mastery you kindled me, heap of ashes that I am, into fire—a fire, however, inseparable in its nature from myself, quickening nothing, lighting nothing, doing no service, idly burning away."

Carton's interactions with Lucie, Darnay, and their children develop his character. Originally, he describes Lucie as a "golden-haired doll." Soon, however, he comes to love her so devotedly that, as he tells her, "'there is a man who would give his life, to keep a life you love beside you!'" (bk. II, ch. 13). By the end of the story, Carton has effectively passed through the neoplatonic stages of love articulated by Peter Bembo and quoted in *The Renaissance in England* (Hyder E. Rollins and Herschel Baker, eds. [Boston: D. C. Heath and Co., 1954]): from the love of the particular to that love of the universal, which create the transcendent aura of the last pages when he is absorbed in the idea of the "Resurrection and the Life": "'I am the Resurrection and the Life, saith the Lord: he that believeth in me, though he were dead, yet shall he live: and whosoever liveth and believeth in me shall never die'" (bk, III, ch. 15). Lucie might, then, be viewed as the *anima* guiding him.

Carton develops similarly in his relationship to Darnay, from indifference, through ambivalence ("'Do you particularly like the man? . . . A good reason for taking to a man, that he shows you what you have fallen away from, and what you might have been! . . . Come on, and have it out in plain words! You hate the fellow'" [bk. II, ch. 4]), to such identification with his double that he becomes an alter ego. When, in the final scene, Carton changes clothing with Darnay and sends him back into the world to restore him to life in one sense, he is simultaneously "restored to life" by his sacrifice. Psychoanalytically, his "bad" self dies, and his "good" self is freed to live.

So far as his own life-in-time is concerned, its fulfillment is limited like Louisa's. Although Lucie was lost to him, "her children had a strange sympathy with him—an instinctive delicacy of pity for him. What fine hidden sensibilities are touched in such a case, no echoes tell; but it is so, and it was so here. Carton was the first stranger to whom little Lucie held out her chubby arms. . . . The little boy had spoken of him, almost at the last" (bk. II, ch. 21).

Carton's change from the man of indifference to the man of total commitment is emblematized by his altered view of the meaning of the fire in the fireplace. As he gazes at the fire now, he suddenly "lifted his foot to put back one of the little flaming logs, which was tumbling forward. . . . His indifference to fire was sufficiently remarkable to elicit a word of remonstrance from Mr. Lorry; his boot was still upon the hot embers of the flaming log, when it had broken under the weight of his foot. 'I forgot it,' he said" (bk. III, ch. 9). His indifference to the fire threatening him signifies the difference between a life "idly burning away" and one committed to burning for the light and warmth of others—a far cry from the life burning away into ashes "quickening nothing, lighting nothing."

12. A suggestion here of the undeviating monster to which he is related.

13. Note the distinction made here between the promise of persisting vitality in the "live-*coals*" and the reminder of death in the *wood* fire crumbling into ashes.

# *Bibliographical Essay*

Axton, William. *Circle of Fire* (Lexington, KY: University of Kentucky Press, 1966).

Axton discusses Dickens's uses of theatrical modes and traditions as going far beyond simple exploitation of dramatic forms and techniques. "Dickens argued," Axton writes, "that the conventions of the popular theater contain an inherent truth to life . . . obscured from the man in the street by his own dullness of vision, and that it was the function of the creative artist to revivify this vision by depicting the commonplace—as it really seemed to Dickens—in all the glowing color, light, movement, and surprise of the playhouse" (p. 8).

Axton's discussion, then, presents the devices of the theatre as (frequently hyperbolic) resources Dickens used for recharging language. Axton's defense of such devices extends readily beyond the "theatrical" to include the closely related "melodramatic," "sensational," and "sentimental"—all descriptive of action heightened and exaggerated by the imagination to make us see what has been dulled by familiarity.

This book reenforces my own arguments to the same effect, but from a different point of view.

Carey, John. *The Violent Effigy: A Study of Dickens's Imagination* (London: Faber and Faber, 1973). American edition: *Here Comes Dickens: The Imagination of a Novelist* (New York: Schocken Books, 1974).

Carey's book enlarges upon ideas that are underlying assumptions of my study: that Dickens's view of life is essentially comic, that the violent and the orderly aspects of his nature are equally and uncompromisingly real, that his spontaneous responses to experience are childlike in their honesty and in their lack of inhibition by conventional expectation (a consequent "literalism" is a crucial aspect of his humor)—and that all of these characteristics somehow define the special quality of his genius.

In the chapter on "Corpses and Effigies," Carey explores the relentless interest Dickens maintained in dead bodies and their accoutrements, as well as in their facsimiles in dolls, dummies, masks, and the like; his seeking out of mortuaries and waxworks; his repeated appearances at hangings and beheadings. I believe that our separate discussions significantly complement one another.

I find the chapter on "Dickens' Children" one of the most enlightening in the book for the illumination it throws on the contrast between Dickens's childlike and totally honest portrayals of experience and his moralizing distortions of it. Most of the chapter draws the sharp contrasts between his "model children, pious little monsters, moribund and adult"—dwarfs—and his very different fully imagined children who have not yet been civilized. Their responses to the realities around them are honestly complete without a moral or social censor telling them what would be the right or proper response. They therefore frequently appear heartless to well-trained adults. Because they are children, their perceptions and interpretations are still largely tied to sensory responses. What Carey says of Dickens's children can equally well be applied to Dickens himself.

Toward the end of the chapter, I believe that Carey takes a wrong turn when he says that "Dickens produces dwarfs because he stops remembering what it was like to be a child" (p. 146). Carey does not draw the most important conclusion immediately at hand. In the chapter on Dickens's humour, he argues that the humour *is* a child's humour. This chapter offers further convincing evidence that the "secret" of Dickens's imagery is not the "obsession" claimed by psychoanalysts, but rather the childlike nature of his imagination. He does not have to "remember" responses he made before he was civilized out of them: they are still his responses. He himself might be called a "natural" adult. This idea, in fact, makes more sense to me than anything else I have encountered on the subject.

Cockshut, A. O. J. *The Imagination of Charles Dickens* (New York: New York University Press, 1962).

Cockshut's book is included in this review largely because of the insistence of its title. Only peripherally can it be regarded as a study of the "imagination" of Charles Dickens. Although Cockshut discusses "symbols" and "myths," it is mainly as they attach to the external rather than the internal world. The "mythical" elements he explores belong to "the revolutionary and even the reforming Dickens." The source of the myth's abiding strength he finds, "not in Dickens's opinions, nor in the actual political tendencies which can be discerned in his books, but in his hypnotic power over the reader's imagination" (p. 55). Cockshut thus tends to suggest that the informing imagination belongs to the reader rather than to the author: that Dickens employs such things as fantasy, fancy, and melodrama to manipulate the imaginations of his readers for persuasive purposes, instead of writing into his novels the genuine products of his own imagination for purposes of expression or communication.

The final sentence in the book reiterates Cockshut's "performing" emphasis, and his overall failure to understand Dickens's imagination: "So, in the end, his lack of intellectual consistency, already castigated in these pages, and the neurotic instability of the man's feelings, hardly matter, because the vivid journalist, the entertainer and the artist are triumphantly at one" (p. 186).

Daleski, H. M. *Dickens and the Art of Analogy* (New York: Schocken Books, 1970).

The emphases and directions of Daleski's study are clearly set forth in the preface. Having selected texts that seem to him representative of stages in Dickens's development, he tries to show (taking his lead from Steven Marcus's observation [see p. 223] that Dickens has an "analogical imagination") "how our perception of the play of analogy in Dickens both directs us to the focus of a given work and makes manifest its structure" (p. 13). Daleski has been concerned to demonstrate both the increasing complexity of the cluster of ideas that is at the thematic centre of the novels, and the increasing comprehensiveness of vision that results from Dickens's more and more skillful use of analogy as a structural principle.

We are so far in agreement. Our paths diverge when he states that it also discloses "a traditional Dickens who is preeminently concerned with money and love" (p. 14). Appropriately, then, his discussion primarily explores analogies as devices rather than natural products of Dickens's imagination. The book is based on careful and detailed readings, which instructively parallel readings in this work, but they are based on different premises and lead to different conclusions except for a shared belief in Dickens's developing control of his analogies and art.

Ford, George H. "Dickens and the Voices of Time," in *Dickens Centennial Essays,* Ada Nisbet and Blake Nevius, eds. (Berkeley: University of California Press, 1971), pp. 46–66.

Ford's article extends my own limited discussion of time into the larger context the subject deserves. While restricting his discussion to Dickens, Ford begins his article with a helpful review of previous studies on the general question of the Victorian "senses of time."

Ford finds in Dickens and other major Victorian writers at least two of the attitudes accounting for the different voices we hear in their literature. The public Whig voice of Dickens is the future-oriented Victorian belief in evolutionary change and progress. The personal voice of Dickens, on the other hand, his "secret prose" invoking "the music of memory" (Graham Greene's terms) in anticipation of Proust, is a private, past-oriented vision. Accepting this simplification, "we can say that his prose moves between these two poles of public and private, each with its own wavelength" (p. 51).

Throughout much of his detailed development of these instructive observations, Ford tends in a direction I find troublesome. Critical approaches that are primarily biographically or historically grounded tend to blur the distinction between *a* period in the past and *the* past as a universal concept. This distinction I consider pivotal in evaluating Dickens's imagination. In his discussion of the conflict between past and future, for example, the specific historical context influences his judgment, which stops with the statement that "the conflict between past and future was never resolved" (p. 55). The larger view would perhaps include the further thought that it is of crucial importance for human development to maintain the uneasy tension between past and future rather than to seek a more comfortable resolution. Although Ford's conclusion can be interpreted to include the larger interpretation, much of the discussion seems to point in the other direction.

Franklin, Stephen L. "Dickens and Time: The Clock without Hands," *Dickens Studies Annual* 4(1975), pp. 1–35.

I have included Franklin's solid little essay as an interesting companion piece to Ford's entry reviewed above. Franklin takes issue with critics who find in Dickens's acceptance of time either a rejection of the past or a "vigorous Whig tone" (Ford), a "Macauleyesque cheerleading" equating with progress the changes taking place around him. His title is meant to suggest that "Dickens' undoubted fascination with clocks rests on what they record, the flow of time and the action of time on existence, rather than on any particular form of time, such as history of the past. . . . [T]o Dickens that the clock ticks on is of the utmost relevance, where its hands point means little" (p. 2). I totally agree.

Franklin also finds a "surprisingly strong resemblance" between Dickens's and Henri Bergson's views of free will and time. Both reject what Bergson describes as the spatialization of time, envisioning it as discrete blocks lying side by side. Bergson's *durée* is "the temporal continuum that Dickens signifies so often by the ticking of a clock or the chiming of a bell" (p. 3). But unlike Bergson, Dickens locates duration in the exterior universe rather than solely in the consciousness.

In his analysis of *The Old Curiosity Shop*, Franklin quite rightly challenges conventional views regarding Dickens's rejection of the historical past. But Dickens was not a champion of the historical present either. His "own attitude toward temporality simply precludes consideration of time in terms of periods or eras, except insofar as . . . linguistically convenient" (p. 9). To live in good acts and to die in peace of mind, he concludes, are the "Christian" lessons of time in the book.

The extended discussions of the various novels from Franklin's point of view are stimulating, instructive, and solidly based. And there can surely be no argument with his conclusion that "this clock without hands sums up Dickens' creative incorporation of time into his novels, and it expresses both the moral implications Dickens attributes to temporal attitudes and also the deliberate, intellectual affirmation of life that is Dickens' career-long response to the problems inherent in temporality" (p. 34).

He adds, however: "And if, as Dickens' many symbolic clocks suggest, duration is the mode of time in the exterior universe as well as in the human mind, then that duration—to which man is free to conform and which he must confront to function for the good—must be an expression of the consciousness of a greater mind, the mind of God" (p. 35). In this statement, Franklin has taken his own "leap of faith" to find in Dickens a "supernatural" Christian, a conclusion for which he has produced no real evidence. Dickens's affirmation of life, so far as I can see and so far as Franklin has presented evidence, simply does not warrant the larger conclusion.

Holloway, John. "Dickens and the Symbol," in *Dickens 1970*, Michael Slater, ed. (New York: Stein and Day, 1970), pp. 53–74.

Holloway's discussion accepts the definition of Dickens's language as "symbolic" in nature. Within this definition, the essay draws a number of important and valid conclusions I believe my own study supports. Reviewing preceding treatments of Dickens's symbolism, Holloway identifies "two main directions in which the symbolism has been explored" (p. 53), both of which rely upon the idea that Dickens "uses" symbolism in some way; this idea indicates that the critic "is beginning to think about him mechanically" (p. 56). In a great work of the imagination, Holloway says, this is not the right language. The power of the symbolic image "lies in what is mysterious, enigmatic and contradictory about it" (p. 57)—where it somehow escapes from the trite. This power cannot be explained away.

Holloway explains that previous symbol criticism tends toward an analytical, Benthamite model. In introducing his own predilection for a synthetic Hegelian view, Holloway points out that this view was available to Dickens through Carlyle's Teufelsdröckh ("In a Symbol there is concealment and yet revelation") (p. 58), as well as in statements by Coleridge (". . . by a Symbol I mean, not a metaphor or allegory or any other figure of speech or form of fancy, but an actual and essential part of that, the whole of which it represents"). The logic of this paradoxical structure "invites us to become aware of fuller significance in . . . revelation and concealment" (p. 59).

Holloway opposes any implication in his predecessors that by using symbols Dickens has provided a means of simplifying meanings; any suggestion that the "symbolic dimension of the novel in question . . . could be expressed merely by *an other and simpler version of the tale*." Dickens "seems almost at pains to invest whatever could look like a symbol with a dialectical, self-contradictory potentiality" (pp. 61, 63, emphasis Holloway's). Consequently, the "symbolic message (if message it can be called) is one only to behold, not to de-code" (p. 64).

Hornback, Bert G. *"Noah's Arkitecture" A Study of Dickens's Mythology* (Athens, OH: Ohio University Press, 1972).

Hornback proposes in this book to examine the inseparableness of imagination and society in the art of Charles Dickens, and to conduct an exploration of the vision of the world he creates from it, a vision both realistic and mythic. Dickens's "mythology" consists of his use of mythic symbols from Genesis. In later novels, the myth is directly realized in the story.

In Dickens's world of change, says Hornback, the opposing forces are growth in his characters and decay in civilization. Whereas in early novels, the "degeneration often overwhelms him, and he takes his characters away into their retreats to save them" (p. 5), later novels (though his vision of chaos/disorder is darker) exhibit more opportunity for changing things for the better by making the best of this world and making new beginnings in it.

Two of these mythic elements—Eden and the Flood—obviously relate directly to this study. In my judgment, Hornback's thesis leads him to too narrow a view of the materials he isolates for treatment and throws his conclusions askew.

Kearns, Michael S. "Associationism, the Heart, and the Life of the Mind in Dickens' Novels," *Dickens Studies Annual* XV (1986), pp. 111–44.

Kearns's article presents in a clear and cogent fashion how nineteenth century ideas of associationism can contribute to a better understanding of Dickens's character development and related themes.

David Copperfield is a paradigm showing how the *heart* can be strong to oppose the external forces, with a complex of associations leading to convictions and acts of will. While Dickens did not have the twentieth century concept of an "unconscious realm," he did acknowledge processes of the mind continuing without direct attentiveness. The life of David's associationally structured mind moves "toward a character determined by his heart rather than by chance impressions from the external world" (p. 124).

Kearns considers Dombey an excellent example of Dickens's "radical revision of association psychology" (p. 132), showing that while Dombey has "perverted his best nature and hardened his character" by the association principle, Dickens "holds [him as well as every other] individual fully accountable for how the principle is applied" (p. 135). The process through which he develops control of his own life involves first the necessity to wipe the slate clean. Kearns demonstrates that each of the characters surveyed must wander in his "own tremendous region" (p. 120) and then become a child again before this reformation can take place.

The dilemma of psychology at Dickens's time was "how to reconcile the data of psysiology with a dominant belief in an immaterial mind and the general commitment to the divine analogy" (p. 141), maintaining that a structural similarity between the mind and the external world disposed the former to replicate internally "all the works of God." Kearns concludes his essay with the argument that Dickens solved this problem very logically by showing that if the mind could have shapes impressed on it, it could also be returned to a state of smoothness. He presented a version of death and resurrection that did not rely on divine intervention but made use of what all human beings knew they possessed, because they could feel its urgings—the heart (p. 142).

Kligerman, Charles, M.D. "The Dream of Charles Dickens," *Journal of the American Psychoanalytic Association* 18 (1970), pp. 783–99.

I have included Kligerman's essay in this bibliography because I think it is strikingly revealing about Dickens's relationships with women and throws light on some of my discussions, particularly with regard to Arthur Clennam. It possesses the rare virtue of having been written by an M.D. for publication in a professional journal of psychoanalysis. It has the added virtue of careful analysis (until the last novels) relating Dickens's life to the literary text.

Kligerman defines as his subject Dickens's tendency to idealize a certain ethereal kind of young girl, along with the consequences of a series of narcissistic disappointments in relation to them. His specific purpose is to contribute to understanding two puzzling features of

Dickens's life: first, that "this supremely successful writer, a man of vitality, good will, virile charm" had such an unhappy love life and, secondly, that in later years he turned increasingly from writing to public dramatic readings "which he pursued in demonic, quasi-suicidal fashion that undoubtedly hastened his death" (pp. 783–84).

Kligerman's interpretation takes the reader through a fascinating retracing and associating of the various relationships with women in Dickens's childhood and youth to his conclusion that Dickens suffered from a "split maternal image" creating an ambivalence toward women that he never resolved. On the one hand was a repressed malignant image; on the other, an idealized image of the ethereal young girl.

At the end of his life, as Dickens "apparently began struggling with more aggressive tendencies and the liberation of less neutralized rage" he "worked fanatically as his feminine literary characters became progressively more hateful" (pp. 79–98). (In this statement, though, he is spectacularly wide of the mark.) But with some point he cites Dickens's affair with Ellen Ternan as evidence of his continued psychic distress.

Kligerman attributes the suicidal public performances only partly to the exhibitionist release they provided. The murder of Nancy (in *Oliver Twist*) as the last adaptation in his repertoire of dramatic readings reached into "a deeper, more primitively instinctual motive" (p. 798). When he died shortly thereafter of stroke, Kligerman concludes, "the author and his ideal were finally reunited . . . by symbolic murder and suicide."

McGowan, John P. "David Copperfield: The Trial of Realism," *Nineteenth Century Fiction* 34 (June, 1979), pp. 1–19.

This small study of *David Copperfield*, which considers language in the novel and its relationship to reality, has implications that enlarge into a commentary not only on David as a writer, but, in terms employed also in my study, on Dickens as well. The article argues a disillusionment with *realism* ("that literary mode which stresses language's ability to repeat or represent accurately in words the world of things" [p. 2]). *Fancy*, on the other hand, focusing on the difference between the world of objects and a linguistic world, emphasizes what *imagination* adds when it undertakes to describe the world "out there." As David's memory wrestles with the problem, the "power of the word" becomes evident.

Pointing out its relationship to the "talking cure" of Freud, McGowan says: "The word in art, in repetition, is magic: by merely talking about it the past can be changed, a change which must also influence the present" (p. 19). In writing of a past he had long repressed, Dickens examined this possibility. As his disillusionment with the "real" England grew, he relied increasingly on "fancy" as an escape from that England and as a possible means of changing it. In common with other criticism tying its conclusions to history, this article unfortunately tends to reduce "fancy" to its realistic implications.

McMaster, Juliet. "'Better to Be Silly': From Vision to Reality in *Barnaby Rudge*," *Dickens Studies Annual* 15 (1984), pp. 1–17.

In examining the authenticity of "visions" in *Barnaby Rudge*, McMaster comes to conclusions that reenforce my own on the transcendent reality of the dream world in a novel that perhaps I did not sufficiently consider. In this novel, she writes, "those visions that move on the edge of consciousness—dreams, fantasies, chimeras of the imagination—recurrently leap into the center of the action, and are confirmed as being more real than the rationality that rejects them" (p. 1). While several Dickens novels "expose the illusory nature of mental projections," in this novel, for the most part, the vision is validated. "Illusions recurrently turn real, dreams are prophetic, ghosts are substantiated into flesh and blood, and the wild fantasies of madmen are actually enacted. In the unleashed frenzy of the Gordon Riots we have an analogy for the release of the untamed forces of the unconscious" (p. 2).

McMaster believes that the supernatural—easily overlooked in a novel ordinarily considered historical—has a special place in its exploration of "the uneasy relation between the conscious and unconscious levels of the mind; and it reenforces the vision of the riots as a dreamlike emanation from the unconscious" (p. 10).

McMaster concludes that while "the pattern confirms that this is a novel about the eruption of the unconscious . . . the pattern also suggests that [it is] about the imagination, that shadowy everyman's land that lies between the conscious and unconscious regions of the mind. . . . The imagination, properly recognized, can mediate between the conscious and the unconscious, authority and impulse, the governing and the governed" (p. 16). This conclusion avoids the temptation to "psychoanalyze" Dickens himself, granting him instead the artist's power to convey the workings of the human mind.

———*Dickens the Designer* (London: The MacMillan Press Ltd., 1987).

McMaster here argues that, in "examining the relation between the outward and visible and the inward and spiritual" (p. 3), Dickens reveals a "painter's philosophy." All artists in considering their art must "ponder the relation between appearance and reality." While much great literature, particularly, is concerned with appearances that are illusory or deceptive, there is a sense in which Dickens's art is like the painter's in its declared faith in the invisible as the true. Like Browning's Fra Lippo Lippi, Dickens believes the "outward and visible world 'means intensely.'" Particularly in his creation of character, "there is a consonance between appearance and essence that pertains more usually in the visual than in the verbal arts. . . . He writes as a kind of semiotician, studying visible phenomena as signs—door-knockers as symbols for their owners; houses as signalling their occupants; faces, clothes, carriages, cabs all as telling a story about something else, some inner reality that is accessible only by this language of appearances" (pp. 3–4).

McMaster's book throws light on her declared subject: Dickens as "designer." It therefore has much to say on Dickens's methods and skill as a visual craftsman but quite appropriately does not concern itself with the internal imaginative processes.

I find some difficulty in accepting at face value a statement that Dickens had a "declared faith in the visible as true" comparable to that of Fra Lippo Lippi. The point is rather that Dickens *creates* appearances consistent with the reality, writes as if they are there, and asks a reader to believe in them as trustworthy. Despite Dickens's unquestioned fascination with physiognomy, I believe that his correspondences (like his ghosts) are a product of imagination rather than of his belief system. Indeed, do most artists share Fra Lippo Lippi's belief? Making the internal visual is their only medium of expression (cf. my review of Marten, below).

McWilliams, John R. "*Great Expectations*: The Beacon, the Gibbet, and the Ship," *Dickens Studies Annual* 2 (1972), pp. 255–66.

In this illuminating "small study," McWilliams points out first that recent critics have emphasized how, in Dickens's later novels, beneath the confusion and multiplicity Dickens encourages, the world is gradually reordered for the reader "according to lines of plot which reflect Dickens' conviction that all men are connected with and responsible to one another" (p. 255). McWilliams states his own purpose to argue that the novel's unity also depends upon Dickens's conscious use of a cluster of interrelated images that turn into symbols.

McWilliams's discussion develops the interpretation of beacon and gibbet by relating them to the "governing metaphor" for Pip's *Bildungsroman* as a ship journey. These three images haunt Pip's imagination. Because Pip describes his expectations, failures, and new understandings through these metaphors, the reader is constantly returned to the quality of the boy's imagination. Pip dreams in symbols taken from his experiences. When those experiences lead to greater insight, Pip has the sensitivity to alter the symbols without discarding them.

Although I do not agree with all of McWilliams's discussion, I believe his main points are well taken.

Marcus, Steven. *Dickens: From Pickwick to Dombey* (New York: Basic Books, 1965).

The sheer variety of things Marcus says he is trying to do in this widely quoted book ("relating these novels to each other, to the course of Dickens' life and thought, and to the culture to which they belong" [p. 9]) leads him finally to abandon his original plan to consider all of the novels and to limit discussion to the seven novels from *Pickwick* to *Dombey*. Unfortunately, rather than limiting the scope of his enquiries in order to develop his most provocative and penetrating general observations, he merely introduces what I would consider his intrinsically most significant topics and then dismisses them. Since the topics slighted are all relevant to my own study, I miss what further he might have said, for example, when he briefly comments that the "transcendence" Dickens achieves in "the miracle of *Pickwick Papers*," is "in large measure achieved unconsciously" (p. 18).

Even more buried and stimulating is a single sentence (also picked up in part by Daleski [see p. 215]) that Marcus simply drops into the middle of a very long paragraph: "This analogical imagination is preeminently Shakespearean; it is what G. Wilson Knight refers to when he describes Shakespeare's plays as 'expanded metaphors'" (p. 40). Once more, I find myself waiting for explanation that never appears.

In another instance, Marcus alludes to a topic which fired Dickens's imagination: how to account for the "'peculiar uneasiness' that wax dummies generally arouse" (p. 148). Its origin lies, Marcus says, paraphrasing Ortega Y Gasset's thought, in "the provoking ambiguity with which wax figures defeat any attempt at adopting a clear and consistent attitude toward them. . . . Looking at them we suddenly feel a misgiving: should it not be they who are looking at us? [cf. Carey on 'Corpses and Effigies.']" (p. 148). The habitual regard Dickens held for such creatures of imagination as though they were real people, Marcus says, has much to do with his singular, primitive powers as an artist, an idea he again does not develop.

Finally, in a discussion of "communication," Marcus finds it necessary to clarify what Dickens seemed to have in mind when he employed the term "my meaning" in explaining to his readers why he had decided to discontinue *Master Humphrey's Clock*. Dickens has in mind, Marcus states, "not some abstract moral or maxim, but a complex, enlarging state of consciousness which the novelist dramatizes or 'works out' in the course of the writing, a vision and interpretation of experience" (p. 171). This parenthesis seems to me worth more development than what purports to be his main topic.

"The Changing World" described in chapter eight I find to be the most satisfactory section of the book. His discussion of *Dombey and Son,* focusing on many of the scenes, images, and themes important to my own investigations, goes along lines that interestingly complement my findings, while the total discussion goes to different but not conflicting conclusions.

Marten, Harry P. "The Visual Imaginations of Dickens and Hogarth: Structure and Scene," *Studies in the Novel* 6 (1974), pp. 145–64.

Marten's analyses of the imaginative similarities between Hogarth and Dickens are strikingly identified and persuasively developed in this engrossing article. He argues that comprehension of Dickens's "artistic indebtedness" to William Hogarth provides one way to "recognize the aesthetic framework" for his multitudinous fictional bases: "In matters of total formal construction and treatment of scenic detail especially, the grotesque visual artistry of Hogarth will help us come to grips with the work of the novelist who so much admired it" (p. 145).

Acknowledging the obvious similarities between Hogarth and Dickens, he moves on quickly to what he considers of "greater interest and importance": "the Hogarth-Dickens correlation in matters relating to the creative imagination" (p. 149). The middle of the article is thus of special relevance to the matters explored in my book.

Responding to earlier critical comments by Ford and Monod indicating that Dickens was a "spatial" rather than a "temporal" writer, he points out (as I would) that their remarks must be qualified. Although we respond to most visual art spatially and to most fiction temporally, the work of both Hogarth and Dickens requires us consciously to respond both spatially and temporally, the "impact of the scenes com[ing] most immediately from the relations among the elements within them (scenic details, characters) and then gradually from the relation to the whole" (p. 150).

Specific discussion of "scenes" from both artists is based on Hogarth's own description of his artistic intentions as "intricacy of form," defined as "that peculiarity in the lines, which compose it, that *leads the eye a wanton kind of chace*" (as quoted on p. 151, emphasis Hogarth's). This "chace," says Marten, is a "visual adventure and tremendous fun," in which "nothing stands still. We focus on a multitude of detail, all of it interesting. The eye stops and moves, stops, turns and begins again taking in the tremendous variety of life in the scene" (p. 151). The ensuing discussion is an illuminating lesson in how the "speculation of the artist" moves from particular to particular gathering meaning as it goes.

The remainder of the article examines what Marten calls the "Hogarthian-Dickensian grotesque." In the prints and novels, our familiar world, though rooted in verifiable fact, is "abruptly turned askew. This confusion of the everyday is menacing" (p. 158). At the same time, "straight" details in the scene manage to preserve a precarious balance. Both artists (with some failures) "get the effect of terror and also . . . achieve the comic."

While a number of statements in the article seem to imply—no doubt rightly so—the influence of Hogarth on Dickens, much of the weight of the article points to a natural relationship embedded in their respective natures, which would have drawn Hogarth to Dickens as much as it drew Dickens to him.

Miller, J. Hillis. *Charles Dickens: The World of His Novels* (Cambridge, MA: Harvard University Press, 1958).

This is the first and continues to be one of the best of the comprehensive imagination studies. When, in the mid-1960s, I conducted the original investigation that led to *The Imagined World,* I carefully postponed reading far into Miller's book until my own analyses were secure. I sensed at once the degree to which our thinking was going along parallel lines, and did not want my own perceptions and observations to be swayed by his in any way. In retrospect, I believe that this was a sound decision. As a result, although our separate studies frequently meet and proceed together for a while, they soon part to go in different directions.

Miller's general statements in the introduction are in almost complete harmony with my own opinions. I can take little exception to his statement that "taken all together, all the unit passages form the imaginative universe of the writer. . . . His style is his own way of living in the world given a verbal form. So in literature every landscape is an interior landscape, just as each imaginary man or woman is also a figure in the writer's own private world of perception or memory, longing or fear" (pp. ix–x).

Miller explains that what he means by the "world" of Dickens's novels is the totality of all things as they are lived in by all human beings collectively. For Dickens, its totality is embodied in the great modern commercial city. But how could he reach the real city? Since all of its millions of inhabitants interpret their world in terms of their own fears, fancies, and opinions, any single point of view is both partial and distorted. Dickens's solution is to seek the truth by giving "an exhaustive survey of the surface itself," and "when enough of the isolated parts are described, and their relations discovered, the truth behind each, it may be, will be liberated—a truth at once particular and universal" (p. xvi). Miller thus relates Dickens's method most interestingly to Browning's attempt to tease out the truth in *The Ring and the Book.*

In a general way I find Miller's summaries and conclusions persuasive and agreeable. The idea that each protagonist begins in isolation, moves through successive adventures, essentially attempts to understand the world and integrate himself in it, and thus finds his real self appears unarguable. So is his observation that the frustrated search for a transcendent spiritual power undergirding human values ends in an existential affirmation, though I see little evidence of "the frustrated search" itself.

More specific judgments and conclusions invite argument or a call for clarification. When he says that "the death of Nell near the graveyard of a country church reflects back on Oliver's retreat to a happy rural paradise and suggests that it was an evasion of Dickens's problem, not a real solution" (p. 330), Miller seems to say that Dickens should have sought the latter—yet surely the real point is that the problem itself is insoluble except in a person's/character's belief system.

Most importantly, I find it difficult to accept as real the "changes" Miller finds in the last novels. If the idea that "the transcendent spiritual power glimpsed at the margins or in the depths of the material world is not really a positive support for human values" (p. 333) is a new one, some evidence of a contradictory earlier view must be forthcoming. This evidence I do not believe exists, except perhaps in Dickens's apparent belief in a kind of retributive justice, a belief he still exhibited in the last novels.

Neither can I accept the flat statement that Dickens rejected the past. The discussion in which the statement is imbedded misses what is to me the crucial step of absorbing the past into memory as a part of the process of self-identification.

Newsom, Robert. *Dickens on the Romantic Side of Familiar Things: "Bleak House" and the Novel Tradition* (New York: Columbia University Press, 1977).

In this study Newsom gives fresh insights into the dualistic nature of Dickens's vision of reality by picking up his own expression, "the romantic side of familiar things" from the preface to *Bleak House.* His thesis is that, properly understood, "the phrase explains with extraordinary precision the central imaginative principle of Dickens' art" (p. 2). That is, rather than merge the romantic and familiar into some new synthesis, he sought to keep each intensely alive: "a *mixture* of fact and fancy," both of which must be maintained with their own identity.

Two chapters in particular explore matters of moment to discussions in my book. In chapter two, "*Bleak House,* I, Suspended Animation," Newsom develops the methods by which Dickens succeeds in creating in *Bleak House* a world of mysterious relationships, a world in which "what we have come to think of as the 'familiar' suddenly ceases to be so, and strikes us instead as something the very opposite . . . the 'romantic' [the converse likewise being true]" (p. 18). How does he achieve this? Newsom points to a "chaotic circularity," which returns the reader again and again to a point that seems to promise an action not yet begun. "Reading the opening chapter is like watching the workings of a complex machine when all the gears have been disengaged, but continue to turn under their own momentum" (p. 25) in a state of suspended animation.

In chapter three, "*Bleak House,* II, The Uncanny," Newsom pursues these ideas through discussion of the constant tension between romantic/familiar, eternal/topical, and dreaming/waking created by "the experience of imperfect, circular, and involuntary repetition we know as *deja vu*" (p. 50). This sense of *deja vu* is achieved for the reader in the double perspective provided by the double narration.

In the second section of chapter three, Newsom reviews Freud's essay on "The Uncanny." I found particularly rewarding his account of "the resonance between Dickens' techniques for evoking feelings of uncanniness and Freud's description of the conditions giving rise to and the particular dynamics of the uncanny" (p. 65). He quotes Freud's comments on the uncanny in literature, which Freud thought provides "a much more fertile province than the uncanny in real life." Newsom points out that the tension between two quite different frames of reference, the "commonsensical and rationalistic view of scientific scepticism on the one hand, and the primitive belief in the supernatural on the other, is quite precisely one of the things Dickens has suggested by dwelling on 'the romantic side of familiar things'" (p. 66).

The quality of double perspective is accounted for in psychoanalytic theory by the dramatic cooperation between the conscious, preconscious, and unconscious. This cooperation is a prominent feature of hypnosis, hypnagogic states between sleeping/waking, and neuroses. It is also related to phenomena involving movements into altered states of consciousness followed by amnesia for these altered states (for all of which Dickens had a lifelong interest).

Romano, John. *Dickens and Reality* (New York: Columbia University Press, 1978).

Romano sets the stage for his discussion of Dickens's realism (which he hopes will generalize into a discussion of realism itself) in an introductory chapter with a well-chosen title furnished by Flora Finching:

"The Horizon of *et cetera*." He finds clearly inadequate a definition of realism as representational. Using *Our Mutual Friend* as his illustrative novel, Romano points out that, in contrast to Tolstoy's *War and Peace*, Dickens's novel makes no effort to conform to our "real" world. Its details reconcile primarily only to each other "cohering at last in a significant whole but responsible along the way to no expectations derived from experience outside the text" (p. 3). While thus agreeing with the Formalists, Romano argues that the notion of realist form has recognizable and important implications beyond the formal, in particular for themes and character. A realist such as Tolstoy or Dickens "resents the unreality of the conventions of artistic presentation, such as the posture, the limitation at the edge of the canvas, and the alien frame" (p. 7). In his frustration at trying to get at "the world that lies beyond the farthest border of his power to portray," he seeks a way to explode the forms of his novel to admit this outside world of reality.

Taking issue with the views of such Formalists as René Wellek and Austin Warren that in a successful work of art "materials are completely assimilated into the form" (p. 13), and that only the cohering formal whole is capable of correspondence to the real world, Romano argues further that it is exactly at the points where the novelist momentarily succeeds in destroying the closed form of his novel that his work touches the reality of the world outside and thus, in the most significant sense, becomes most "realistic."

I particularly respond to Romano's example of Charley Hexam's unexpected disruption of the Veneering's formal dinner-party world. His detailed discussion of its "mirrored" surface, as opposed to the "depths" represented by Charley, parallels and complements my own discussion of the novel.

Romano weaves many considerations into his analysis and pursues the implications of his argument into many specific and detailed aspects of form and its disintegration by the momentary intrusion of the "formlessness and sprawl of reality" (p. 46). Dependence on the real world is the first fact of realism, as opposed to the autonomous notion of "pure form," which asserts its radical independence. Bradley Headstone (as well as a host of other characters) tries to reduce his life to ordered forms, only to be "exploded" by the "lurking, primordial" dimensions of existence. Romano calls Dickens an "artist of language in love with his medium, whose use of words protests against the limitations imposed upon them in the service of representational form" (p. 106).

Deriving his terms from Roman Jakobson, Romano considers Dickens's extensive use of metonomy as opposed to metaphor (which is primary in the literary schools of romanticism and symbolism) to be an indication of his "realistic" trend. This metonomy (the "substitution of proximate things") maintains an openness, relating its world to the real world by an "imperfect closure . . . a certain area of experience actually located on the world's horizon" (p. 114). Form is fragmentary rather than whole. Life's reality, for Dickens, is "a contradictoriness that is not equipoise but schism, not harmony but a jangling discordance, as of bells" (p. 116). Both a novel and a person are shaped by "the other"—by what they exclude, by what they are not. What the individual owes to others, what the work of imagination owes to the world, is nothing less than its life.

Stewart, Garrett. *Dickens and the Trials of Imagination* (Cambridge, MA: Harvard University Press, 1974).

Stewart's lively and generally persuasive stylistic study of Dickens's imagination is itself charged with the wit and verbal skill about which he writes. The book could not have happened otherwise. The sharp and detailed analyses in this densely packed book are irreducible: properly, it must be read rather than summarized (as should many of the studies reviewed here).

Stewart calls Dickens the "great writer of modern industrial society," his prose increasingly a response to the London industrial metropolis. "Countering the pull of urban anonymity, the quirks and assertions of its own verbal personality were there constantly to remind us that identity might still vibrantly hold its ground" (p. 225). Dickens's characters struggle to "regain . . . the acute beauties of wit and style from which they have been disinherited" (p. 224). Although he thus relates Dickens's prose to his contemporary world, Stewart does not make the mistake of accounting for it historically. Rather, he considers that it is Dickens's unique gift to show us how the verbal imagination enables any one to retain a center of personal freedom in the midst of an impersonal but imprisoning outer world. "With a furious and persuasive invention unequalled in our fiction," Stewart writes, "Dickens's effortless way with words becomes an access back to their source, an exploratory 'way' into the poetic impulse itself from which language springs." Our views of the essential function of Dickens's language as crystallized in the quoted sentence are so harmonious that I find most of his book singularly relevant to my own interpretations.

Among the profusion of Dickens characters Stewart finds many representations of both true and false artists of the figurative imagination. For the true artists (such as Sam Weller, Dick Swiveller, or Jenny Wren) the imaginative fancy creates inspiriting language fictions in which to believe. Their creations are visionary. The false artists, in contrast, merely "pretend" to believe their fictions for personal aggrandizement.

Stewart carefully "diagnoses" the problems, the "trials" of imagination, that confront Dickens's characters. In *Pickwick,* imagination "quarantined" itself against, specifically, the false public rhetoric of the outside world (Sam Weller entering the novel as the life-bringing force of the true artist of the imagination). "Yet in one of Dickens's novels after another it is the naughtiness of language—its impurities both ethical and esthetic; its moral and metaphorical lapses, confusions, indelicacies, excuses—which is dragged before us in comic review" (p. 114).

After Dick Swiveller, Stewart notes that the characters fall silent (Mark Tapley and, very much later, Jenny Wren are the only exceptions in their revitalization of language). Verbal wit has forsaken them and imagination must go underground in the "romantic" withdrawals of escape artists, both true and false pastoralists. Verbal wit is never for long, however, denied to the narrative voice.

In his chapter on "Escape Artists," Stewart concludes that Dickens's novels show us that the irrational impulse alone can ransom us away from a world that makes neither rational nor poetic sense, a reality of neither rhyme nor reason. They show fancy to be our only deliverance, yet they know too that "the poetry of existence" can be a destructive sham, not honest relief but a mere subterfuge.

My only quarrels with Stewart are based on his view that Dickens totally controlled his novels from the beginning and on his practice of extrapolating on occasion too far for credibility. In *Pickwick Papers* especially I think the novel can be more accurately accounted for as the spontaneous creation of a young genius yet learning to control his craft and working his fiction out of a number of difficulties by his imaginative resourcefulness. The novel therefore changed and grew as he wrote it, rather than having been thought out in all its complexities in advance. Both Pickwick *and* Dickens, I believe, learned a good deal during the course of the story. On the second point, I have already commented on the extended life he provides for Little Nell as unwarranted, though most interesting (see Introduction). All in all, however, in my opinion this is the best and most comprehensive of the stylistic studies.

Stoehr, Taylor. *Dickens: The Dreamer's Stance* (Ithaca, NY: Cornell University Press, 1965).

The first four chapters of Stoehr's book are particularly interesting in relationship to this study. His exploration of the dream elements in Dickens's fiction provides highly relevant theoretical background for many of my discussions.

The first three chapters consider "The Style," "The Vision of Reality," and "The Analogy to Dream." "The Style," as Stoehr convincingly presents it through analysis of the St. Antoine "Hunger" passage in *A Tale of Two Cities,* acquires its characteristic flavor from its use of detail as an active ingredient in setting and plot and from its use of rhetorical devices such as anaphora and metonomy (both interpreted broadly) to order and connect these details. As apparently needless and accidental details weave into a "whole narrative . . . webbed with . . . interconnections" (p. 9), they lead to a denouement of discovery that the apparently disconnected elements are in fact related and even form a logical sequence. Stoehr argues that Dickens's whole procedure (true for the passage analyzed, certainly) may be described as metonymical. The way he catches a moment isolated in time and space exactly identifies his graphic realism of detail. Similarly, the articulation, juxtaposition, superimposition of such details give, by the combination of order and disjunction, the strangely unreal effect we also associate with Dickens: "the sense of a world all in pieces, where every fragment is nonetheless intimately and mysteriously involved with every other fragment" (p. 19). Metonomies of character and plot become "montage-clusters," any part of which, as Kenneth Burke has explained, "may do synecdochic duty for the whole" (p. 20). Stoehr summarizes Dickens's stylistic blend as "dream-like, hallucinatory, superreal" (pp. 32–33).

Chapter two, "The Vision of Reality," gets into "one of the most tangled questions in contemporary criticism" (p. 34), that of mimesis, tracing the movement from style to manner. Critics must first ascertain the way in which any novelist relates the particular fictive world to facts. Theoretically, verisimilitude may appeal to a reader's *judgment* that fiction and life correspond, or to his *impression* of lifelikeness. The first may be called natural; the second artificial. Stoehr locates Dickens's vision between them. He attains a "very high degree of natural verisimilitude," but the devices he uses "although sometimes conducive to artificial verisimilitude are often destructive of it" (p. 41).

A carefully detailed and highly relevant discussion of "The Role of the Narrator" concludes the chapter. Dickens's "negative capability" enables him to project himself into every character to such a degree that he cannot be identified with any of them. This is true even with first-person narrators. As the narrator identifies himself with everything, he himself disappears: he *becomes* the narrative, a natural corollary of allowing the scene to stand alone and to provide its own interpretation. The kinds of choices Dickens makes and the order he imposes on them contribute to the illusion of a story telling itself. Here Stoehr's discussion is particularly complementary to that in other studies. He concludes the chapter by observing that while Dickens's metonymic style particularly creates the impression of the story writing itself, and leads to a judgment of natural verisimilitude, his metaphors do likewise by seeming to have been stumbled upon rather than searched out by an authorial intelligence. The result is a "mythic" reality, with the weirdly hallucinatory effect of dream.

In chapter three, "The Analogy to Dream," Stoehr relates the various features of Dickens's vision to Freudian dream theory (thus pointing out the similarities between poetic work and dream work). Dickens's stylistic devices, in simultaneously concealing and revealing his explosive subject matter, parallel Freud's theory that the elements of dream work both hide and display the dream content. The chapter develops various perspectives related to the analogy.

"The Novel as Dream" shifts from theoretical to practical as Stoehr analyzes the "Dark Novels" of Dickens's later years. He acknowledges at the outset that he will often speak of Dickens "as a psychotherapist might speak of a patient whose dreams he is analyzing" (p. 93). But he insists that the point of this discussion is not to understand Dickens, but his novels—the end not his health, but our pleasure. The distinction, I think, becomes murky. Also, along the way, the connection between the discussion and dream is not clear to me. Nonetheless, the psychoanalytic interweaving of biographical and social influences into Dickens's "nucleus of pain" is interesting in itself. Stoehr further acknowledges that "much of the foregoing discussion might very well have been undertaken without any reference to dreams and the dream manner" (p. 135). But he insists (with some point!) that psychoanalytic interpretation furnishes understandings impossible with ordinary methods of stylistic analysis. He resists calling Dickens an allegorist, and reenforces the idea that his novels "are not mere codes to be deciphered." Each novel must, like dreams, be attended and responded to fully, to be absorbed, rather than to be added up into meanings.

Stone, Harry. *Dickens and the Invisible World: Fairy Tales, Fantasy, and Novel Making* (Bloomington, IN: Indiana University Press, 1979; London: MacMillan, 1980).

In this book, Stone has attacked matters associated with the experiential sources of Dickens's "fabling mind," which I tried to avoid as irrelevant to what I was doing. I therefore have found it a valuable complementary study.

For me, the highlight of the book is chapter three, "Dickens' Fabling Mind: 'A Mist of Fancy over Well-Remembered Facts.'" In this chapter he constructs plausible and probable origins for the fabling mind in the people and experiences of Dickens's childhood. Stone believes that this mind arrived at its final form with Dickens's experiences in the blacking warehouse. He registers his own uneasiness, however, at what may seem "a bald and reductive way of summarizing something that was infinitely more mysterious and complex" (p. 69). Nonetheless, he concludes that by the time Dickens left the blacking warehouse the essential habit of his creativity had been formed. At the center of that habit was the fanciful transformation of life that was not simply a by-product of his creativity but indistinguishable from it.

I must share Stone's own misgiving that the very nature of his investigation frequently results in discussion that tends to reduce his subject to what can be explained and accounted for. His conclusion at the end of the book, however, is unarguable:

> Dickens' universality, like his motifs and techniques, is . . . connected to his commitment to fairy tales. For that commitment helped him tap the same deep reservoir of wishes and urges that fairy stories tap, a reservoir fed by man's immemorial responses to life. Fairy tales, like myths, legends, fables, fantasies, and other correlatives of the invisible world—correlatives that overlap and reflect one another—survive because they embody deep and profoundly attractive or frightening human hopes and fears. At the same time, fairy stories also embody a sense of life's mystery and wonder, a refraction of life's strangeness and wildness; they testify to the weird signatures and correspondences, the enigmatic forces that lie buried deep in the hidden heart of things. (p. 338)

As with Steven Marcus's work, reviewed earlier, I wish that Stone had found a different way to limit his book: namely, that he had decided upon a comprehensive look throughout the novels at "Nursery Tales" alone. I also think that a most crucial aspect of Dickens and fairy tales remains unexplored in his book. Although the progression from fact to fancy is extensively traced, Dickens's deep belief in the need to reverse the process from fancy back to fact again receives no attention; yet final reconciliation between them is essential to complete the story. (This last criticism is probably what Robert Newsom had in mind when he noted the lack of attention to the "critique of fantasy [or fancy] implicit in much of Dickens [and notably in *Great Expectations*]" [DSA, 9, 1981, p. 270].)

These criticisms should not obscure the fact that within the discussion are many illuminating references and insights pertaining to Dickens's imagination that make Stone's book a stimulating and valuable resource. To choose one of these, I am specifically indebted to him for referring me to Dickens's essay entitled "When We Stopped Growing." His conclusions from reading this essay reenforce my own beliefs from other evidence. Stone states that "certain powerful impressions of his childhood fixed themselves indelibly in his mind; his growth, insofar as such impressions are concerned, stopped at the moment of encounter. Throughout the novels, one catches a glimpse of how fixed yet imaginatively free [an] image was when one meets the same detail in a totally transformed context" (p. 40).

Vogel, Jane. *Allegory in Dickens* (Tuscaloosa, AL: University of Alabama Press, 1977).

The title of Vogel's study urges its inclusion in this bibliography. It is an engrossing, extremely clever and ingeniously argued book difficult to evaluate. At one extreme it proceeds on assumptions, goes along a path, and draws conclusions that nobody would or could argue with. At the other extreme, it makes leaps of inference that seem so speculative and so improbable that they are difficult to credit. The very ingenuity of argument by which a circuitous route leads to a triumphant conclusion puts strains on credulity. In between, Vogel piles up the patterned evidence to a degree that seems more than adequate to justify her thesis that Dickens was in studied control of all the threads of pattern pointing to Scriptural allegory.

Dickens was unquestionably and unarguably in deepest sympathy with Christian ethics and principles (though I find it hard to consider him a "devout" Christian), and his familiarity with the Bible provided him with an abundance of analogical resources, which he utilized fully in *David Copperfield.* But the allegory or myth, I would argue, belongs to the Bible rather than to Dickens. In this regard, like Faulkner he is a myth-user rather than a myth-maker. *His* myth (in Jung's terminology, the myth he "lives in") is quite another. Perhaps, then, the problem I have with the book begins with the title (why not *Scriptural Allegory in Dickens*?) and extends through those arguments that try to make Christianity Dickens's own enveloping myth.

# Index